CW01544732

FAR HEADINGLEY
WEETWOOD and WEST PARK

FAR HEADINGLEY
WEETWOOD and WEST PARK

DAVID HALL

with a foreword by
ALAN BENNETT

FAR HEADINGLEY VILLAGE SOCIETY
2000

First published in 2000 by
Far Headingley Village Society

© David Hall 2000

All rights reserved. No part of this book may be reproduced,
stored or introduced into a retrieval system, or transmitted
in any form or by any means (electronic, mechanical,
photocopying, recording or otherwise) without the
prior permission of David Hall and
Far Headingley Village Society.

The right of David Hall to be identified
as the author of this work has been asserted
by him in accordance with the Copyright,
Designs and Patents Act 1988.

ISBN 0 9539312 0 X

Printed and bound by
SMITH SETTLE
Ilkley Road, Otley, LS21 3JP

Dedication: To Sue, John and Becky for letting me hide away in the office, piecing this book together, over so many week-ends.

Contents

List of Illustrations	xii
Acknowledgements	xvii
Copyright Acknowledgements	xix
Foreword by Alan Bennett	xxi
Preface	xxiii

Introduction and the First Millennium:

Roman Britain	1
The Kingdom of Elmet & the Origins of Headingley	1
The Anglo Saxons & the Derivation of the Name "Headingley"	2
Danelaw	4

Dawn of the Second Millennium:

The Normans	5

The Monks of Kirkstall Abbey and the Beginnings of Far Headingley	7
The Dissolution	10

The Tudor Heritage: Weetwood, New Grange and The Manor of Headingley Become Private Estates

Tracing 1. Headingley Moor	12
Tracing 2. New Grange	13
Tracing 3. Weetwood	13

The Seventeenth Century: The Borough of Leeds, the First Headingley Church, and Civil War

Weetwood Hall and New Grange "Hall"	15
The Borough of Leeds	16
First Headingley Church	16
Civil War	18
The Brudenell and Cardigan Connections	18
The Foxcrofts of Weetwood (Part 1)	19

The Eighteenth Century: The Turnpike, Other Road Links, Farm Management and The New Parsonage House

Otley Old Road	23

Land Management	24
The General Perspective	25
The Foxcrofts of Weetwood (Part 2)	25
The Wades of New Grange	27
Church and School Patronage	29

The Nineteenth Century Before Victoria: Headingley Moor is enclosed, New Grange Becomes Kirkstall Grange and we introduce The Beckett Family

The Marshalls of New Grange	32
Kirkstall Parish	33
William Beckett Acquires New Grange	34
The 6th Earl Of Cardigan and The Inclosure Act of 1829	36
The Birth of Far Headingley as a Recognisable Village	38

The Victorian Years: Aspects of Public Health, Transport, Education Law and Order

Public Health	40
The New Turnpike	40
Omnibuses and Trams	44
The Leeds to Thirsk Railway	49
Education	50
Law and Order	51

The Victorian Years: The Cardigan Interest (continued) — 53

The Victorian Years: A Rapidly Changing Landscape, the Establishment of a New Parish and more on the Becketts

The Developing Landscape	54
William Beckett and the Queen's Visit to Leeds	56
The Beckett Patronage and Foundation of St Chad's Church	59
Edmund Beckett Denison QC, the 1st Baron Grimthorpe	62
The Dedication of St Chad's	63
The Becketts and Further Patronage	66
Beckett Family Connections After William	67
Ernest Beckett	68

Triumph and Tragedy	69
Lucy Beckett and the Founding of the St Chad's Home for Waifs and Strays	71
St Chad's School	72
Moor Road Chapel – the Wesleyan Mission	73
St Oswald's Anglican Mission Chapel at Highbury	74
Recalling St Chad's in the 1880s	77

The Victorian Years: Umbrageous Foliage and Rich Gardens.

Castle Grove	79
Moor House (demolished)	83
Samuel Smith's Vacant Moor Road Plot and his Patriotic Neighbour, Mr Ramsden of Albert House	85
Moorfield Lodge and Moor Grange	86
Burton Crescent	86
Grove Lane: Oakfield Terrace Building Club and early Building Societies	88
Hollin Lane	90
Shaw Lane	93
Oxley Hall and Spenfield	94
Bardon Grange, The Hollies and Fox Hill	97
Bardon Hill and Joseph Pickersgill	99
Weetwood Hall	105
Meanwoodside (demolished)	107

The Victorian Years: Peg-it-up Baths and a Yard for the Duck

George Merry Reminisces	112

The Victorian Years: The Prince and The Professor

The Prince – The Extraordinary Story of Prince Alamayou 1861 – 1879	117
The Professor – His famous son and another Princely Tale	123

Into The Twentieth Century: The Beginnings of a New Age and The End of an Old Order

Ernest Beckett and The King's Mistress	129

Gervase Beckett – the last Beckett at Kirkstall Grange	131
Kirkstall Grange is sold and a College Established	132
The Great War	132
The Children's Home	135
Schools in the Twentieth Century	136
Past Times and Pastimes – Cricket	139
Golf	140

The Twentieth Century: Enlarging the Parish Church — 143

The Twentieth Century: Towards The Modern Age – Business and Pleasure
Some Well Known Far Headingley Establishments

Bryan's Modern Fisheries	149
The Picture House	151
Glendor (Do-It-Yourself) Ltd	152
Mansfield Garage	152
Cottage Road Washhouse	155
Moor Road Dairy	156
Walker's Dairy and Convenience Shopping in the 1940s	156
The Catholic Care Home	161
Personal Banking in the 1950s	161
More Memories	163
Public Houses in Far Headingley	167

The Twentieth Century: New Roads and New Development. From Rich Gardens and Large Estates to Public Parks and Housing

The Ring Road and Residential Expansion North	175
Local Transport and Far Headingley Depot	177
Beckett's Park	178
West Park and Reservoir Hill	179
Castle Grove and The Masonic Hall Company	185
Moor Park Housing Estate	186
The Hollies and Meanwood Park	188

The Twentieth Century:
More Surprising Literary Connections	190

Into the Twenty First Century: Care for the Present and Regard for the Future

    Far Headingley Village Society   198

Who's Who and Who Was Who   202

Bibliography   221

List of Patrons   223

Index   224

And finally – make this book unique   231

List of Illustrations

Portraits

David Hall	inside book jacket
Cuthbert Brodrick 1822-1905	56
William Beckett. Oil on canvas by Sir Francis Grant	60
Lord Grimthorpe in 1889. A Spy cartoon	65
Ernest Beckett	68
John Kirk 1835-1908	80
James Walker Oxley at Spenfield in the 1920s	96
George Corson 1829-1910	96
Alf Cooke 1842-1902	106
Prince Alamayou 1861-1879	120
Arthur Ransome 1884-1967, his mother Edith and his father, Cyril.	125
On the steps of Kirkstall Grange in December 1905: Lady Betty Balfour, Mabel Beckett, Gervase Beckett, Arthur Balfour, Gerald Balfour, Mr Saunders and Mrs Oliver Howard	133
Marion Beckett and unknown companion in a carriage outside Kirkstall Grange c1905	133
'Far' Headingley golfing pioneers at the Spen Lane cubhouse in 1898	140
George Thomas Johnson 1878-1954	165

Maps and Plans

A picture map of Far Headingley Village in 1990 by James Brown	xx
An extract from the Baines and Newsome map of the Borough of Leeds 1839	xxii
Headingley Manor, surveyed for Lord Cardigan in 1711	22
A plan of New Grange, Headingley, surveyed by S Wilkinson of Darlington in 1766	28
An extract from John Tuke's map of Leeds, 1781	30
The development of Headingley Moor 1829-1846, a map by Colin Treen.	37
An extract from the 1851 Ordnance Survey.	43
An extract from the 1909 Ordnance Survey.	142
The 1972 planning brief prepared by Leeds City Council showing the original Conservation Area boundaries	199

LIST OF ILLUSTRATIONS xiii

The Beckett Family Tree 204
The Simpson, Smith & Oates Families of Meanwood 217

Drawings and Prints

The Otley Road horse trough drawn by Mike Smith.	xxv
Samuel Buck's "Prospect of the Ruins of Kirkstall Abbey" in 1723	8
St Giles Church, Headingley.	17
93 Otley Road in 1917 drawn for the Yorkshire Post. Demolished in the 1960s	31
A plan of Far Headingley tram depot and stables 1874	46
Hollin Lane school 1840. Artist unknown	50
Kirkstall Grange. A drawing by Mike Smith	58
The Wesleyan Mission Chapel. A 1974 sketch by Mike Peace	73
St Oswald's Church, Highbury. A 1989 sketch by W John Varker	75
A view of the Salon at Castle Grove in 1896	81
Castle Grove. A 1996 sketch by E RIchard Vaughan	82
Spenfield. An early sketch	95
Bardon Hill. The Ground Floor plan in 1899	102
St Chad's Church floor plan 1869-1909 showing the east end after 1909 in outline	144
Weetwood Lane Forge. Drawn from a photograph by Mike Smith	153
The Three Horse Shoes. The ground floor plan taken from a surveyors report dated May 25th 1903	169
No tick at The New Inn. A sketch by Mike Smith	171
Moorville, Moor Road. A detail of the gate arch sketched by Michael Smith	193
Mazebrook. A sketch by Mike Peace	197

Photographs

A Far Headingley greetings card c1900	xxv
Harvesting at Weetwood in 1887. A photograph by Godfrey Bingley	27
The gates and lodge to Kirkstall Grange c1903	35
Cardigan Cottage, St Chad's Road, date unknown	38

LIST OF ILLUSTRATIONS

A three horse drawn tram standing outside Far Headingley depot about 1880	45
A double-decker horse car outside Far Headingley Depot about 1899	45
The Depot Staff at Far Headingley Depot about 1899	46
A steam tram, engine and trailer, about 1890	48
An electric tramcar on the Otley Road in thE 1930s	48
Hollin Lane school 1920s – by this time a working mens club	51
Victoria Terrace in 1971	55
St Chad's Church 1868	64
St Chad's Vicarage date unknown	66
St Chad's Home for Waifs and Strays opened by Ernest Beckett in 1894	71
Highbury Working Men's Club, 1905	75
The heart of the old common. A view taken from Cottage Road in 1971	78
Castle Grove lodge and Moor Road in 1906	83
Burton Crescent, a post card view. Date unknown	87
Oakfield Terrace, Grove Lane.	89
Grove Lane 1923	89
Hollin Lane in 1915	91
Shaw Lane in 1904	92
Shaw Lane in 1917	92
Weetwood Villa in 1916	94
Spenfield fron the south east c1890	96
The Hollies, Weetwood, c1920s	98
Bardon Hill. The 1999 sales particulars	100
Bardon Hill lodge before 1920	103
Weetwood Hall in 1927. South elevation	104
Weetwood Hall in 1927. West elevation	104
Weetwood Lane in 1907	106
Meanwoodside, as built by Edward Oates in 1838	108
Aerial view of G W Atkinson's Beckett's Park Training College campus c1950	134
The Second World War air raid and ambulance station, Weetwood Lane, in 1995	135
Moorlands School at St Chad's Villas Otley Road. Date unknown	136

Otley Road, West Park near Leeds Modern School in 1941	138
St Chad's Church in 1936	143
The Otley Road frontage to St Chad's Church in 1926	146
The stone screen from St Chad's original chancel at Meanwoodside c1920	147
Headingley Picture House with its original glass canopy	150
Headingley Picture House. The interior	151
Mansfield Garage 1971	153
Tomlinson's Dairy, Moor Road in 1935 just before it was altered	157
Tomlinson's Dairy, Moor Road with new shop front in 1935	157
Victoria Buildings, Weetwood Lane and Moor Road in 1930	158
Weetwood Lane from Otley Road in 1930	158
Two views of the Otley Road shops above Cottage Road c1900 and c1911	160
St Chad's Parade Otley Road in 1934	162
Leeds Industrial Co-operative Society, the Co-op, at West Park in 1937	162
5 and 7 Weetwood Lane c1910	163
Weetwood Lane and Otley Road junction c1905	166
Weetwood Lane and Otley Road junction in the 1920s	166
A three horse drawn tram outside the Woodman Hotel. Date unknown	172
The Otley Road/Old Otley Road junction c1910 above the present day Lawnswood roundabout	174
New suburban "homesteads" fronting the Otley Road c1915	174
Far Headingley Depot in 1935	176
Demolishing Far Headingley Bus Depot in 1992	176
The Otley Road entrance to Beckett's Park and the laying out of St Chad's Drive in 1932	178/179
Thoroughly in the country – the Otley Road in 1904 just above the Spen Road junction	180
The tram terminus at West Park c1910	180
Aerial view of Reservoir Hill in the 1920s/30s	182
Spen Road, West Park c1910	182
West Park housing and the incomplete shopping parade in 1914	183
A closer look at West Park shopping parade in 1913	183
New suburban housing at West Park c1915	184

The Otley Road, Reservoir Hill (the filter beds) facing south c1900	187
The Otley Road, Reservoir Hill facing north c1900	187
Woodland Walk at Hollis Park c1920	189
Meanwood Valley 1887	189
Spen Road West Park c1910	190
Claremont Drive, New years Day 2000	194
St Chad's Gardens, Otley Road.	195
Moorville, Moor Road in 1976. The home of Professor Kettle and his family.	197
Nicholson's Cottage Road/Heathfield Terrace corner shop in the 1970s	201
Churchwood Avenue in the 1940s/50s	222
Victoria Terrace Garden	230

Acknowledgements

My thanks to all those who have helped me in the production of this book. The list will inevitably be incomplete. Given the long period of time that I have been collecting material, the number of people who have assisted in a small but often crucial way is endless. However, I must record my gratitude to:

Ann Alexander
Ian Ballantine, for giving me access to his Leeds post card collection
Sir Martyn Beckett
Brian Beevers, Leeds Reformed Baptist Church
Jim Bright, Business Manager, Leeds Museums and Galleries
James Brown
Albert Bryan
Mr Edmund Brudenell
Kathleen and Neville Bush
Fred Casperson
Dr Hilary Diaper, Curator Leeds University Gallery
David Dixon, Leeds University Media Services
Joe Dodgson
Janet Douglas
Ann Farr, Leeds University Brotherton Library Special Collections
Robert Finnigan, Leeds Diocesan Archives
Barry French
Dr Kevin Grady, Director of Leeds Civic Trust
David Grindrod (and Robert Merry) for access to the George Merry interview
Lord Grimthorpe
Chris Hammond
Donald Hood
Arthur Hopwood, for the benefit of his Meanwood and Weetwood research.
Richard Irving
Alfred Johnson
Kathleen Johnston
Mrs Cecily Ledgard
Michele Le Fevre, Leeds Library and Information Services
   (abb. Leeds City Library)
David Lloyd Hughes for his work on the Oates, Simpson & Beckett family trees
Huon Mallalieu
Mrs McMeeking, St Agnes School
Dr Tony Moyes, for reviewing the section on Kirkstall Abbey
Yvonne and John Oughton
Mike Peace
Bob Preedy
Margaret Ratcliffe, The Arthur Ransome Society

John Richards
Martin Rigg for helping me bring this book to publication
Michael Smith for his pen and ink illustrations specially produced for this book
John Spencer LL.B
John Townsend
W John Varker
Mrs Lucy Warrack
Keith Wilson
Geoffrey Wooler
Mrs Paula Woolnough, Moorlands School
Members of Far Headingley Village Society

Copyright Acknowledgements

For use of copyright material, acknowledgements are due to the following writers and publishers etc:

Rosemary Ashton, *George Eliot A Life*
Alan Bennett, *Writing Home*
Asa Briggs, *Victorian Cities*
F P Casperson, *Leeds Lantern Slides*
J M Collinson, *Weetwood and the Foxcroft Family*
Saul David, *The Homicidal Earl*
The Arthur Ransome Estate
Martin Seymour Smith, *Hardy*
Harley Sherlock, *Cities Are Good For Us*
J Soper, *Leeds Transport*
Diana Souhami, *Mrs Keppel and Her Daughter*
John Tolkien, *The Tolkien Family Album*
Colin Treen, *The Making of the Lost American Garden at Meanwoodside*
Colin Treen, *The Story of Oakfield Terrace*
University of Leeds Media Services, photographs by Godfrey Bingley
E Richard Vaughan, *A History of Castle Grove*
Matthew Winterbottom, *Leeds Art Calendar* No 115 1994

Every attempt has been made to acknowledge copyright and obtain the requisite consent. Where this has not been possible we hope that the persons concerned will support us in our decision that the work was worthy of inclusion.

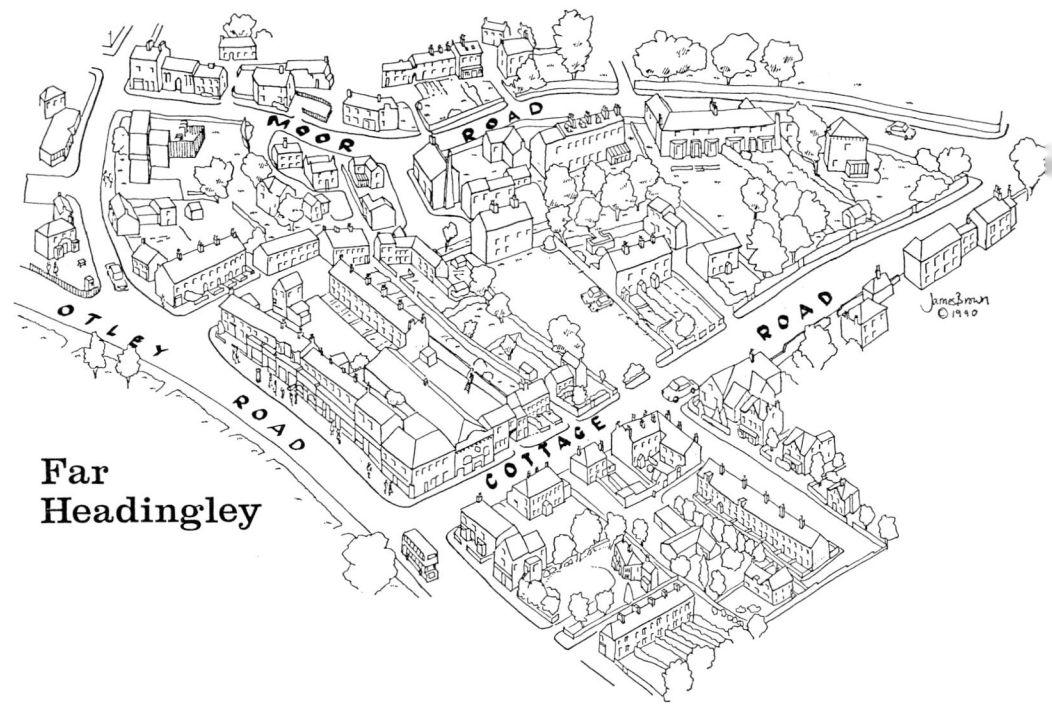

Far Headingley Village, the heart of the Conservation Area on Headingley Moor drawn by James Brown in 19[...]
Courtesy: James Bro[...]

Foreword by Alan Bennett

I lived in Far Headingley from 1946-57, my father having bought the butcher's at 92A Otley Road where we lived above the shop. I was always ashamed of our constricted social circumstances because being above the shop meant we had neither hallway nor front room so that one stepped straight into the kitchen/living room from the passage outside. Indeed one night a couple did just that, and without knocking, under the impression that they were coming into the backdoor of the Three Horse Shoes.

The shop had a big old-fashioned walk-in fridge, run by a motor with a fan belt. It was a temperamental machine and was always threatening to break down, particularly when Dad had the fridge full of meat or poultry as he did at Christmas, when the ruin of the contents of the fridge would have meant bankruptcy.

Rationing was another worry, particularly in the late forties, when the meat ration was lower than it had been during the war. There was never enough to go round and there was fierce competition between the three butchers in Far Headingley; us, Cook's and Demaine's, one of which was thought to be 'on the twist' i.e. dabbling in the black market, but with the stipendiary magistrate and the chief constable as customers there was little risk of conviction. Some of this small time corruption eventually found its way into my film *A Private Function*.

Far Headingley was a sheltered community in which to grow up, every need catered for except for a library for which one had to go down to North Lane. In outward appearance it seems to have changed very little, though I'm still mildly surprised that Hirst's is no longer a confectioners (the manageress a gravelly-voiced Miss Dove, her speciality bridge rolls) or that Hopper's the grocers no longer exists or Wildsmith's the greengrocers next door, both at the start of Weetwood Lane.

I'm always pleased, though, that the Cottage Road cinema is still here, the cinema manager in the fifties always in a dinner jacket and with his pencil moustache thought by me to be the smartest figure in the community. Smart too was Doctor Denton whose NHS surgery was next door to the Three Horse Shoes but who lived in Burton Crescent where his daughter kept a horse on which she would occasionally parade at a stately pace up Weetwood Lane.

I'm glad that so much of the area has survived and that it's more valued for its character and interest now than it ever was then. Leeds is full of such submerged villages. Armley, Bramley and Kirkstall are others, with buildings often of remarkable antiquity and it's right that their history should be told as David Hall tells Far Headingley's here It will enhance the pleasure of living in such a definite community and foster its sense of identity.

I'm just a little disturbed though, to find that I've passed so soon into history.

Alan Bennett

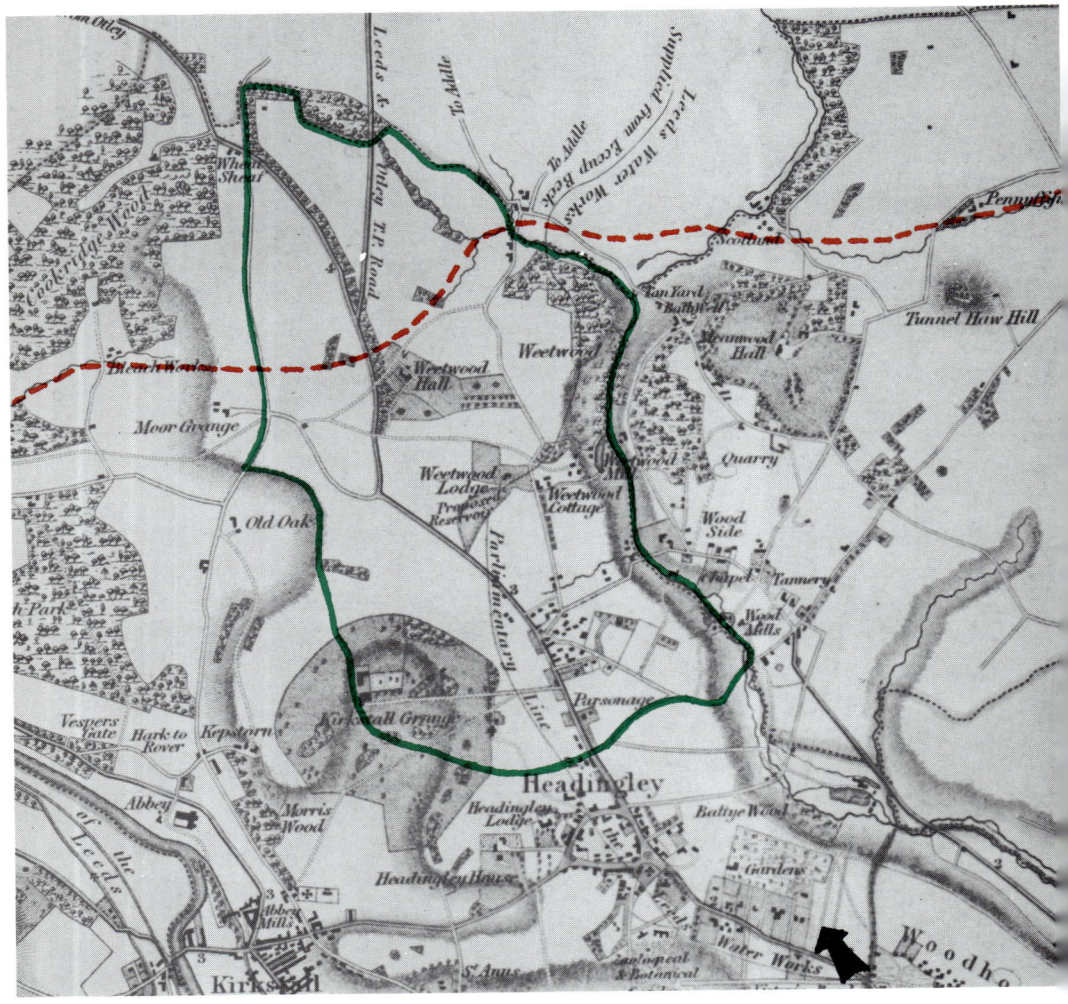

An extract from the Baines and Newsome map of the Borough of Leeds 1839. Alfred Austin's house is show arrowed. Far Headingley Parish boundary & the line of the Leeds outer ring road have been superimposed assist orientation.
Courtesy: The Thoreseby Socie

(- - - Ring Road 1921)
(—— Far Headingley Parish Boundary 1868)

Preface

In the context of a two thousand year span of history, Far Headingley is a young parish formed in 1868 after completion of its parish church, St Chad's. It was called Far Headingley because it was on the farther side of Headingley from Leeds, and in the mid 19th century, Leeds was a place to move farther away from if you valued clean air and decent sanitation.

There had been a steady migration from the burgeoning smoke stacks of Leeds to the rural out-of-townships from the 1820s, firstly by wealthy merchants building imposing villa houses at Headingley Hill and later by artisans attracted to cheaper building plots at Far Headingley which the omnibus had, by then, made increasingly more accessible.

Two contemporary views give us the picture. Alfred Austin was born in 1835 at Ashwood, Headingley Hill – now 48 Headingley Lane opposite Leeds Girls High School. He was the son of a prosperous Leeds woolstapler and rose to become Poet Laureate, succeeding Alfred Lord Tennyson in 1896. In his biography, published in 1911, Alfred Austin remembers the Headingley of his youth as …

> 'an outlying rural parish in the neighbourhood of Leeds, itself more like a very quiet provincial town than what it has since become. My home, built by my father shortly after his marriage, was thoroughly in the country; no other houses intervening between it and the farther side of Woodhouse Moor. One small cluster of lowly buildings could alone be seen on the Moor, which I have heard my father say he remembered as having been the kennels for the local hunt. No tall chimney, no volumes of smoke, could be seen from our grounds, nothing to indicate the proximity of unpicturesque mills and furnaces. Adjoining meadows, the playground of my brothers, my sisters and myself, widened our boundaries'.

By the turn of the century, the pressures of population growth and industrial expansion had made a considerable impact. Far Headingley, still in the countryside, is a separate parish. Edmund Bogg a local historian writing in 1902, describes the area as …

> 'not nearly so delightful as a generation ago (but) still the most charming suburb of the great city. Beautiful residences, half hidden in umbrageous foliage and rich gardens, peep out here and there all along the route, and ever and again castle-like halls and towers stand forth stately and imposing in luxuriant grandeur, a veritable paradise for the homes of our city merchants. (At Far Headingley) the church of St Chad's rests in pleasant surroundings, with its tall commanding spire, rising above the treetops forming another pleasing and interesting object.
>
> The extreme contrast to the above is only too apparent yonder in the valley. One sees smoke, there are hideous noises, the creak, clang and shriek of machinery, and belching fumes and flame from forge and factory, with grime dirt, and the sky pregnant with evidence of the commercial enterprise of this great manufacturing centre, and the dark, turbid river of Hades rolling through.'

That same dark, turbid river of Hades, today flows through the now fashionable Leeds waterfront where converted old, industrial wharf buildings and newer, pastiche Victorian look-a-likes accommodate offices, flats and restaurants; and where the somewhat cleaner waters of the River Aire are navigated by pleasure boats rather than coal barges.

In 1902 Edmund Bogg was already anticipating some improvement,

> 'the evils and transgressions which our city fathers tolerated in the past are now fast being remedied. We shall soon have a purer atmosphere and consequently more sunlight.'
>
> Round and About Leeds and the Old Kingdom of Elmet, Edmund Bogg

In fact it was not to be until the 1960s that, as a result of the Clean Air Act, industrial smogs in the centre of Leeds became a thing of the past, many civic and institutional buildings had their soot-blackened walls washed and the richness of the city's Victorian heritage began to be more widely appreciated.

At the end of the 20th century Headingley (including Far Headingley), however, can no longer be called Leeds' 'most charming suburb'. Its popularity became too much for it and in the course of a hundred and fifty years it went from open farmland centred around two small hamlets, to prime building land for wealthy Leeds businessmen, and finally to almost unrestrained speculative development. The once quiet Headingley Lane which tracked its way up Headingley Hill following the curved lines of field boundaries is now a principal arterial road out of the city, crowded with daily commuters. It is motorised horse-power which sweeps past the old gatehouse to Mr Beckett's estate on the Otley Road and it is a long time since working horses pulling dog-carts, landaus, phaetons, or an omnibus have paused to drink at the water trough which stands nearby.

St Chad's church still rests in pleasant surroundings set well back from the main road, and the mid-Victorian village of Far Headingley remains largely as its late Victorian residents would have known it, but for the loss of surrounding wheatfields and pasture land to 20th century housing estates and municipal parkland.

This then, is the story of Far Headingley, including Weetwood and West Park. It touches on Headingley and Meanwood but makes only passing reference to that part of Far Headingley parish north of the Ring Road. It recounts the history and introduces the reader to the characters and the personalities who have lived in this area or whose lives have been connected with it.

It has been researched and written to celebrate the new Millennium and brings together all sorts of references and material collected over a number of years and now woven into narrative form. It is not an academic work, nor a definitive history. However, I hope it will help maintain an interest in, and appreciation of, a remarkable local heritage.

PREFACE

XXV

The horse trough on Otley Road near 'Mr Beckett's gatehouse'. Victoria Terrace is seen on the other side of the road in this sketch by Mike Smith. *Courtesy: Mike Smith*

A turn of the Century greetings card from Far Headingley. *Courtesy: Ian Ballantine*

Introduction: The First Millennium

Since this is a 'Millennium Book', marking the full passage of time from the birth of Christ, we should begin with the first Millennium, a thousand years of obscure history, at the end of which Far Headingley was probably no more discernable than it had been at the start. Nonetheless, we must set the context, note the physical and human landscape, and acknowledge the great tide of events which first deposited Headingley and its neighbouring communities on the beach of time.

For this was wild territory, part of the ancient British Kingdom of Elmet, fought over and subdued sequentially by the Romans, Saxons, Danes and Normans. It was the Normans who endowed the catholic church in gratitude of the spoils of conquest, and the establishment of Kirkstall Abbey in the 12th century really marks the first beginnings of the monastic estates which would eventually define Far Headingley.

However, in writing about Far Headingley, we cannot ignore its parochial parent, Headingley, nor the surprisingly reversed importance 2000 years ago of Leeds and Adel ...

Roman Britain, The Kingdom of Elmet and the Origins of Headingley

If Leeds existed at all at the time of the Roman invasion (1st century AD), there is little evidence to suggest that it was ever an important place to the occupying army. Having conquered the south of England, the Roman legions marched northwards subduing all opposition before them. North of the Humber, in the North Humber-land, the ancient celtic tribes of Brigantes fought the Romans as they pressed on past Doncaster, crossing the River Aire at Castleford (not Leeds) and on to York.

York was founded in AD71 as the most northerly of the Roman fortresses of the empire. By that date, the Crucifixion (AD33) had taken place, St Peter had been crucified as a common criminal (c64AD), and St Paul executed by the sword outside the Ostian gate of Rome (AD67). The time of the foundation of York was the era when the four gospels were beginning to be written down[1].

Once established in the region, the Romans opened up their own trade routes and built roads radiating from York. One in particular crossed the Pennines to give access to the Irish Sea. The road passed through Adel and Ilkley, both fortified Roman encampments and trading posts. At first it was necessary to defend the road from marauding tribes, but during the course of the Roman occupation, local tribal society developed into more peaceable communities, stabilised by the occupying forces who offered trade, administrative control and protection from other invaders. During this time Leeds became a recognised settlement where the River Aire could be forded, and just to the north, early habitations became established west of the Meanwood tributary, Adel Beck, in an area which would become known as Headingley.

The Romans had fought the Brigantes through wild country, covered by immense forests. The great Forest of Elmet spread over the region from the Don valley to the Nidd where it merged with the Forest of Knaresborough. In Headingley, the dense woodland was predominantly oak and one oak tree, in particular, was to become a landmark of special significance.

Clearings were made in the Headingley woods, the land was cultivated and grazed upon. Felled timber and outcrops of rock provided building materials and tools, forest game was hunted and there was fresh water in the the beck. Gradually two small but distinct settlements formed in this district, one where ancient forest tracks converged on a cleared moor, now Far Headingley, and one a little further south where a singularly large oak tree marked the meeting place of tribal elders, Headingley.

The Roman occupation lasted for over 350 years and, in that time, a civilised and mainly stable society developed but when the Roman legions finally withdrew early in the 5th century AD the old order was already breaking down. There was no strong government and local chiefs had to form new alliances. The two Headingley hamlets lay centrally within the Celtic British Kingdom of Elmet (remembered today in other placenames – Barwick-in-Elmet, Sherburn-in-Elmet) but the region generally was soon prey to new invaders and another turbulent period of British history unfolded.

The Anglo-Saxons and the Derivation of the Name 'Headingley'

First across the North Sea came Angles and Saxons from northern Europe, landing and settling all along the east coast of Britain, driving the surviving Britons westwards. Elmet remained an independent and inhospitable mainly Celtic kingdom 'shut in by rivers, surrounded by forest swamp and dreary moorland', but eventually early in the 7th century it was absorbed into Northumbria under the rule of the Saxon overlord, King Edwin.

Fierce battles ensued between the British Celts and the Saxons which claimed the lives of Edwin and his successor Oswald[2]. It was Oswald's brother Oswy who finally routed the Celts at Whinmoor near Leeds in 655 when Penda, King of the Celtic Mercians was killed.

The Anglo-Saxons, having regained supremacy, slowly began to re-order the country into governable divisions. The English shires date from this time. Each shire was an amalgam of smaller districts called 'hundreds'[3], and each hundred had a court, a local assembly which administered law, collected taxes and maintained the peace by protecting the right to hold land and property.

The large oak tree at Headingley, already an established meeting place, and by now renowned for its majestic size, became the site of the local hundred court – within the scire of Ervic (Yorkshire) – the Scyre-ac or Shire Oak.

At some point during these post Roman times the place name, Headingley, began to evolve, for it is generally accepted that the word has its root in Saxon English and means 'The Field of the Son of, or family of, Hed, or Hedda'. The true derivation, however, does remain open to some conjecture:

Ley, leigh or lee in a place name usually means 'glade', a forest clearing, and is close to the modern word – lea, a meadow[4].

Ing was commonly used to form a patronomic – a surname, and so denotes 'son of' or perhaps 'of the family of'. 'It was the custom of those ages' wrote Ralph Thoresby, in 1714, 'to form a patronymique *(his spelling)*, by adding 'ing' to the father's name, which way was much used in their pedigrees. Thus we have Heding - the son of Hed'. Note the letter 'a' was not introduced, or perhaps reintroduced, into the name until the 19th century. In Thoresby's day this was Hedingley.

In his book *Ducatus Leodiensis (The Topography of Leedes)*, Ralph Thoresby goes on to some intriguing speculation:

> 'Who this Hed was, or the name of his son, I will not pretend to discover at the distance of so many ages; though considering the humour of those times why may not 'St Hedde' put in for it? Who, though he was Bishop of Winchester XXVII winters (to speak in the dialect of our saxon ancestors, who numbered the years by winters), yet was he a north countryman, and educated at Whitby Abbey of which he was first monk and afterwards Abbot. He was so celebrated for miracles that the credulous people made a considerable trench, by scraping away the hallow'd dust where he was buryed, which, mingled with water, they sprinkled on such as were sick, both men and beasts'.

Saint Hedde was a product of the religious development at this time which evolved around celtic missionaries moving through Scotland and into northern England – St Aidan of Iona established Lindisfarne Abbey (651); St Chad of Lindisfarne founded the monastery at Lastingham; St Wilfred founded the abbeys of Hexham and Ripon; St Hilda founded Whitby Abbey and 'chaired' the Synod of Whitby where Wilfred convinced the others to turn away from the celtic religion and to become part of the Roman church.

But Thoresby has another suggestion to make:

> 'The interposition of the letter "l" in Hildin or Heldingley, would tempt us to deduce the name from Helden, a Danish king in these northern parts, from whom the Lowe, or hill here, might be called "Hedinglow", or "law", as it is sometimes pronounced. And I find it so writ in the parish-registers, in the time of the very learned Robert Cooke A.D. 1592. The difficulty is not in the termination, but in the former part of the name, whether from that pagan, King Healdine, or from Heddeing, that is Hedde junior. That king indeed seems probable because he was the first who in the year 876 divided these parts of England amongst the Danes, who thereupon began to plough and sow the land. This king was slain by Edward senior A.D. 911.'

Christian Saint, pagan king or local Saxon patriarch – take your pick.

Danelaw

In the 9th century it was the Danes who plundered and colonised much of eastern England establishing by treaty in 873 their own territory, the Danelaw, which for a time, included the whole of Yorkshire, Lincolnshire, East Anglia and the East Midlands.

Onto the system of shires the Danes imposed their own divisions. In Yorkshire they created the Ridings (lit: thrithing – third part), and throughout Danelaw the local administrative divisions were known as wapentakes, the word wapentake meaning 'weapon touch' denoting an act of allegiance to the overlord by the symbolic touching of weapons. Decisions made at a public assembly would be confirmed by the flourishing of weapons.

In Headingley the hundred court became the Wapentake Court of the Scyre-ac, 'so denominated from some remarkable oak to which the inhabitants repaired upon public occasions.'[5]

Today, the name Skyrack remains familiar enough though many may not know the origin of the word, nor that the very tree itself, which gave broad leafed shelter to the earliest Headingley settlers, lived on into the 20th century. It was located, of course, near the two inns named after it, The Original Oak and The Skyrack. Its wasted hulk finally collapsed in a gale in 1941, and from its ancient wood Robert Thompson, the mouseman of Kilburn, carved a figure of the Madonna and child. This fragment of the great Oak, a relic of the dark ages, is now in the lady chapel of St Michael's church. And on the Otley Road, by a plaque marking the site of the 'original' oak (near the HSBC Bank), a new oak grows.

During this period attempts were made to suppress the Saxon monasteries. Indeed the opening salvo of the Viking age is generally regarded to be the storming of the monastery at Lindisfarne on June 8th 793. Lastingham Abbey, near York was closed down by the pagan Danes and not restored to the monks until after the collapse of the Danelaw.[6] Under Norman rule there would be an avalanche of new monastic foundations in Yorkshire.

Notes

[1] Several Roman emperors spent time at York. Hadrian, to review the construction of the Roman wall (AD122-128); Septimius Severus, to plan the EXPEDITIO FELICISSIMA BRITANNICA against the Scots (AD212); Constantius who came to York with his wife St Helen of the True Cross, and who died in York; Constantine, his son, who was declared emperor in York. It was Constantine who later converted to Christianity and took the capital to Byzantium, which ultimately led to the schism between the Eastern Orthodox Church and the Holy Catholic Church of Rome. A J Moyes.
[2] St Oswald, in whose name the mission church at Highbury is dedicated.
[3] The 'hundred' being a hundred hides – an ancient measure of land 'enough to support a family' – The Oxford Dictionary
[4] In the Aire valley around Leeds we find Morley, Tingley, Cottingley, Farnley, Wortley, Armley, Bramley, Headingley, Burley, Rodley, Farsley, and Calverley.
[5] Ralph Thoresby writing in his *Topography of Leedes* 1714.
[6] In 1088 the Lastingham monks founded the great benedictine abbey of St Mary's by Bootham Bar, York.

Dawn of the Second Millennium

The Normans

The power of the Danes waned in the 11th century as the Saxon kings began to unite England. In 1066 the Vikings were finally defeated by King Harold at Stamford Bridge, near York. His personal triumph, however, was short lived, for within three days a new invasion was underway. William, Duke of Normandy, Viking Normandy *(Vikings: French Normands)*, had crossed the Channel and landed with his forces on English soil. Harold marched his weary army south and met the French at Hastings. In a six hour battle Harold's army was defeated and he himself famously fell to a stray arrow.

William the Conqueror, aided by five thousand French knights and continental mercenaries quickly invaded and suppressed the south of England. He redistributed the land among his followers and, as king, imposed strong government from London where the language of the court was now French. In 1069 he turned his attention to the more rebellious north of England. In the latter half of that year Willam marched north with his army and advanced into Yorkshire. He forded the River Aire at what is now Ferrybridge where he broke through the Saxon resistance, commanding his best lieutenants to subdue and lay waste the whole region[1].

One of these men, the Norman baron Ilbert de Lacy took control of the western territory and, as his reward, he became possessed of vast lands including the West Riding of Yorkshire. At Pontefract he built a magnificent Castle from where he governed his extensive jurisdiction which became known as the Honour of Pontefract. De Lacy in turn sub-granted the feudal lordship of confiscated estates and manors between the Aire and the Ouse to his companion in arms, Ralph Paynel (or Paganel) who built his castle at Drax (between Selby and Goole – now better known for its power station). In this way, Ralph Paynel became Lord of the Manor of Leeds and the Manor of Headingley.

> 'William the Conqueror made sure there was no resurgence of the squabbles between Saxons and Danes by transfering manorial power from the motley thanes to the Norman barons and knights, who owed William a more direct allegiance than was owed by the thanes to their Saxon kings. Nevertheless, in spite of the centralised power of the Norman monarchy (epitomised by the organisation brought to bear for the Domesday survey), much that was Saxon and Danish survived: in particular the Saxon village and shire and the Danish burgh, together with the ecclesiastic parish which generally followed the boundary of village or burgh'.
>
> *Cities Are Good For Us* by Harley Sherlock, Paladin 1991

A great patron of Marmoutier Abbey near Tours in northern France, Ralph founded for a local order of Benedictine monks, the priory church of the Holy Trinity in York, and gave to it the revenues from the churches of both Leeds and Adel (adjoining parishes since Headingley, although a separate manor, was a chapelry within the Parish of Leeds).

Ralph died in 1109 and his feudal estates passed down the Paynel family line. During the 12th century Norman churches replaced the old Saxon buildings at both Leeds and Adel, the latter still extant. Leeds, however, although only a hamlet on the banks of the Aire, had a bridge over the river and was becoming a focal point for trade. In 1207 Maurice Paynel, now Lord of the Manor of Leeds founded, by charter, the manorial Borough of Leeds, recognising the right of self government through elected officials. He sold off thirty burgage plots on either side of a new street, just up from the bridge gate, thereby establishing Briggate and the beginnings of a new township of freeholders.

But what of Headingley Manor — further subinfeuded it seems by Ralph Paynel to a Walter Paytefen. In 1152, nearly a century after the conquest, William le Peitevin de Haddingeleia was invited to grant land in West Headingley to a local prior and his twelve apostle monks for the founding of another great monastery. Setting up the deal was the Lord Baron of Pontefract himself, Henry de Lacy.

Notes

[1] In 1069 York Castle was sacked for the second time by the English. William's reaction was swift and bloody. His subjection of the north was achieved through the most appalling destruction of villages, crops, men, women and children. A huge proportion of the population perished. Some estimate up to 90%. Much of the land shared out among the Norman war lords was derelict. Headingley, however, was comparatively unaffected although the Domesday Book records its fall in value from 40s to 4s between 1066 and 1086. Leeds increased marginally in value during the same period £6 to £7. A J Moyes.

The Monks of Kirkstall Abbey and the beginnings of Far Headingley

Whilst the Benedictine monks at Holy Trinity, York, had found a great benefactor in Ralph Paynel, their brothers from the newer and stricter Cistercian order found an even greater benefactor in Henry de Lacy, Ilbert's grandson.

In 1147, Henry agreed to honour his vow to endow a new abbey in thanksgiving for his recovery from a sickness. Generous to a fault in such matters he donated, we are told, the entire village of Barnoldswick-in-Craven 'with its appendages' to prior Alexander and his twelve apostle monks, purposefully dispatched from Fountains Abbey to establish a new daughter abbey. The monks, together with ten lay brothers, endeavoured to establish the new monastery at Barnoldswick but they were harassed by dispossessed villagers and other raiders. In addition, it seems they were not suited to the climate. They elected to move on and followed the River Aire downstream until they found…'a place covered with woods, and unproductive of crops, a place well nigh destitute of good things save timber and stone but a pleasant valley inhabited by certain pious anchorites (*hermits*) with the water of a river flowing down its centre'[1].

The new location of which Henry de Lacy approved, was at West Headingley. Possession was granted by William le Peitevin and soon timber was being cut and stone quarried. During the next thirty years there arose on the forty acre site the great Norman church of St Mary, Kirkstall, a magnificent Cistercian Abbey within the Parish of Leeds. Unlike the Parish Church, however, it had no ties or obligations to the more humble Benedictine Priory at York.

In 1723 Samuel Buck, agent to the Earl of Cardigan, Lord of the Manor of Headingley-cum-Burley, inscribed a picture of the Abbey for his master, giving a third alternative spelling to William Pietevin:

> 'Henry de Lacy having instituted at Barneldswick in Craven a convent of Cistercian monks from the Abbey of Fountains under Alexander their first Abbot AD 1147. They found means to transplant themselves six years afterwards to Kirkstall in Aredale upon the brink of the River Are inhabited at that time only by hermits. Where having obtained of William Pietavensis, the soil, at the yearly rent of five marks, this pleasant Abbey was erected.'

For nearly four centuries Kirkstall Abbey prospered and expanded, albeit knowing some dark and turbulent times in that period. Kings, archbishops, and the only English pope, Adrian IV, offered it protection and conferred grants and charters. It received gifts from men of all 'ranks and kinds' and came to own lands, not only around the present City of Leeds, but in the East Riding, Lincolnshire and Lancashire.

Supporting the Abbey's commercial interests were many farms or granges, each grange overseen by a small number of lay-brothers. The first, not surprisingly,

Prospect of the ruins of Kirkstall Abbey dated 1723 by Samuel Buck for Lord Cardigan.

was at Barnoldswick but others were established more locally and are now remembered in neighbourhood place names – Moor Grange, Allerton Grange and, in particular, New Grange at Headingley which was later to become Kirkstall Grange (now Beckett's Park).

All around the Headingley district, ancient woodland was cleared for timber and fuel. Crops were raised and livestock reared. The Kirkstall economy was based on sheep and cattle and extensive animal pasturage was required. Coppiced wood was used for fencing, charcoal was burnt as part of the iron extraction process and oak bark was used for leather tanning. The monks worked coal seams at Woodhouse Moor, quarried stone at Bramley Fall, smelt iron at Weetwood, and ground corn at Headingley Mill in Meanwood Valley.

The common grazing land north of Headingley settlement and to the east of New Grange had already became devoid of timber and taken on the appearance of open moorland. This was **Headingley Moor** which would remain an open common until it was enclosed for building in the 1830s to form the nucleus of modern day Far Headingley. It was still known as Headingley Moor when, in 1868, St Chad's church was built on the old monastic Kirkstall Grange estate (by this time William Beckett's domain) and the new parish was named Far Headingley. Today, Heathfield Terrace and Moor Road recall the centuries old common and the Monk's Bridge over Meanwood Beck is still remembered in the name Monk Bridge Road. The bridge crossed the fast flowing beck in the 'mean' – or common – woods. It was on the monks' cattle drove route between the Abbey's Chapel Allerton pastures and the monastery precinct where the annual audit of livestock took place. Near the bridge the monks built a corn mill. Mill buildings have stood on the site ever since[2].

The earliest record of **Weetwood** appears in 1240 in connection with the Abbey. In that year, the court in York upheld the Abbot's absolute rights to the 'Whettwoods' and threw out a counter claim made by a John de Bermingham. The Kirkstall monks had an iron bloomery at Weetwood where raw iron was made before being taken to be refined at the forge in the abbey precinct[3]. Timber was an important resource and it would have been necessary to protect it against opportunist claimants. The Abbey's 'Whettwoods smethe' or smithy stood at the bend in Leeds Ring Road where the road passes over Meanwood beck, a location until recently known as Smithy Mills. A short walk down stream in Meanwood is the site of a second early bloomery. This was Hazelwell (or Hesylwell)[4].

For four hundred years Kirkstall Abbey dominated the local scene. By the turn of the 14th century it had clearly become a major corporation in its own right. The monks provided local employment, they managed their lands and property, they produced and sold cloth, they provided board for passing wayfarers, they ran an infirmary.

However, in spite of their early missionary zeal, their quiet pastoral life, their daily religious devotions and their pious doctrine it seems that eventually power and wealth corrupted the monks and abbot of Kirkstall. T Hargreaves, writing his History of Kirkstall Abbey in 1848, tells of 'the luxurious and debauched manner of living' and how it became customary 'to inveigle females from the path of piety into that of profligacy. They (the monks) pretended miracles and used most barefaced imposture – typical relics included God's coat, Our Lady's smock, the cloak of St Lawrence, St Edmund's nails, an angels wing and enough pieces of the holy cross to make a man-o'-war'[5].

It was all to end in the 16th century.

The Dissolution

When Henry VIII, Defender of the Faith, but not his marriage vows, divorced Catherine of Aragon in favour of Ann Boleyn, he defied Rome and appointed himself head of the reforming catholic church in England. He ordered the dissolution of all monasteries assuring the people, through Archbishop Cranmer, that they 'had no cause to be grieved' because by suppressing the abbeys, the King would 'gather such an infinite treasure that from that time he should not need, nor would not put the people to, any manner of payment or charge for his or the realm's affairs'[6].

On the night of November 22nd 1539 an armed detachment of the King's men arrived at Kirkstall and 'invited' Abbot Browne to sign a contract handing over the Abbey and all its estates to the Crown. The monks were turned out and the property confiscated. The inevitable end had been anticipated and the eviction was peaceful. There was, in fairness, some consolation. The abbot was allowed to retire to the Gate House (now Abbey Museum) on a handsome pension whilst the monks, who received much smaller pensions, were found other places in the Yorkshire church. The servants dispersed locally[7].

Details of the Abbey's property were recorded in a survey of lands of dissolved religious houses and included 'farms of the site of the monastery of Kyrkstall and demesne lands with two corn mills, granges called **Newgrange** and Cukrige, lands in Burley and Heddingley, a fulling mill, lands in Westheddingley and Capstone,[8] two smethes called Whettwoods and Hesylwell …'[9]

We are not told how the closure of such an important institution affected the lives of the inhabitants of East and West Headingley (which now included the settlement of Burley) many of whom were no doubt dependent on the Abbey for their livelihood. The monks of Kirkstall, having always produced their own wool and agricultural produce for sale, had contributed in some measure toward the local economy, but not particularly to the development of Leeds as a market town. The Abbey's wool was sold directly to European merchants until export restrictions were imposed and it is thought that very little, if any, was sold through the local market on Leeds Bridge.

In fact, the disappearance of Kirkstall Abbey, had little impact on the welfare of the local population. On the contrary it resulted in land sales that were to attract not only titled estate owners into the district but also 'a new race of gentry, raised by trade'. These land sales would create three distinct parcels of ownership immediately north of Headingley village which, combined, make up present day Far Headingley – Headingley Moor (within Headingley Manor), New Grange, and Weetwood. And with new landowning interests came a whole new level of squirearchy …

Notes

[1] A much used quotation, drawn from the founding documents.
[2] In 1994 Highbury Works, then a fellmongery, closed and was converted to 'Mill Race' apartments. A Leeds Civic Trust Heritage Plaque records the importance of the site and its medieval beginnings.
[3] Not the ironworks that grew into Kirkstall Forge but small refinery workshops. R A Mott in his article for the Thoresby Society (Misc Vol 15 Pt 2) asserts that there were no iron works on the Kirkstall Abbey site until after the Dissolution and perhaps not much earlier than 1600.
[4] A J Moyes '*Kirkstall Abbey's Iron Bloomery at Hazelwell*' Medieval Europe 1992.
[5] Good quote though this may be, monastic life in the 1530s is a matter of considerable debate and Mr Hargeaves may be attributing to Kirkstall the worst exesses of *some* English monasteries.
[6] From a sermon preached by Thomas Cranmer, Archbishop of Canterbury, in March 1536 backing the King's proposal then before Parliament to cull the monasteries.
[7] Pensions were related to the assessed value of the monastery. Kirkstall's assessment amounted to about £450. Accordingly the Court of Augmentations, which had the responsibility of paying the pensions, fixed Abbot John Browne's pension at £66 per year whilst most of the monks were granted between £5 and £7 per year each. Kirkstall was wealthy compared to Jervaulx, Byland and Rievaulx (assessed at between £200 and £230), but Fountains was in another league altogether, being assessed at £1,100. 'It was a paying game', Dr A J Moyes.
[8] **Capstone, or Kepstorn**. Residents of Kepstorn Road in modern day West Park may be curious about the naming of their road. Writing at the beginning of the 18th century, when Capstone (or Kepstorn) was part of the Wade estate, the Leeds historian, Ralph Thoresby, notes:

> 'Kepstorn. This place also belonged to the said monastery and is now the inheritance of Benjamin Wade of New Grange. The Saxons rarely used the letters K or Q. I presume it was of old writ 'Caepstorn' from 'ceapan' a market place, and the Norman 'torn', a circuit. That such marts not only belonged to religious places but were often celebrated in the very church yards is notoriously known; and in many places (particularly at Burnley in Lancashire) I have seen crosses yet standing in the churchyards with as many steps round for the convenience of the sellers of provisions, as in any of the modern market places'.
>
> *Ducatus Leodiensis*, Ralph Thoresby 1714

[9] The 'smethes' at 'Whettwoods and Hesylwell' were iron bloomeries in the Meanwood Valley. Weetwood bloomery was on the site of Smithy Mills where the Ring Road now passes over Meanwood Beck.

The Tudor Heritage:
Weetwood, New Grange and the Manor of Headingley become Private Estates

In 1541 Robert Pakeman 'of the King's Household' became a tenant of the Crown by leasing, for 21 years, the forfeited monastery site plus 'two watermills for grain, a grange called Newgrange and a close of pasture adjacent called Oxemore ... all in the the Parish of Leeds'[1].

When Edward VI came to the throne six years later he granted the Abbey lands, with the benefit of Robert Pakeman's lease, to the protestant Archbishop of Canterbury, Thomas Cranmer[2]. However after Edward's short reign, the property returned to the Crown when Cranmer, dispossessed by Roman Catholic Queen Mary, was obliged to 'surrender his own life'. In 1556 he was burnt at the stake for heresy.

Tracing 1. Headingley Moor:

Elizabeth I made some reparation in 1568 and restored the Crown's interest in the Abbey estate to Cranmer's son, also named Thomas. This gift appears to have been limited to the property originally leased to Robert Pakeman since, four years earlier, the Crown had disposed of part of the Headingley lands to Robert Savile of Howley including the settlements of Headingley and Headingley Moor. When Thomas Cranmer II decided to sell his holding in 1583, which included New Grange, Weetwood and the Abbey site, Savile stepped in again and acquired the Abbey site. Savile's enlarged Headingley estate became the reconstituted Manor of Headingley-with-Kirkstall, and Savile ... Lord of the Manor.

Sir Robert Savile was the illegitimate son of Sir Henry Savile of Thornhill – for a period High Sheriff of Yorkshire and himself a large landowner, whose property included the Manor of Howley near Morley. Sir Henry had a daughter and a son, the latter dying without issue. He also had eight illegitimate children. In one of them, Robert, he took such great interest that he allowed him to take the name of Savile and left him a considerable part of the family estate. Sir Robert settled at Howley (near Batley) and built Howley Hall, where he lived until his death in 1585.

Succeeding to Sir Robert's estates, including the Manor of Headingley-with-Kirkstall, was his son, John. By all accounts, John Savile (1556-1630) was a remarkable man, influential throughout Yorkshire and Lincolnshire – an eminent politician, a lawyer, a large land owner and a patron of the church. He continued to own Headingley Manor (with Headingley Moor) although his seat remained at Howley Hall, a property he extensively improved and augmented. He was to become a prominent figure in the history of Leeds, in later life, as we shall see, but for the moment we will leave Sir John here and return to Thomas Cranmer II's remaining (Far) Headingley interests – New Grange and Weetwood.

2. Tracing New Grange

The first wealthy merchant family to actually settle in the (Far) Headingley district was the Foxcroft family of Kebroyd near Halifax. Thomas and Joanna Foxcroft had married in 1563 and, in 1569 moved to New Grange, after a short time living at Barre Grange adjoining the old Abbey. Initially tenants of the younger Cranmer they eventually purchased the New Grange property in 1583.

There seems to be no recorded description of the house, no doubt converted from the monks' original grange buildings. It must have been spacious enough though, for Thomas and Joanna had seven children. The eldest, Isaac Foxcroft, inherited New Grange in 1596 but, not wanting to live there himself, he sold it to his brother-in-law, Anthony Wade of Halifax. In this way the Wade's Far Headingley connection was established. The Wade family would remain at New Grange for the next 200 years.

Anthony Wade of King Cross, Halifax, had married Isaac's sister, Judith Foxcroft of New Grange, in 1590. The Wades of Halifax were another merchant family who had prospered during the reign of Queen Elizabeth I. Like the Foxcrofts they were large South Pennine landowners, and we are told that, 'much rivalry appears to have existed between the two families … concerning the acquisition of land in the Halifax area'[3]. Around 1590 a Samuel Wade was murdered by one of Judith's cousins, Michael Foxcroft of Kebroyd, and so it is perhaps not surprising that Judith and Anthony Wade wanted to live well away.

3. Tracing Weetwood

Cranmer sold all his Headingley interests together in 1583. Sir Thomas Cecil was the immediate purchaser but he quickly re-disposed of the three principal parts, no doubt taking an early property speculator's profit. We have seen that the Abbey site was acquired by Sir Robert Savile; and Thomas Foxcroft bought New Grange. William Arthington Esquire, of Arthington and Adel, purchased the remainder – 'all of the woods called Whitwoods alias Weetwoods'.

Known to the early monks of Kirkstall as 'Wetwude', the Weetwoods of 1583 were broadly bounded by Headingley Moor (in Headingley Manor) on the south side; 'Lemeenewude' (Meanwood, Chapel Allerton Manor), to the east side; the Lawn Wood to the north, and the New Grange estate to the west.

The Arthingtons, originally Abbey tenants, had purchased the Manor of Adel from the Crown after the dissolution. In 1583 William Arthington seized his opportunity to acquire the valuable timber of the Weetwoods, but financial difficulties obliged him to quickly mortgage three quarters of the holding, and sell the remaining quarter, just north of Headingley Moor, to Richard Meynell of Thirsk. Richard Meynell moved to Weetwood and built himself a house, probably on the same site as the later Weetwood Hall, from where he managed his woodland.

Towards the end of the 16th century, therefore, we find the small hamlet at Headingley Moor within the fiefdom of John Savile of Howley, Lord of Headingley Manor. The Foxcroft/Wade alliance of Halifax occupy the New Grange estate, bordered by the Headingley lane and Spen lane, and Richard Meynell of Thirsk is husbanding his part of the Wet-woodlands through which passes the road to William Arthington's extensive Adel estate (Weetwood Lane).

So the new 'Far' Headingley gentry were incomers. Certainly the modest small holders and tenant farmers already living in the district had not the cash to buy up monastery land.

Notes

[1] It is possible that Pakeman's two mills were those for grinding corn and a fulling mill in the former inner precinct.

[2] The grant of monastic property to the Archbishop was made 'to fulfill the verbally expressed wishes of Henry VIII before his death (in 1547)'. The gifted properties 'were oddly miscellaneous, and still an austere selection in comparison with many of the mammoth handouts to (Lord) Somerset's cronies in the wake of Henry VIII's death. The plum among them was Kirkstall Abbey in Yorkshire; there was also a little ex-Cluniac nunnery near Kirkstall called Arthington, an obscure Kentish benefice, and a clutch of property around Cranmer's childhood home at Aslockton (Notts)'. *Thomas Cranmer, A Life*, Diarmaid MacCulloch, Yale University Press 1996.

[3] J Sprittles: *New Grange, Kirkstall*, Thoresby Society Vol 13 Part 1 1958.

The Seventeenth Century:
The Borough of Leeds, the first Headingley Church, and Civil War

Weetwood Hall and New Grange 'Hall'

The first significant change of local land ownership occurred in 1620 and, with it came a new branch of the Foxcroft family from Halifax.

Daniel Foxcroft was Judith Wade's cousin. His business interests were wide and varied. He dealt in flax, dyes, soap and groceries, and he shipped cheap cloth across the Baltic with a return trade in corn. He bought the Meynell property in 1620 and in 1625 built himself a new house more befitting a rich Yorkshire merchant. This was Weetwood Hall part of which stands to this day and bears the date 1625 carved over the south entrance.

Perhaps not surprisingly, the rivalry between the Wades and Foxcrofts, still persisted for in the following year, 1626, Benjamin Wade, successor and son of Anthony Wade, rebuilt the house at New Grange in grander style. Nothing is thought to survive of this building, the house being rebuilt again in the 18th century and then substantially altered in the 19th century. However, Thoresby writes that Benjamin Wade, a deeply religious man, had the following inscription carved on his new house above the back door where alms were received by the poor:

> If thou shalt find, A house built to thy mind,
>   Without thy cost,
> Serve thou the more, God and the poor,
>   My labour is not lost.

This inscription, a later copy of the original, can still be seen over the rear entrance to The Grange at Beckett's Park. As J Sprittles points out in his essay on New Grange, published by the Thoresby Society in 1958, this inscription might properly by attributed to hymn writer and poet, George Herbert (1593-1633), for outside Bemerton parsonage near Salisbury where George Herbert was incumbent vicar between 1630 and 1633 one can read the following lines:

> If thou chance to find, A new house to thy mind,
>   And built without thy cost,
> Be good to the poor, As God gives thee store,
>   And then my labour's not lost.

Benjamin Wade and Daniel Foxcroft were now the local squires with Sir John Savile, an absentee landlord. All three however, were influential men in the life of the burgeoning town of Leeds.

The Borough of Leeds

In the same year that we find Benjamin Wade rebuilding New Grange, 1626, Leeds received its first Royal Charter creating a municipal Borough of Leeds. A 1993 West Yorkshire Archive publication 'Leeds City Charters' explains:

> 'By 1600 Leeds had developed from a prosperous rural village into a growing industrial and mercantile centre. Cloth was the staple trade and the merchants were anxious to control it, maintain standards, and exclude competition by forming a self-governing corporation. They obtained a charter from King Charles I creating a new borough to be coterminous with the parish of Leeds, to be administered by an Alderman, nine principal burgesses and twenty assistants, with power to acquire property, to hold courts, to have a common seal, to make and enforce bye-laws and regulations and to collect fines'.

The Borough, being coterminous with the parish of Leeds, included the district of Chapel Headingley-cum-Burley and Kirkstall, and the other Chapelries of Leeds Parish, which now came within, and under, the civic control of Leeds municipal corporation.

The first Alderman of the new Leeds Borough was Sir John Savile of Howley and Lord of the Manor of Headingley with Kirkstall. He was a much favoured, as well as rich, public servant for he could add to his jobs, titles and honours – MP for Lincoln and High Sheriff of Lincolnshire (later becoming MP for York), Master of the Rolls of the West Riding, High Steward for the Honour of Pontefract, Trustee of Batley Free School and Governor of Wakefield Grammar School.

As a further honour to Sir John, the first Leeds Charter bore a seal incorporating three owls, taken from the Savile coat of arms, and a fleece (symbolic of the Leeds wool trade), a measure of Sir John's importance no doubt, particularly when we learn from Rev R V Taylor, in his *Biographia of Leodiensis* published in 1865, that although first Alderman of Leeds Sir John 'did not, however, formally discharge the functions of the office'. Notwithstanding, the owl has been an emblem of Leeds ever since and three owls remain the prominent feature of the City's present coat of arms.

The First Headingley Church

Sir John did, in fact, leave a particular legacy to Headingley. During his year of office as Alderman, 1626, he gave land for the erection of a church. A stone building, similar in size to the Norman church at Adel was built and dedicated to St Giles. It stood for over 200 years. It was rebuilt in 1838 to designs by William Chantrell who became renowned as the architect of Leeds Parish Church. Within 50 years however, Chantrell's Headingley church was replaced by a new and much larger church which still occupies the site gifted by Sir John. This, of course, is the present day St Michael's.

St Giles Church, the first church in Headingley, built on land donated for the purpose by Sir John Savile in 1626. It was demolished in 1833. Benjamin Wade endowed the curacy. Almost certainly a small chapel of ease already stood on the site, part of which may have been incorporated into the new church. *Courtesy: Ian Ballantine.*

Two years after his appointment as the first Alderman of the Borough of Leeds, Sir John was elevated to the peerage as Baron Savile of Pontefract. In 1630 he died at Howley Hall. He is buried near his father in Batley parish church.

Sir John Savile was succeeded by his son Thomas whose entry in the Dictionary of National Biography makes intriguing reading:

> Sir Thomas Savile (c1590-1653?). 2nd Baron Savile of Pontefract, created Earl of Sussex in 1644. He succeeded to the English peerage at his father's death and, on the same day he endeavoured to seize some property his father had left to his sister, Mrs Anne Leigh, and compelled the tenant to sign a deed 'with a dagger at his breast'. He was a bitter enemy of the government and was recognised as the organ of the English malcontents. He was, however, favoured for a time by the Court. His first wife was Frances, with whom he had no issue. His second marriage was to Lady Ann Villiers with whom he had a son, James and a daughter, Frances.
>
> 'Throughout his shifty intrigues his one fixed purpose was to establish his own fortune whichever party triumphed'. Between 1646 and 1658 he passed 'in retirement' at Howley Hall.

Clearly a disappointment to his upright father (had he known), but he seems to have married well. Lady Ann Villiers was the daughter of the Earl of Anglesey and eventually her father's sole heiress.

Civil War

Sir Thomas was 'advanced to the dignity of Earl of Essex' according to Mr J M Barber a 19th century Heckmondwike chronicler, in 1644. This was no doubt in return for attending King Charles 'in his troubles' – the English Civil War. Apparently Sir Thomas Savile was with the King at Oxford when that city was beseiged.

Leeds, itself, was lost to Cromwell in January 1643. There was, by all accounts, no very great resistance since the main battle at Leeds Bridge lasted only two hours. Those loyal to the King, having made ready to defend the bridge, were surprised by Sir Thomas Fairfax's ploy of crossing the River Aire west of Leeds and directing his main forces on the town from the north.

Three thousand foot soldiers are said to have marched over Headingley Moor and through Headingley, on January 23rd 1643, confronting Royalist sympathisers at Woodhouse Moor and Meanwood Valley before storming the town[1]. The King's men were under the command of General Sir William Savile[2]. Casualties were recorded thus:

> 'January 23rd 1643. Leedes was taken by Sir Thomas Fairfax, eleven soldiers slain, buried 24th; five more slain two or three days after; six more died of their wounds.'

Sir Thomas Savile was succeeded as second Earl of Sussex by his son James. James married Ann Wake and had a son who died in 1670 and was buried at Batley. A year later James joined his son in Batley church and the Howley inheritance, including the Headingley estate, passed to his sister Frances, and in particular her husband Francis Brudenell.

The Brudenell and Cardigan Connection

Lady Frances Savile had married Francis Lord Brudenell in 1668[3]. It was a match which joined two extremely wealthy landowning families. The Brudenell fortune had been laid down by Sir Robert Brudenell, who at the time of his death in 1531 owned estates in seven counties, including the family seat at Deene Park in Northamptonshire. Like the Saviles, the Brudenells were also staunch Royalists. When imprisoned in Carisbrooke Castle, Charles I offered Sir Thomas Brudenell an earldom if he would send him £1000, a promise honoured by Charles II at the Restoration, for in 1661 Sir Thomas Brudenell was created Earl of Cardigan 'in consideration of his loyalty and eminent service to the King'.

On the death of Sir Thomas two years later, the Earldom passed to Francis Brudenell's father Sir Robert. In 1668 therefore Lady Frances Savile must have anticipated a future life at Deene Park as wife of the 3rd Earl. That title, however, was to belong to their son George. Francis Brudenell, already very rich and now possessed of the Savile estates including the Manor of Headingley-with-

Kirkstall, continued the family tradition of trumpeting the Royalist cause. He was a catholic and a Jacobite. He fought for the restoration of James II and was imprisoned for four years in the Tower of London on charges of high treason. He died in 1698, outlived by Sir Robert, who followed in 1703 at the grand age of ninety six.

So it was that through Frances Savile's marriage to Francis Brudenell, The Manor of Headingley-with-Kirkstall became part of her son, George Brudenell's inheritance in 1698, five years before he succeeded as the 3rd Earl of Cardigan on the death of his grandfather.

The Foxcrofts of Weetwood (Part 1)

The Foxcrofts of Weetwood, by contrast to the rising prospects of the Brudenells, were not caught up in the Civil War. Daniel Foxcroft had died in 1639 leaving Abigail, his widow and four young boys. One of the boys, another Daniel, baptised in 1631 eventually came into his father's property. In 1653 he brought his new wife to Weetwood Hall, Martha daughter of Francis Layton, Squire of Rawdon, and in 1661 he was appointed an alderman under the new Leeds Borough Charter. This Charter, issued on the restoration of the Monarchy, provided that the borough of Leeds was to be governed by a mayor, twelve 'honest and discreet' (no doubt meaning 'loyal to the King') aldermen and twenty four 'able and discreet men' as councillors. Daniel Foxcroft was mayor of Leeds[4] in 1665, but after an active career in municipal affairs he 'retired' in 1679. He died in 1691.

Local historian, J M Collinson, gives us this impression of Weetwood Hall as it was in 1639, much of the detail being gleaned from the settlement papers of Daniel Snr:

> Downstairs was a 'hall house' with an iron range, a great table with two forms and a little round table, a best parlour, a little parlour, a buttery and a kitchen. On the first floor were four chambers with beds, tables and cupboards. Above there was an uppermost chamber with a great chest at the stairhead – apparently an attic used for storage. Outbuildings are not mentioned but must have existed. It was a handsome new house but probably smaller than New Grange.
>
> *'Weetwood and the Foxcroft Family'*, J M Collinson, University of Leeds Review 1987/8

There were nine estate tenants including William Phillipp who held land and a cloth fulling mill 'presumably' says J M Collinson 'the predecessor of the now vanished mill near Weetwood Mill Lane'. He is referring to Weetwood Mill which later became a paper mill, then bleach house and 19th century dye works before its eventual closure and demolition. Today it is the site of a market garden although the old mill pond is still easily recognised.

But back to the late 17th century, during which Daniel Foxcroft II made further extensions to Weetwood Hall. Ralph Thoresby writing in 1714, describes the Hall as now having 'nine lower rooms, including a milk cellar, and eight upper rooms, five with ranges, plus a garret'[5]. According to J M Collinson 'later deeds mention a brewhouse, bakehouse, barn, stables, oxhouse, garden and orchard'.

Mr Collinson also refers to Manklin's Farm[6], 'as it was then called', south of Weetwood Mill and to the north of Headingley Moor. Mounting debts which, perhaps significantly, followed his retirement from the civic scene, caused Daniel Foxcroft to dispose of this farm plus six smaller tenanted farms, and the mill.

The eastern border of the Foxcroft estate was marked by the Meanwood Beck and the Weetwood Mill streams. This was all 'Weetwoodside'. On the other side of the beck was Meanwoodside (otherwise Weetwoodside), Thomas Whalley's estate. Thomas Whalley was a prosperous tanner and gentleman farmer. His family would retain Meanwoodside until 1834. Originally tenants of Kirkstall Abbey, the Whalley family were long established in the area and continued to enlarge their estate by piecemeal acquisition during the early 18th century[7].

Francis Brudenell had also found reason for disposing of part of his Headingley estate, no doubt to sustain his Jacobite interests. In 1673 he sold almost three hundred acres of farmland on Headingley Hill to his tenant John Walker. As we shall see the pattern of piecemeal land sales was to gain momentum during the 18th and 19th century.

But if, for the moment, we could return with Ralph Thoresby to the end of the 17th century and to what he described as that 'decent chapel' in Lord Cardigan's Manor, St Giles at Headingley, we might now recognise the names of a number of notables at rest, for in 1714 Thoresby recorded the following memorial tablets:

> A stately monument of white marble inscribed: Herein is deposited the mortal remains of Benjamin Wade of New Grange who gave the benefit of £200 to the curate of this chapel for ever. He departed this life (leaving no issue by Edith his wife) Feb 5th A.D. 1671 in the 81st year of his age.
>
> Also the body of Anthony Wade of New Grange who died 14th Dec 1683 aged 49 leaving 1 issue – Benjamin Wade who erected this tomb A.D. 1694.
>
> Also the body of John Walker of Hedingley, gent, who departed this life 8th Nov 1698, likewise four of his children.
>
> Also the body of John Killingbeck of Moore-Grange, alderman, once mayor of the Burrough of Leedes, who departed this life 19th Sept 1696 in the 79th year of his age[8]. And his wife Beatrix.
>
> Also Martha, wife of Daniel Foxcroft of Weetwood who died 1st July 1688. Also Daniel who died 6th Aug 1691 aged 60.
>
> *Ducatus Leodiensis*, Ralph Thoresby 1714

Notes

[1] Many musket balls have been found in living memory in the steep bank of Meanwood Ridge above the beck.

[2] Part of the extended Savile family, Sir William died of camp fever in York in 1644.

[3] Francis Brudenell's sister Anna Maria was notorious for being wife to the Earl of Shrewsbury, whom she married at eighteen, and mistress to the Duke of Buckingham. The liaison provoked a bloody duel between the two men in 1668, the year of her brother's marriage to Frances Savile. Samuel Pepys famously recorded the incident. Each side had two supporters in attendence – Talbot and Howard for Lord Shrewsbury, and Holmes and Jenkins for Lord Buckingham:

> 'They met yesterday in a close near Barn Elms, and there fought. And my Lord Shrewsbury is run through the body, from the right breast through the shoulder, and Sir John Talbot all along up one of his arms, and Jenkins killed upon the place and the rest – all in a little measure – wounded. This will make the world think that the King hath good councillors about him, when the Duke of Buckingham, the greatest man about him, is a fellow of no more sobriety than to fight about a whore'.

[4] The first Mayor of Leeds was Thomas Danby 1661.

[5] 'Ducatus Leodiensis', Ralph Thoresby 1714

[6] **Manklin's Farm** is largely that tract of land which today would be bounded by Hollin Lane, Weetwood Lane, Weetwood Mill Lane and Meanwood Park. It was bought by Joseph Oates in 1796 and became known as **Snow's Farm** after Thomas and Betty Snow, the farm tenants. 'Snow's Farm' remained a working farm well into the 20th century, until house building created the Hollin estate. According to Arthur Hopwood's researches the original farmhouse stood on the site of present day Hollin House.

[7] There were six successive Thomas Whalleys at Meanwoodside between about 1600 and 1750. On May 12th 1656 Thomas Whalley the elder of Chapel Allerton, a tanner, left to Thomas Whalley, his son 'the Tanhouse with the pits' and 'the low parlour in which I now dwell with chamber over'. The tanhouse stood at the foot of Hollin Drive and later became Holmes Farm, (subsequently converted to three stone dwellings). The 'low parlour with chamber over', was the original structure on the site of the house later known as Meanwoodside, demolished in 1954. A deed of 1690 confirms the Whalley freehold purchase of 'messuages or tenements and several closes bounded ... by The Meanwood ... Headingley Moor and the lands of Daniel Foxcroft'. Source: Arthur Hopwood and Fred Casperson, *Meanwood*, 1986.

[8] This John Killingbeck incidentally, a tenant of Lord Brudenells who had also resided for a period at Headingley Hall, was the father of John who became Vicar of Leeds in 1690.

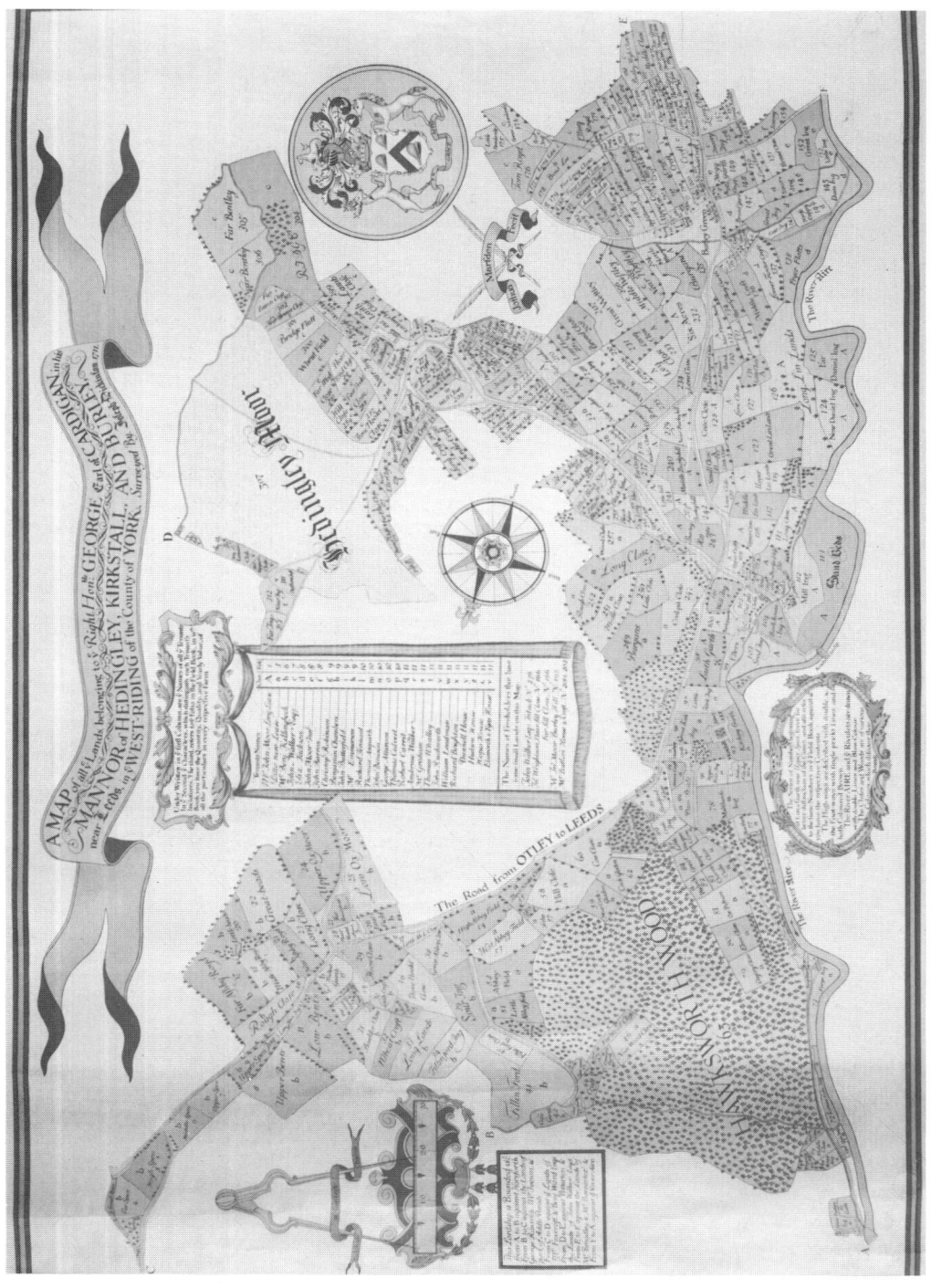

The Eighteenth Century:
The Turnpike, Other Road Links, Farm Management, and the New Parsonage House.

The beginning of the 18th century marked a significant change in the importance of Leeds as a commercial centre. In November 1700 the Aire and Calder Navigation opened, establishing the town as an inland port accessible by cargo ship and barge from Hull. As a consequence commercial traffic on the main highways into Leeds began to increase substantially – not that there was much change to note at this time in the quiet, rural village of Headingley and the nearby hamlet of Headingley Moor.

While Ralph Thoresby was busy researching his own local history of Leeds and its out-townships (*Ducatus Leodiensis* published in 1714), the new 3rd Earl of Cardigan, George Brudenell was sensibly getting the measure of his Yorkshire property holdings. He instructed his agent, Joseph Dickinson, to survey and map the family's *Hedingley* estate.

Accordingly, in 1711 Mr Dickinson completed a 'MAP of all ye Lands belonging to ye Right Honourable GEORGE, Earl of CARDIGAN in his MANNOR of HEDINGLEY, KIRKSTALL, AND BURLEY, near Leeds'.

The cartographer carefully plotted and identifed each close and field. Furthermore he listed the tenants' names, and made cross references to a separate 'Folio in the Field Book, in which Book you have the quantity, quality, and yearly value of all the particulars in every respective farm'.

Although extensively cultivated, there were within the Manor boundaries two large unfarmed tracts of land – Hawksworth Wood to the north of the Abbey site (still well forested), and '*Hedingley Moor*' common, (later Far Headingley village). The very noticeable gap in between is Mr Wade's New Grange estate.

Otley Old Road

The road pattern is also interesting to note, for far from being on the Otley road, Headingley is well by-passed. In 1711 'The Road from OTLEY to LEEDS' followed the Burley Road and Spen Lane, passing through the small settlements of Burley Green and Kirkstall, and keeping west of New Grange.

In 1754 when the Leeds-Otley-Skipton road was turnpiked, a Major Forster exercised some influence, for the enabling Act specifies that 'no tollgate shall be let near to a certain house in Burley West Lane called Major Forster's House'.

On present day Kirkstall Hill the road from Headingley crossed the Leeds road to Otley at Morris Lane and continued down to Kirkstall bridge (the first river crossing west of Leeds Bridge) from where it continued as a busy commercial route from the port of Leeds to Bramley and to Halifax – a road 'much used and frequented for the carriage and conveyance of wool, woollen manufactures, dying ware, corn malt, fruit and other commodities'.

Incidentally, a field marked Coal Pit Close at the Morris Lane crossing tells of the search for mineral deposits as well as the usual agricultural pursuits. Coal was prospected at every opportunity around Leeds and by the end of the 18th century, the Cardigans were enjoying large revenues from their collieries on the south side of the town.

During the 18th century the track crossing Headingley Moor from Headingley to Moortown Leys via Monk Bridge and Stonegate Lane would become increasingly well used as a cross country route from Kirkstall Bridge to the Harrogate road putting Headingley at something of a cross roads. The Monk Bridge Lane is shown crossing *Hedingley Moor* on the 1711 map, but Moor Road itself and Cottage Road do not yet exist.

The Moor is wholly within the Cardigan Estate bounded on the east by Meanwood Beck and to the north (from Hollin Lane) by the Weetwood Hall estate. Both *Hedingley Moor* and the adjacent *Mean woods* were ancient common land whereby commoners could share the grazing, cut turf and take certain amounts of stone and timber. A track across the Moor, unmarked in 1711, became the main thoroughfare for driving cattle and sheep, and the curious bends in 20th century Moor Road near Weetwood Lane almost certainly date from this time.

At Moor Grange on the Spen Lane from Otley to Leeds, a quieter lane (now Spen Road) probably no more than a farm track, crossed the Ox Moor, north of New Grange and continued south to join the *Addle* Lane at a fork in the road on Headingley Moor. The lane continued through Headingley and onto Leeds, and so it could be said that Headingley was 'on the way' to Otley, although it would not become the main commercial route for another hundred years.

Moor Grange (and Ox Moor), was also part of the Cardigan estate and farmed by tenants. Indeed Mr Dickinson's plan of the Manor indicates that in 1711 a traveller on the old Otley road did not get passed the Earl's fields until he was beyond the High Spen (north of what is now New Adel Lane).

Land Management

The day to day estate management devolved from Lord Cardigan's head steward at Deene to the under-steward in Wakefield who collected and remitted the rents. Agricultural leases, often for only a few acres, were carefully drawn to ensure good husbandry. For his 1977 University treatise, Colin Treen cited one such lease – a 1793 lease of four and a half acres at Headingley to Samuel Waddington stipulating that no more than a third of the land was to be in tillage at any time, no 'meadow or ancient ground' was to be ploughed up without the Earl's consent and the tenant was to 'well and effectually summer fallow each part of the said lands once at least in every six years. And furthermore, he shall not have more than two crops of white corn without the intervention of a summer's fallow'.

During the fallow period, meliorating crops could be sown – coleseed, turnips, beans and clover – to be eaten by cattle and sheep, and the land was to be further replenished by twelve cart loads of manure or twenty five horse loads of lime per acre.

Concessions were given to those tenants who put up new buildings or undertook major repairs. In addition there were non-agricultural tenants on the Cardigan estate – tradesmen, labourers, millwrights.

Those who were not formal tenants of the Cardigans would subsist as best they could building shacks on *Headingley Moor* and fencing off small areas to pen pigs and other animals. In time, these common land encroachments became more substantial and by the end of the 18th century a number of stone cottages were standing on the Moor. Lord Cardigan's agent seemed to have been fairly relaxed about this trend, concerned no doubt to stop the unsightly spread of hovels and degenerating land, and happy to collect some additional rents.

The General Perspective

So, although a very small hamlet in 1711, Headingley was a well established settlement, focussed on the area around its small church and the ancient oak. Most of Cardigan's *Hedingley* estate lay to the west, taking in Burley and Kirkstall down to the river as far as Hawksworth Woods.

The path across Woodhouse Moor from Leeds winds up Headingley Lane passing through the late John Walker's three hundred acre farm before arriving at Headingley. Among the assorted buildings and smallholdings is Headingley Hall, close to the shire oak and until recently tenanted from Lord Cardigan by gentleman farmer John Walker who was also Recorder of Leeds. Continuing north, the track soon leaves the village behind and opens onto the heathfields of Headingley Moor with the gates to Mr Wade's New Grange estate on the left, and a few cottages on the Moor where the road forks to Addle.

The Foxcrofts of Weetwood (Part 2)

Immediately to the north of *Hedingley Moor* was the Weetwood Hall estate. Daniel Foxcroft, that distinguished alderman and one time Mayor of Leeds Borough had died in 1691 leaving Weetwood to his eldest son, Samuel. But although well connected the family fortunes were in decline and when Samuel died in 1713 he left borrowings on the property and only a small farming interest.

Samuel was succeeded by his brother Francis, a versatile scholar according to Ralph Thoresby, who had emigrated to Cambridge, Massachusetts (Harvard). Francis had also inherited through his mother, part of the Layton estates in Rawdon, and when he transferred his English property to his son, another Daniel, in 1719, Daniel was already living at Rawdon.

J M Collinson in his study of the Foxcroft family, doubts that Daniel Foxcroft ever settled at Weetwood Hall, and noted that 'besides the hall and adjacent fields, there were at this time two large farms, one the later Weetwood Farm with a tannery, and the other, in which Samuel's widow had a life interest, near Spen Lane with clothworker's shop'.

Through his father's connections, Daniel became a merchant in the North American trade, and was living in the then fashionable London suburb of West Ham when Weetwood Hall, and seventy six acres of land, were offered to let in 1735. John Geldard, the tenant of Weetwood Farm and tannery acted as agent.

Daniel died without issue in 1741 and his aunt, Samuel's widow, died the following year, bringing to an end the Foxcroft Weetwood connection. Francis Foxcroft's family were by now well established in New England and had no interest in Weetwood Hall. According to J M Collinson, efforts were made to sell the freehold – no doubt to clear mortgage debts – but when these failed the estate was offered for lease by the mortgagee, a Leeds businessman, John Noguier.

Within a few years the southern part of the estate, excluding the Hall, was bought by Sir Henry Englefield Bart. Sales of Englefield land nearly one hundred years later would provide building plots for several stylish Victorian mansions – Bardon Hill, Oxley Hall, The Hollies, Spenfield – but in the middle of the 18th century Weetwood Hall stood in tranquil rural isolation. The cartographer, John Tuke, notes on his 1781 map that Lady Anne Denison was living at the Hall at the time of his survey.[1] This is the widow of Sir Thomas Denison, the eminent and wealthy Leeds High Court judge who had died in 1865. Sir Thomas may have bought Weetwood Hall from the legal successors of the Foxcrofts but, in any event, after his death we know that Lady Denison was the owner of the Hall and 249 acres of land.

On the demise of Lady Anne, the Hall was offered for lease and Joseph Oates became its tenant. The freehold passed to the trustees of Lady Denison's estate and later devolved to Edmund Beckett on his marriage to Sir Thomas' heiress, Maria Beverley of Beverley. Throughout the 19th century, as we shall see, the house was occupied (and further improved) by some distinguished families. All however, or so it seems, were tenants. The freehold, did not pass out of the Beckett family ownership until a conveyance to Leeds University in 1919.[2]

From the 1790s the little water mill at the bottom of Weetwood Mill Lane was let to William Martin and his son James – as papermakers[3].

> They lived at the ancient Weetwood Farm nearby, and it was there, according to family tradition, to avoid payment of duty they would wine and dine the Excise

Harvesting at Weetwood. This photograph was taken by Godfrey Bingley in August 1887 and is simply entitled "Weetwood Lane Far Headingley". *Courtesy: Leeds University.*

man so well that while he slept they could purloin his official stamp and frank a good stock of paper. In 1858 Edward Oates, the owner of Meanwoodside, purchased the property from the Englefield trustees to protect the water rights to his estate, and in correspondence refers to 'the most delicate white paper formerly manufactured by Mr Martin'.

All trace has now gone and the only reminder of this little industrial site is a stone arch over the tailrace where it emerges opposite Hustler's Row.

F P Casperson, *Leeds Lantern Slides*, The Thoresby Society

The Wades of New Grange

New Grange, meantime, belonged to the Wade family through most of the 18th century. Benjamin Wade had built his house in 1626 and little was to change until the middle of the 18th century, when in 1752 Walter Wade, decided to rebuild the house in a somewhat grander style. Parts of the 1752 house are still discernible notwithstanding its 19th century remodelling by William Beckett.

As we have seen from the tombstone in Headingley chapel yard, Anthony Wade of New Grange had died in 1683 aged forty nine succeeded by his son,

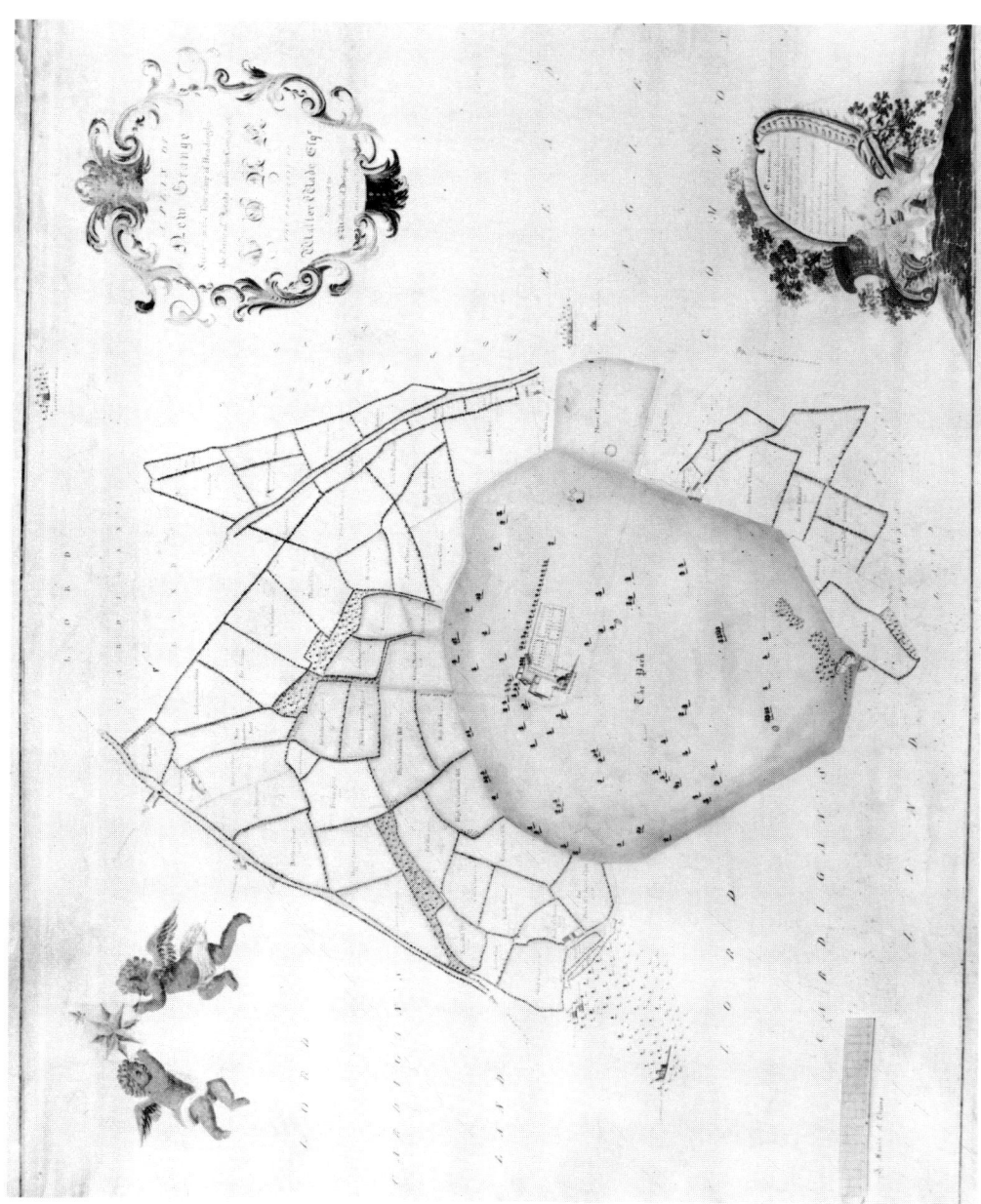

Benjamin. Benjamin and his wife had no children and consequently New Grange passed to Anthony, a nephew. At the beginning of the 18th century, Anthony's son Benjamin was in possession. This Benjamin was the father of Walter who rebuilt the house in 1752.

Since 1590 therefore we have followed the Wade descendants in this order: Anthony, Benjamin[4], Anthony (who died 1683), Benjamin, Anthony, Benjamin, – Walter. Walter was his father's fifth son, and no doubt had fate been kinder to his brothers, yet another Anthony would have taken proprietorship of New Grange.

Walter's own first born, Benjamin, died in infancy and so the new, New Grange was to pass to his second son, another Walter, who had married Ann Allanson of Halifax. This Walter died of a bilious fever in 1771 aged only forty nine leaving the property in the care of his son, another Benjamin. Ann continued to live at New Grange, presumably with Benjamin and his family. But when he died in 1792, the decision was taken to move to smaller accommodation and seek a tenant for the estate. In 1795 the contents of New Grange were auctioned and before the end of the century, Samuel Buck, the Recorder of Leeds was in residence on a lease from the Wade family.

Walter's widow, Ann died in 1809 and was buried at Headingley chapel.

Church and School Patronage

Before leaving 18th century Headingley, we should return to the Cardigan inheritance and note what small but significant changes have occurred in the *Hedingley* Manor.

In particular, a very fine Georgian house has been built on the common, just before we reach the gates to New Grange. It fronts on to the east side of the lane and has a south facing wing looking back toward the village. It is the new parsonage and replaces the old vicarage at Burley. In addition, the Minister has been provided with his own coach house, stable, formal gardens and a not inconsiderable parcel of glebe land.

In 1770, George, the immensely wealthy 4th Earl of Cardigan (now also Duke of Montagu through his marriage to Lady Mary Montagu) allowed forty one acres of 'waste and common lands' at Headingley Moor to be enclosed for the benefit of the curate of Headingley. Holly Dene parsonage was built on part of the site in 1777.

Further north, at *Hedingley Moor Side* – near the junction of Addle Lane and the now well defined track which will become Moor Road – half an acre of the common has been enclosed and built upon. A house, mistal and stackyard stand on the site.

At Headingley there are two schools. In 1783 Lord Cardigan endowed the first public elementary day school next to the small church of St Giles (later St Michaels) – Benjamin Wade of New Grange made a donation – and in 1798, James, 5th Earl of Cardigan, agreed that rent from Mr Martin's paper mill[5], upstream from Monkbridge, might be held in trust to provide for a schoolmaster to teach six poor children at a small free-school in Wood Lane. All signs that Headingley itself, had developed into a cohesive and sizeable community.

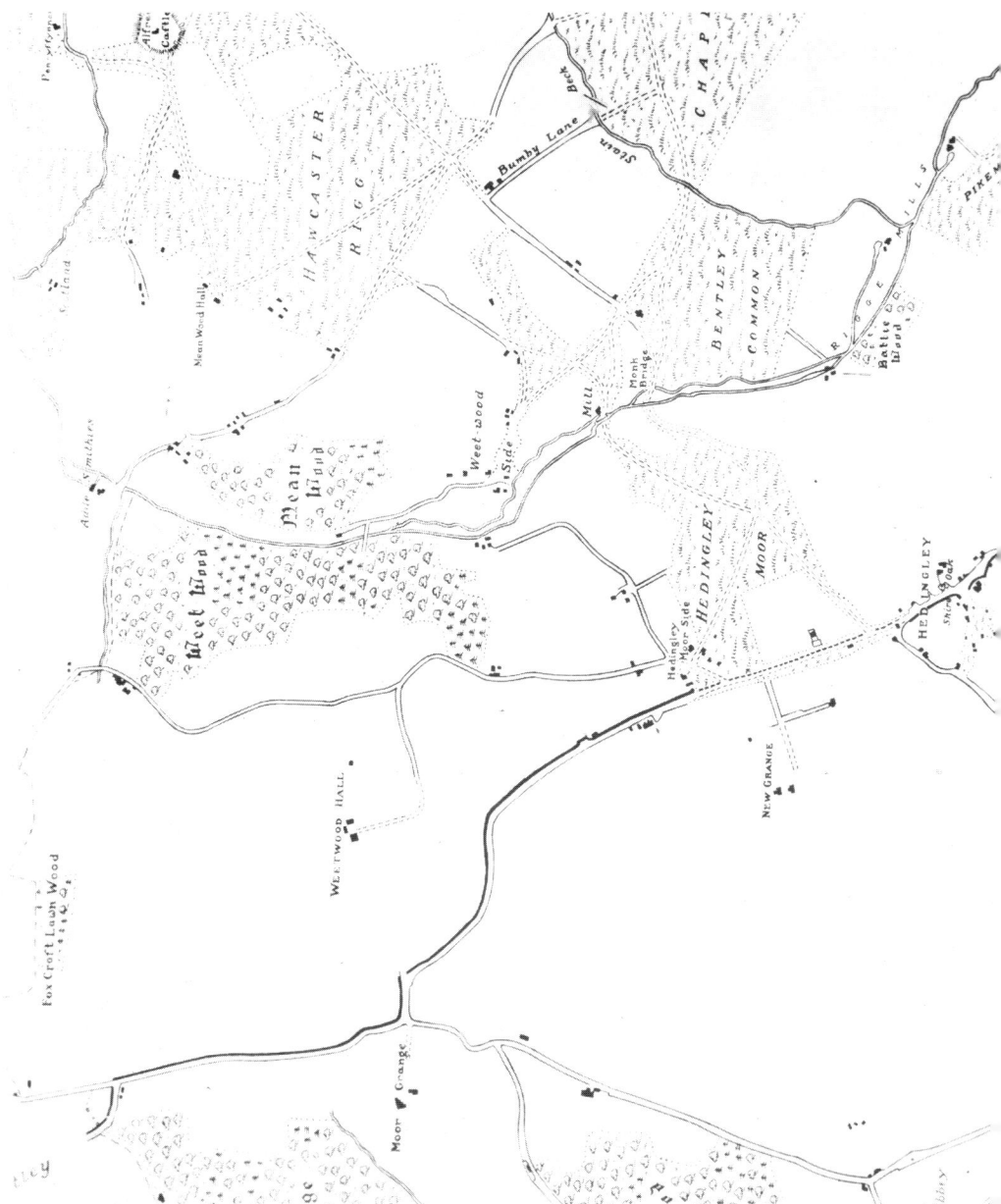

1781 John Tuke's map of Leeds. Lady Denison is resident at Weetwood Hall and Benjamin Wade is at N Grange[1]. The parsonage house and glebe land takes a fair slice out of Hedingley Moor and one or two encroachm buildings can be seen on the moor at Headingley Moor Side. Addle Smithies are shown as is the mill at M Bridge. The road through "Hedingley" becomes present day Spen Road at West Park and connects to the Leeds and Otley turnpike at Moor Grange.

Courtesy: Leeds City Lib

Meanwhile, in Leeds, commercial trade flourished, new businesses were constantly being established which attracted a fast growing population. By the end of the 18th century, all the principal roads out of Leeds had been turnpiked, and the extraordinary engineering feat of linking Leeds to Liverpool by canal had been completed. This latter enterprise was to be the catalyst for the rapid growth in textile manufacturing which would cause both Leeds and Bradford to boom in the 19th century.

Notes

[1] This copy of John Tuke's map does not record Lady Denison or Benjamin Wade. Other copies do.

[2] Arthur Hopwood's researches indicate that Weetwood Hall and thiry three acres (tenanted by Joseph Oates) plus 249 acres of land occupied by other (farm) tenants was sold by Edmund and Maria Beckett-Denison to Edmund's brother Christopher Beckett by a deed of conveyance dated August 8th 1821. Three years later Christopher Beckett bought the Meanwood Hall estate where he lived with his sisters Mary and Elizabeth until his death in 1847. Meanwood Hall itself, was built by another member of the Denison family. All very interwoven!

[3] This William Martin was the son of Thomas Martin, paper maker of Wood Mills (on the site of Highbury Works).

[4] This Benjamin built the first New Grange 'Hall'. He died in 1621, aged 81.

[5] Formerly the monk's cornmill, now a paper mill, called Wood Mills, on the site of what would eventually become Highbury Works, a tanning mill and not to be confused with Weetwood Mill at Weetwood Mill Lane, also a paper mill and also operated by a branch of the Martin family. Wood Mills was made into a paper mill by Thomas Martin in 1785. It was the enlargement of the mill pond, at the request of Thomas Martin that created a lease and provided the annual five guineas ... 'for the education of six poor children in reading, writing and arithmetic to be nominated on Michaelmas Day by the majority of inhabitants, resident householders, in Headingley'. Extract from the *21 year lease dated March 25th 1797* between the Earl of Cardigan and Thomas Martin of Wood Mills. Researched by Arthur Hopwood.

Cottages in Otley Road on the way out of Headingley drawn in 1917 for the *Yorkshire Post*. Built on a thin strip of Headingley Moor Common west of the 'main' road and possibly the building noted at this location on John Tuke's map of 1781 (page 30). Demolished in the 1960s to make way for another new shopping parade. Salvo's Restaurant now stands on this site.

Courtesy: Michael Smith.

The Nineteenth Century Before Victoria:
Headingley Moor is enclosed, New Grange becomes Kirkstall Grange and we introduce the Beckett family, but first …

The Marshalls of New Grange

'New Grange is a cheerful place,' wrote Dorothy Wordsworth in 1807, 'and the Abbey – how beautiful'.

Dorothy and William Wordsworth together with Mrs Rawson, their aunt from Halifax, were the house guests of John Marshall. He had taken over the lease from Samuel Buck, and installed his family at New Grange some three years earlier. Dorothy Wordsworth and John Marshall's wife, Jane, were old schoolfriends.

Reflecting on their return journey home to the Lake District, Dorothy noted the distinction between the very different settings of Bolton Abbey and Kirkstall Abbey, Bolton Abbey being 'in the most beautiful valley that was ever seen. The river is greatly inferior to Kirkstall, but the situation infinitely more beautiful – a retired, woody winding valley with steep banks and rocky scars – no manufacturers – no horrible forges and yet the forge near Kirkstall has often grand effects'[1].

John Marshall was forty years old when he moved to New Grange. A self made man, his fortune came from flaxspinning. He was one of the first to succeed in the spinning of flax by machinery, following Arkwright's example in spinning cotton. He staked everything on this enterprise and became immensely rich. Setting up firstly at Scotland Mill on Adel Beck in 1788 with Samuel Fenton and Ralph Deartone, he had the good fortune to employ a young and brilliant engineer from Darlington, Matthew Murray. The business expanded rapidly and within three years Marshall re-located to larger mills at Water Lane in Holbeck. His protegé, Matthew Murray, went on to establish an engineering foundry, also in Holbeck, and became world renowned for his many engineering inventions.

A large house, away from the bustle and grime, was very much what the Marshalls required in 1804. They already had six children and a further six were to follow. John Marshall also wanted a household establishment which befitted his advancement in society. That year he moved his family to New Grange from Meadow Lane, Hunslet. The house was large, and costly. More than a dozen servants were employed, and household expenses ran to over £3,000 per year.

Dorothy Wordsworth was nothing if not candid. In 1797 she had written to Jane Marshall congratulating her 'upon the health, strength, liveliness and activity' of her little boy. Just as well really, because 'you can perceive he is not handsome'. She also approved of the eventual move to the countryside near Headingley village, 'for there is not half the comfort in children when you are in or very near a town'.

John Marshall landscaped the grounds near the house and raised sheep and cattle in the surrounding fields. It is also generally thought to be John Marshall who joined in the national celebration of the final defeat of Napoleon in 1815, by ordering trees to be planted in representation of the troops at the Battle of Waterloo.

In this same year, 1815, with his still increasing wealth, John Marshall bought a large estate in Cumberland. This was Hallsteads, which he soon began to consider his country seat. He gave up his New Grange tenancy from the Wades and looked for a smaller Leeds residence. He selected Headingley House, a sizeble villa, in Kirkstall Lane, which he bought from Mr Bischoff, a woollen merchant, for £7,500, and immediately further enlarged by adding a west wing costing £2,500, and twenty five acres of farm land (ten leased from Lord Cardigan). This was to be John Marshall's new house 'in town'.

The lease of New Grange, meanwhile, was taken up by John Marshall's former partner, another wealthy flaxspinner, Thomas Benyon with his wife Jane.

John Marshall died in 1845, five years after the completion of his architecturally fantastic and voluminous Temple Mill at Water Lane.[2]

Kirkstall Parish

In these early years of the new century we can see the beginnings of the pattern of development which was to gain rapid momentum over the next few decades. Commerce and industry were expanding in Leeds, money was to be made and new homes required both for workers and the rising industrial barons. The rural landscape of Headingley-cum-Kirkstall was especially attractive and well located.

By 1820, a whole range of mills had grown up in Meanwood Valley, all harnessing the Adel beck as it flowed down to Sheepscar. The flax mill, paper mill and ancient corn mills we know about. But now there are four tanneries, a further paper mill, and Wood Mills where oil seeds are ground for linseed oil.

It was still a harsh age in many ways. In 1819 a Leeds butcher, William Smith stole two sheep from a Rothwell farmer and was executed by hanging for his crime. As a punishment, it was no doubt considered a necessary warning to the rapidly growing population of poorly paid Leeds factory workers, most of whom lived in appalling conditions. The luckier ones moved into terraced cottages hurriedly built in the out townships including Kirkstall.

In 1818, William Avison began to run regular omnibus services by accommodation coach from Potternewton, Chapel Allerton and Kirkstall villages into Leeds and back. The Leeds Intelligencer noted that 'the fashionable villages adjacent to Leeds, it seems, are about to have A REGULAR DAILY SERVICE at stated hours, quite on the London plan'. Timetables were produced and given out on printed handbills, but William Avison was a little ahead of his time. Three months after the launch of his new business, he was obliged to abandon the regular daily service and return to operating a service 'as orders may suit'.[3]

Mr Avison also offered 'a handsome open landau happy to convey passengers to neighbouring watering places at the price for posting'. In 1820 the cost of sending a letter from Headingley to Leeds was 3d, and to York – 1 shilling.

During the ten year period from 1821 to 1831 the population of Headingley-cum-Burley nearly doubled from 2154 to 3849 and with a growing number of residents there were demands on spiritual as well as temporal life. The small chapel at Headingley could not accommodate the large number of parishioners now living at Kirkstall and Burley. The church authorities and Lord Cardigan were petitioned. A site was found near the Kirkstall Lane/Morris Lane junction and a new church was built. St Stephens Church was consecrated in September 1829, in the new Parish of Kirkstall. Within twenty years nonconformist Methodist and Baptist churches would also be established in Headingley, and a few years later a small Wesleyan Mission chapel at Headingley Moor.

William Beckett Acquires New Grange

Whilst St Stephens was under construction in 1828, Jane Benyon died and her grieving husband Thomas chose to leave New Grange. During the same year the last of the male line of Wades, Thompson Wade (Benjamin's younger brother), also died, and the decision was taken not to relet, but to sell the property.

New Grange was offered for sale in 1829 by a London auctioneer who recorded the "prospect" in these terms:

> 'A panorama is presented which must be seen to be duly appreciated, there is so much of hill and dale, and such a delightful regularity in the Park, such variety and beauty in the distant prospect, while the intermediate space is occupied by quiet rural villages in the valley, appearing in all their unpretending simplicity and character. On the verge of the Park walls is the new church (St Stephens) which appears as an essential appendage, while the hanging woods and venerable Abbey of Kirkstall rise in majestic grandeur, and complete a landscape of inconceivable beauty and interest.
>
> The Earl of Cardigan's fine woods (Hawksworth Woods) appear almost identified with this property and the River Aire which silently pursues its irregular and circuitous courses in the valley below to heighten the scene in the vicinity of the Abbey.
>
> The mansion is erected in stone and partakes of the time and style of Inigo Jones. The approach is by a stone colonnade and portico. In front of the best chamber is a stone gallery overlooking the Park.
>
> In the occupation of Thomas Benyon Esq. With a domain of 450 acres'.

The estate realised £37,000 at auction, according to Colin Treen's researches, but the transaction was not completed. However, by now William Beckett, the forty six year old son of Sir John Beckett had his eye on the property and a new deal was soon negotiated. The house was modernised, new entrance lodges and a gardener's house built. The name was changed from New Grange to Kirkstall Grange, and when William married Frances Adeline Ingram coheiress of Temple Newsam in 1841, he was truly well established.

William Beckett's fortune was made through the family's bank, Beckett's Bank in Leeds. In 1772 John Beckett, William's father, himself the son of a wealthy Barnsley merchant, settled in Leeds and joined the Old Bank, established in Briggate some twenty years earlier. He quickly won the respect of the town and rose to senior partner at the Bank, Mayor of Leeds (in 1775) and Chief Magistrate of the Borough. His influence became so great that a contemporary said of him towards the turn of the 18th century, *'John Beckett governs the country, inasmuch as he governs Leeds, Leeds Governs Yorkshire and Yorkshire governs Pitt'*.[4] In 1813, he was created a Baronet in recognition of his services to the commercial community of Leeds.

Sir John Beckett, Bart., lived very handsomely at Gledhow Hall and raised eleven children. Two of his sons followed their father into active management

The Otley Road gates and Lodge to Kirkstall Grange c1903. *Courtesy: Peter Snodgrass.*

of the firm of Beckett and Company, as the Bank was known from the 1840s – Christopher Beckett of Meanwood Hall, and his younger brother William of Kirkstall Grange. They also became local landed gentry in their own right, and from this time Kirkstall Grange, formerly New Grange, would be forever associated with the Beckett family. Today, the 20th century inter-war housing estate developed on part of the 450 acres, the municipal parkland, and Leeds Metropolitan University's north Leeds campus (which includes the mansion house) are all known simply as Beckett's Park.[5]

The 6th Earl of Cardigan and The Inclosure Act of 1829

We will be returning to the very Victorian William Beckett and his successors a little later, but for now we remain in King William IV's England, and in particular with the 6th Lord Cardigan who had a steady desire to capitalise on the increasing development value of his Headingley estate. In the 1820s a new pocket of exclusive villa homes was taking shape at Headingley Hill, overlooking the Aire Valley. Wealthy Leeds merchants were especially attracted. In 1832 a cholera epidemic in Leeds would confirm the good sense of moving to the unpolluted out-of-townships, if money and opportunity allowed.

As we have seen, up to this time the area north of Headingley remained sparsely populated with only a small community living on Headingley Moor Side enjoying rights 'in common' – principally grazing livestock, cutting turf and sometimes wood. On a map of 1822 the Headingley Moor 'Common' lies between present day Hollin Lane to the north and what was to become Mill Lane, before being renamed Grove Lane, to the south. Monk Bridge Lane is shown as a track crossing the Moor and descending as it does today in order to cross the Meanwood Beck at Monk Bridge[6].

By the late 1820s there existed some thirty encroachment cottages mostly around the Moor 'road' and the Addle lane junction including Smiths Cottages, Sowdens Yard, part of Ellis Terrace, part of Mansfield Terrace and Park Terrace. Encroachments onto common land were generally tolerated to encourage good use of the land which might otherwise become wasted, overgrown and waterlogged. Nationally the general stringency produced by the long wars with Napoleonic France had made it necessary to improve land under cultivation to feed a rapidly growing population.

On the same grounds, large estate owners could petition Parliament for consent to enclose and sell common land. Lord Cardigan now sought the support of the local gentry and in 1829 Royal Assent was given to an Act of Parliament *'inclosing Lands in the Manor and Township of Headingley-cum-Burley'* and appointing Jonathan Taylor of Leeds as land surveyor for *'surveying, planning, valuing, dividing, allotting, inclosing and otherwise improving all the commons and waste grounds in the said manor and township'*.

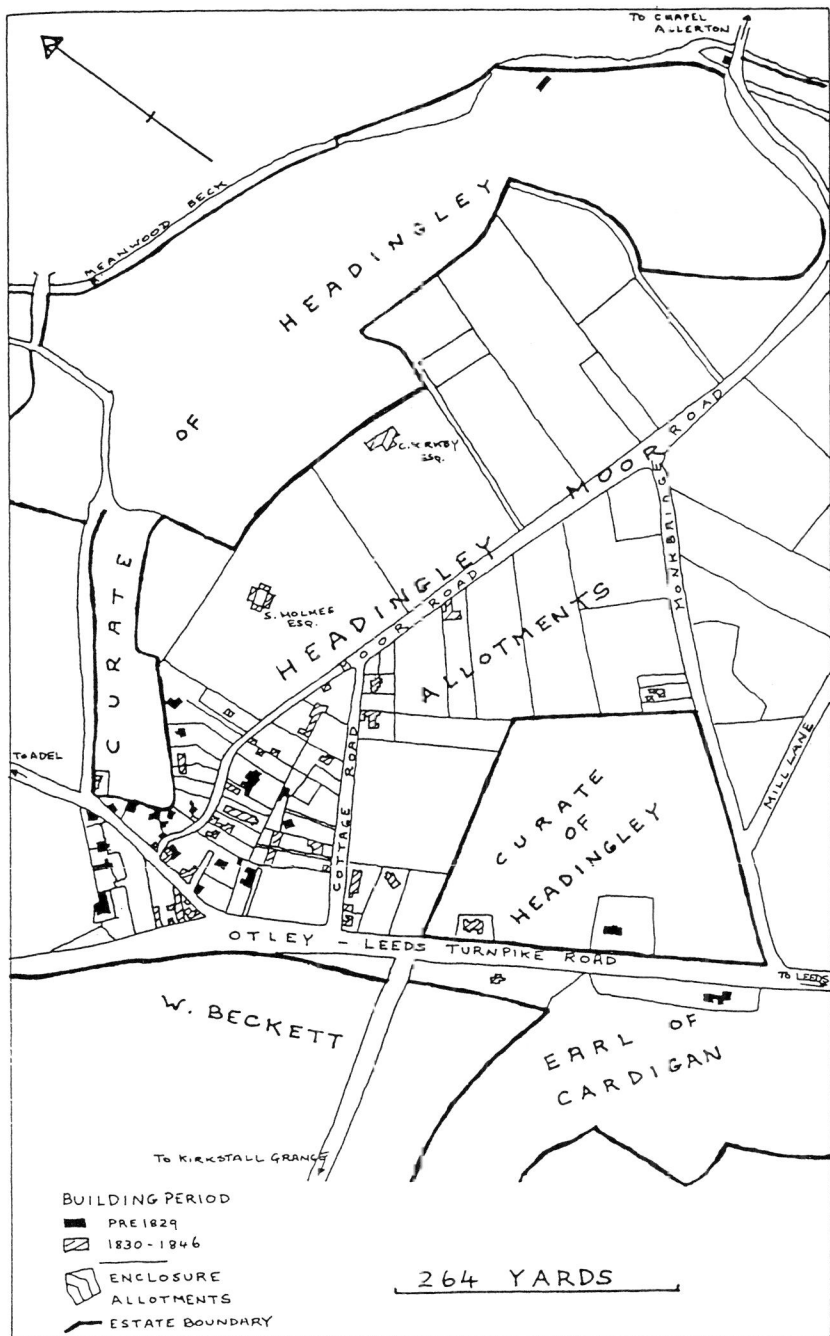

The development of Headingley Moor 1829-1846.
   Colin Treen: Building and Estate Development in the Northern Out-Townships of Leeds.

The Birth of Far Headingley as a Recognisable Village

During the course of the next five years, one hundred and thirty acres were partitioned. Part came directly to the Rt Hon Robert, Earl of Cardigan & Lord of the Manor, 'in lieu of his rights'; part was given to the perpetual curacy of Headingley in lieu of certain glebelands; part was given in compensation to owners of *'ancient messuages'* with rights in common; and part was sold immediately *'to defray expenses'*. This latter part, near the Addle lane, was because the *'concentration of encroachment cottages made it unsuitable for villa development'*.

Two new roads on the old common were now formally created:

> 'The Moor Road, of the width of 30 feet commencing at or about the Centre of the Addle Road (Weetwood Lane) and extending from thence in an eastwardly direction over Headingley Moor to and into Monk Bridge Road; and …
>
> The Cottage Road, of the width of 30 feet commencing at the south east corner of a Garden now or late in the occupation of Mr Farrar or his Undertenants and leading from thence in a north eastwardly direction over part of Headingley Moor and into Moor Road.'

Cardigan Cottage, an early small holder's house on Headingley Moor, built around the time of the enclosure award. St Chad's Parade now stands on part of the site. The 1930s tram depot extension filled the rest of St Chad's Road (north side) and was itself cleared in 1993 for new sheltered housing constructed in 2000. *Courtesy: Ian Ballantine.*

Land was offered for house building at half the price paid at Headingley Hill, acknowledging that it was just that bit farther out of town along a poorly maintained stone and earth road. Notwithstanding, individual property deals were struck, building plots staked out, locally quarried stone brought to site and a recognisable village was rapidly created.

The nucleus of Headingley Moor Village existed from way back, as we have seen. However it was the formal release of land for house building and the creation of the two new roads (The Moor Road and The Cottage Road) which attracted a mini boom in property speculation and an influx of new residents.

Many houses were built at this time, around and within the Headingley Lane (Otley Road), Moor Road and Cottage Road triangle. Some were for investment – William Oddy the local cowkeeper turned shopkeeper owned fourteen cottages, Mr Joseph Longbottom, warehouseman, owned seven and William Scott the local butcher owned a further four. Some were for owner occupation on the grand scale – Mr Samuel Holmes of Park Lane, a wealthy linen merchant, assembled several plots on Moor Road and built Castle Grove between 1831 and 1834. Then there were houses with carriage space and stable to suit the pockets of aspiring gentlemen – Roughstones, and Moor Cottage on Cottage Road, Moorville on Moor Road, and for those with more modest pretensions who kept their horse but hired their carriage – Mazebrook and Wheatlands on Cottage Road.[7]

To serve the community, Mr John Askey, blacksmith and victualler, established his business at The Three Horse Shoes Inn and Mr Wood began a regular horsedrawn omnibus service of five journeys a day between Mr Askey's inn and Upper Headrow in the centre of Leeds.

The name, however, remained unchanged. Until 1868, the new hamlet was simply known as Headingley Moor.

Notes

[1] Marshall of Leeds, Flax-spinners 1788-1886 W G Rimmer *Cambridge University Press* 1960.
[2] When the Egyptian styled mill opened in June 1840, two thousand six hundred workers were entertained to a Temperance Tea.
[3] It was not until 1838 that another stage coach proprietor, John Wood, introduced regular omnibus services between Leeds and The Three Horse Shoes at Headingley Moor.
[4] Quoted from 'Westminster Bank in Leeds', a Westminster Bank publication 1966.
[5] Readers may wish to follow the Beckett line by referring to the Family Tree on page 204.
[6] Map of the Town of Leeds and the Countryside Circumjacent, by Joshua Thorp.
[7] Roughstones is now 50 Cottage Road. Moor Cottage is 46 Cottage Road with a datestone over the carriage block doors '1835'. Mazebrook and Wheatlands are directly opposite. To the latter list one could add 17 Cottage Road, once known as Rose Cottage.

The Victorian Years: Aspects of Public Health, Transport, Education, Law and Order.

The 1829 Inclosure Act was bound to precipitate rapid development during the 1830s, but two factors in particular, helped to consolidate demand – the availability of clean water, and the arrival of comparatively cheap public transport. The latter combined with the construction of the new Leeds to Otley Turnpike.

Public Health

In 1832, a cholera epidemic had spread through Leeds taking over seven hundred lives before coming under control. Drinking untreated water pumped from the polluted River Aire was now a major health risk to town dwellers. Headingley Parish donated alms to relieve the suffering, its own small population being unaffected. Clean underground water supplies became a major selling point for those relocating out of town. The 'beauties of Headingley and its neighbourhood, and the salubrity of the air' were already 'too well known to require any observation'[1]. It also had good local underground water supplies.

Within two years of the epidemic, plans had been made to dam Eccup Beck south of the Harewood Estate and pipe fresh water through Weetwood and Headingley to a new storage reservoir at Woodhouse. Before it reached Woodhouse, Leeds' new water supply was to be filter cleaned, and in 1837 the Leeds Waterworks Company began construction of seventeen filter beds to the north of Headingley Moor (325ft above sea level). The scheme, which included building the Seven Arches aqueduct at Adel, was largely completed by 1843, and in 1844 one landlord of a house to let at Headingley Moor was advertising that 'the Leeds Waterworks main runs near the buildings and water may easily be obtained', notwithstanding that the house already had 'a pump with excellent water upon the sink'[2].

The Leeds Waterworks Company was taken over by Leeds Corporation in 1852. In 1860, drainage and sewer pipes were laid, and four years later the Corporation spent £25,000 enlarging the fresh water conduits and associated pipework between Eccup and Weetwood filterbeds, and onto Woodhouse Reservoir[3]. The pipes had been originally constructed to carry only 1,200,000 gallons per day. By 1864 the daily consumption was 4,300,000 gallons.

In 1860 sewer drains were being laid and in 1896 the Leeds Improvement Act allowed the Corporation to levy a main sewer rate on householders[4].

The New Turnpike Road

In the 1830s, the road out to Headingley from Leeds, was still a quiet rural lane which tracked across Woodhouse Moor, and wound its way up Headingley

Hill, following field boundaries. Through traffic to Otley and beyond took the old turnpike road through Burley to Spen Lane continuing on what is now the Otley Old Road. The Turnpike had several steep gradients particularly descending off The Chevin into Wharfedale, and was itself unsuitable for 'modern' commercial traffic. Road engineers now began looking at an alternative route which would put the Otley Turnpike onto the ancient lane through Headingley.

On June 8th 1837, an Act of Parliament was passed creating a new Turnpike Trust with responsibilities for 'repairing, maintaining, and improving the Line of the Road from Leeds to Otley in the West Riding of the County of York.'

In particular, the Act granted the Trustees powers to develop a new road through the Lawns Wood just north of Weetwood Hall to Bramhope and on to Otley 'in lieu of the old Road' affording 'a more convenient and commodious Communication between the Town of Leeds and the Towns of Otley, Ilkley, Addingham and Skipton, by avoiding a very steep Hill, more than a mile in length, called the Chiven *(Otley Chevin)*, in the Township of Otley, which now forms Part of the present Turnpike Road, and would be of public Utility.'

The road between Lawnswood and Bramhope was completed in 1840 and opened up Headingley as the principal arterial route out of Leeds to Otley. The 'new' turnpike was laid with consolidated stone, but such was the flow of traffic that within five years it had become 'a soft, muddy and indeed exceedingly dangerous road'.

Litigation was commenced against the Trustees for abandoning the road 'from end to end' and leaving it 'to the mercy of the traffic and the weather, both being very severe'.

In 1845, the Trustees retained the services of Richard Bayldon, a road surveyor, who demonstrated the viability of the Turnpike by analysing toll gate returns at the Woodhouse, Headingley and Otley bars. He estimated the annual value of the Tolls at £2,838.

> 'This Account does not include all the Traffic now passing on the Road – for instance, much of the night Traffic (being a large amount) we have not been able to obtain.' *Furthermore*, 'in consequence of the Road being in an exceedingly bad and dangerous state of repair, a portion of the Traffic usually passing on it has left, and gone on other Roads. This being one of the winter months, there are very few (if any) parties going from Leeds to the Zoological Gardens *(at Burley)*, or making excursions of pleasure to Ilkley or other places. As summer advances and the Road improves, it will undoubtedly be found, that considerably more Traffic will be brought on to it, whilst there is no reason to suppose that any portion of the present Traffic will desert it'.
>
> Extracts from Richard Blaydon's letter to the Trustees of the Leeds and Otley Turnpike Road. Jan 21 1845

This latter remark may be regarded as somewhat surprising since work started on the Leeds to Thirsk Railway in 1845, routed through Headingley and intended to take traffic formerly carried by 'coaches, gigs and stage wagons'.

Notwithstanding, the Trustees appointed Mr Bayldon as manager of the Leeds to Otley Turnpike Road and the change he brought about was generously noted by Mr H J Hare of Bramhope Hall, in a letter dated July 13th 1850,

> 'Sir, When in 1845 you undertook the management of the Leeds and Otley Road, the Trust was, as you are aware, in a state fast approaching insolvency, and the Road itself may without exaggeration be said to have been the worst in the Riding. There are now few better'.

On a map of Leeds surveyed by Captain Tucker in 1847, the Leeds and Otley Trust's road is shown crossing Woodhouse Moor, passing the approach to the Leeds Zoological and Botanical Gardens (opened in 1840), and continuing up Headingley Lane where the landscape remains rural in spite of the imposing Headingley Hill villa development. North of Headingley, the road passes the parsonage with its associated glebe land on the south side of the old common; the gates to Mr Beckett's Kirkstall Grange; and the growing hamlet of Headingley Moor where there are now two schools, two large villas (Castle Grove and Moor House), Mr Askey's Inn (The Three Horse Shoes) and several houses in well defined garden plots between Moor Road and Cottage Road. Then, continuing up Reservoir Hill passed Weetwood Hall, the turnpike follows the new road alignment to Bramhope and Otley.

On January 1st 1867 Leeds Town Council agreed to take over the interests of the Leeds and Otley Turnpike Trust within the Leeds Borough District and at midnight on January 31st 'all tolls ceased to be levied'. Toll-gates, toll-houses and bars, 'within the said borough on the said road' were removed and, according to the local press, the 'obnoxious impost' was terminated[5].

This put the road maintenance firmly in the control of the Town Council and reduced the cost of travel. Beyond the Borough limits, tolls were still collected until November 1st 1873 when the three remaining toll-bars on the road to Otley were finally abolished.

On this extract from the Ordnance Survey, surveyed by Captain Tucker in 1847 and contoured in 1851, the "new" Leeds and Otley Trust turnpike is clearly marked as is the conduit pipe of the Leeds Water Works which runs from Eccup to Weetwood reservoir and onto a pumping station at Headingley. A horse trough is shown near the gates to Kirkstall Grange and the farmhouse (Ivy House Farm) that would become St Chad's vicarage is also shown. The village of Headingley Moor is already well formed with Castle Grove and Moor House occupying the prime sites overlooking Meanwood Side. A well is shown on the west side of Otley Road near the Three Horse Shoes. Alpha Cottage is an amalgam of two small cottages.

Reproduced from the 1851 Ordnance Survey

Omnibuses and Trams

After William Avison's failed attempt to run regular omnibuses into Leeds from the borough outskirts in 1818, twenty years elapsed before a new service was introduced which effectively gave birth to the modern Leeds bus network. In June 1838 John Wood of Headingley Moor[6] began plying a conveyance for twelve passengers (eight seated inside) drawn by three horses and operating between The Upper Headrow in Leeds and Mr Askey's inn at Headingley Moor. Mr Askey was both victualler and blacksmith. Appropriately, he named his inn The Three Horse Shoes, a traditional pub name but made doubly apt by being the terminus of Mr Wood's three horse omnibus[7].

The creation of a new turnpike through Headingley and a fast growing local population, assured Mr Wood's early success. Only one month after beginning his Headingley Moor service, he was being supported in court for forcibly throwing a difficult customer off his bus, by 'a great number of gentlemen from Headingley and the neighbourhood, who are in the habit of using the omnibus'[8]. The shamed customer, Mr C.S. Jackson, was a merchant who had objected to the seat he considered his own, being occupied by someone else. The case established the first rule of bus travel – first come, first served.

By the end of the following year John Wood had competition, possibly due to a split with business partners. From 1840 John and William Atkinson's omnibus service also operated between Headingley and Leeds, although originating its journey from Spen Lane rather than Headingley Moor. Colin Treen notes that 'Wood's omnibus had the advantage of a superior standard of hostelry halts and a cheaper fare of 6d between Leeds and Headingley Moor, whereas the Atkinsons' bus was cheaper over shorter distances with a fare of 4d for each of two stages, Leeds to Woodhouse and Woodhouse to Headingley'[9]. John Wood eventually bowed to the competition. He was declared bankrupt in 1845 and his place was taken by William Morritt 'whose bus left The Wheatsheaf as before'[10].

As patronage increased, so extra daily services were added making the three mile journey into Leeds convenient and comparatively comodious. By the early 1860s, there were twelve journeys daily from Leeds to The Three Horse Shoes. This new public mobility, of course, made Far Headingley increasingly more accessible. It was another encouragement towards suburban life. Demand for housing rose, speculators began to build to greater densities, and the Leeds business gentry looked farther out of town for new villa sites.

After the abolition of road tolls in 1867 local services were stepped up again and competition became more fierce as major public transport operators moved in. In 1871, William and Daniel Busby of The Liverpool Road and Railway Omnibus Company, successfully applied to Leeds Corporation for a licence to build and run the town's first tramway system. Metal rail tramways were laid and horse drawn tramcars ran for the first time in September of that year. The

A three horse drawn tram standing outside Far Headingley depot about 1880. St Chad's vicarage is in the background.
Courtesy: The Leeds Transport Historical Society.

A double-decker horse car outside Far Headingley Depot about 1899.
Courtesy: The Leeds Transport Historical Society.

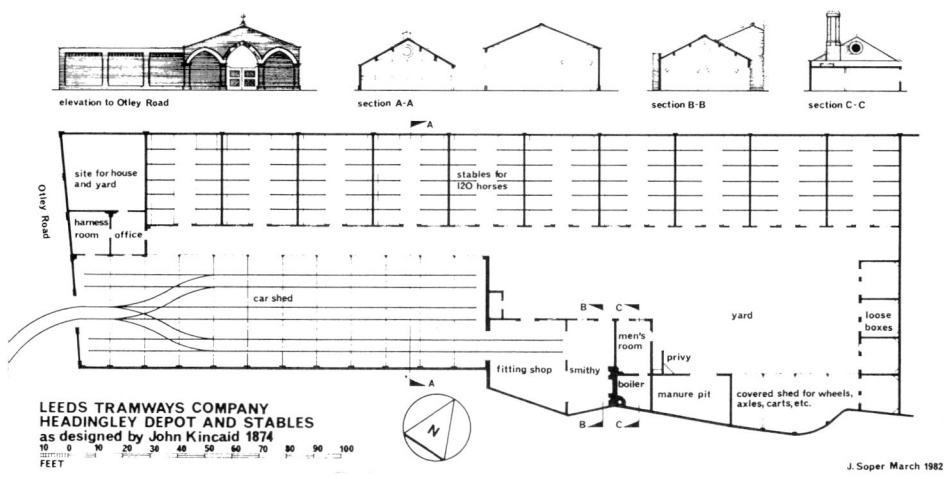

A plan of Far Headingley tram depot and stables as designed by John Kincaid 1874 (redrawn here by J Soper in 1982).   *Courtesy: The Leeds Transport Historical Society.*

The Depot Staff at Far Headingley Depot about 1899
Courtesy: The Leeds Transport Historical Society

first route was from Boar Lane Leeds, to The Shire Oak Inn at Headingley. The Otley Road route would ultimately become route 1 when route numbering was established in the 1920s – and has remained so to this day[11]. Tramcars were to put conventional omnibuses pretty much out of business on competing routes. Over steel rails, one horse could pull three to five times the load carried on normal road surfaces of the day, due to the lower rolling resistance of steel wheels on steel rails. Commuting to Leeds became cheaper.

In 1872, the Busby's transferred their business into the Leeds Tramways Company. The following year the tram rails were extended to Far Headingley and a plot of land acquired from the Cardigan Estate[12] just opposite the gates to St Chad's Church, for tramcar sheds and one hundred and twenty four horse stables. A tram and later bus depot would stand on this site for the next one hundred and twenty years.

Horse-power began to give way to mechanical traction when steam driven trams came into service alongside horsedrawn trams on the Otley Road route in January 1883. The depot at Far Headingley was enlarged and tram workers' cottages built on the adjoining site fronting Weetwood Lane.

The steam engine literally replaced the three horse team, being a steam powered pulling car onto which the passenger tramcar was hitched. The Yorkshire Post reported on an early preliminary trial test run between Hunslet and Kirkstall in October 1877:

> 'It is about half the size of the ordinary cars (ie the horsedrawn cars), and in the engine of it is a vertical boiler, with funnel passing through the roof. The wheels and brakes are shielded by sheet iron to within about four inches of the ground. The upper half of the engine-car except of course the top, is glass, so that the driver can see in any direction. Having been attached to one of the ordinary cars a start was made, the passengers being the Hackney Carriages Committee. They were driven (from the Hunslet depot) at about the ordinary speed and reached the bottom of Briggate in little over a quarter of an hour'.

The population of Far Headingley at around this time was 1402[13]. It had risen from 150 over fifty years and would reach 2500 by the turn of the century. Kelly's directory of 1881 refers to St Chad's church and the Wesleyan Mission in Moor Road (with '150 sittings'). It also mentions trams running to and from Boar Lane every ten minutes on weekdays and every fifteen minutes on Sundays. 'The terminus at Far Headingley includes a depot with a foreman's house'. Fifteen years earlier coaches and omnibuses had been every half hour according to White's Directory of 1866.

During the 1880s, however, rapid advances were being made in the development of electric traction. In October 1891 electric trams, powered from overhead wires, came into service in Leeds:

> 'The cars are attractive, well lighted and ventilated, free from advertisements and complete even to the smallest details. At night they are brilliantly lighted, so that

A steam tram, engine and trailer, about 1890. St Chad's Church gates and vicarage can be seen in the background.
Courtesy: The Leeds Transport Historical Society.

An electric tramcar on the Otley Road between Weetwood Lane and Shaw Lane in the 1920s. Passing Holly Dene and the tree screened villas of Burton Crescent.
Courtesy: Leeds Transport Historical Society.

reading is easy. In fact they run so smoothly and are so comfortable that one is often sorry to be so soon at journey's end, a feeling not ordinarily exited by a tramcar ride. They start punctually, easily average 8 m.p.h. up hill, including stoppages, and rarely or never lose time. If one misses a Headingley car in Park Row, the chances are one may walk to the (Woodhouse) Moor before being overtaken. But if you miss an electric car and walk, the next speedily glides after you and overtakes you. The driver stands on a low platform in front where he can clearly see everything. His foot is on a warning bell and his hands on the controlling gear'.

Leeds Mercury 15th February 1894

Leeds Tramway Company was taken over by the City Corporation in 1894 and horse drawn trams were finally phased out of service at the beginning of the new century (1901). Electric trams had become the standard mode of public transport in Leeds and would remain so until 1959.

The Leeds to Thirsk Railway

Another symbol of progress was the coming of the railway age. The establishment of new railway corridors would help to determine the next phase of suburban growth, in the booming Victorian towns of northern England. Leeds was no exception. In 1845, land was bought from Lord Cardigan enabling a new railway to be built, which avoided William Beckett's Kirkstall Grange estate – William no doubt bringing some influence to bear on his brother Christopher, a director of the Leeds to Thirsk Railway Company. After completion of the massive engineering challenge of Bramhope Tunnel, 'Headingley & Kirkstall' Station was opened in 1849, on a site close to St Stephen's church at Kirkstall. Keeping west of Kirkstall Grange, the railway remained some way from Headingley. A mile long footpath, across the open fields of Mr Beckett's Grange Farm between Headingley Moor and St Stephen's Church, now became the most direct route for those on foot to the station. It is a mark of William Beckett's financial security, that he showed little interest in selling land for house or rail road building himself, no doubt satisfied to let the bank lend the money for nearby development, while land within his own estate rose in value.

The railway took a considerable amount of commercial traffic off the road, although as we have seen, the 'new' Otley Turnpike had been greatly improved under the management of the enterprising road surveyor, Mr Bayldon.

Nonetheless, the coming of the railways marked the end of an era in Britain's development. The end of 'stage coaches, more or less swift riding horses, pack horses, highwaymen, Druids and Ancient Britons', was the impression left on William Makepeace Thackeray[14].

Hollin Lane School and the old Glebe School

Returning pre-railway age, to the late 1830s, we can easily imagine a well established, and growing, community at Headingley Moor. In 1839 a small parish school was erected in Hollin Lane by the curate of Headingley, the Rev William Williamson, on land given by the Oates family of Meanwoodside. A church orphanage school was built the following year in 1840 on a six hundred square yard plot of glebe land close to the parsonage nearly opposite the gates to Kirkstall Grange. The latter was known as the Glebe School and little is known about this establishment except that it was combined with an early lending library and an orphanage for girls. The 1861 census records ten orphan girls living there at the time, all between eight, nine and ten years old. It closed as a school in 1869, the newly created Parish of Far Headingley not wanting (or able) to take over two school buildings nor, at that time, an orphanage. It was finally sold in 1874 when much of the glebelands were disposed of for further housebuilding and the laying out of Burton Crescent. Proceeds from the sale of the Glebe School went towards the building of a new parochial church hall

Hollin Lane school as originally built – one large room with mistress' house attached. Artist unknown. A larger classroom was added in 1872 seen in the photograph (page 51). This view is of the south elevation and is now largely hidden by Glebe Terrace (1877). The Glebe School may have been a similar building.

> Delightful task! to rear the tender thought,
>   To teach the young idea how to shoot,
> To pour the fresh instruction o'er the mind,
>   To breathe th'enlivening spirit, and to fix
> The generous purpose in the glowing breast".

An anthem to teachers if ever there was one.

Hollin Lane school 1920s - by this time a working mens club. Subsequently converted into two shops. *Courtesy: Colin Stewart Hairdressing for Men.*

in Bennett Road to designs by George Corson, and a new house Fairfield was built on the old school foundations.

Little is known about the early development of the school at Hollin Lane. The buildings have survived, but not the teaching records prior to 1869 when it was transferred into the care of Dr Smyth and the church-wardens of St Chads. In the early years the building was shared by Methodists for mutual improvement classes for young men, and a local Methodist leader, Tommy Waite, held a weekly class in the school.

At the time of the transfer in 1869, Hollin Lane school had an enrolment of eighty nine children with an average attendance of sixty nine. There was one teacher and the children were taught the three Rs, Religious Knowledge and Needlework (for girls).

For more on Hollin Lane school after it became St Chad's Church School see page 72.

Law and Order

The wealthy incoming residents of Headingley and Headingley Moor found themselves vulnerable to hardened criminals as well as opportunist thieves. House burglary and street robbery were the main threats. In 1834 Leeds Mercury noted that 'Headingley, not having the benefit of a nightly watch has attracted the attention of a set of vagabonds'. Groups of residents would employ a private watchman. In 1835 one such watchman, James Brown, discovered two men in the back yard of a Headingley house 'and fired at them a pistol'.

Home Secretary Robert Peel's 1829 Metropolitan Police Act had established the London Metropolitan Police and introduced the British Bobby. It was to be a few years, however, before there were police forces in all the major towns. Leeds Police Force was founded in 1836 with ninety three men when the population was 123,393. By the middle of the century the population had risen to 172,270 and the constabulary numbered one hundred and forty one.

In 1855, fifty men were appointed to a Reserve Leeds Police Force 'who would be liable to be called upon for duty at any time, fill vacancies as they occur, and trained in the use of the cutlass'[15]

The first record of a resident police presence in Far Headingley is in 1857 when a police station was established at 3/5 Cottage Road. It was still there in 1890 under the superintendence of Sergeant William Wright[16]. The Far Headingley police station closed in 1891 when larger constabulary premises opened near the corner of Bennett Road and North Lane.

Notes

[1] From local directories of the time.
[2] *Leeds Mercury* 1844.
[3] The aquaduct at Adel came out of use at this time as it was unable to cope with the increased demand. This well known structure, a major engineering feat in its day was, surprisingly, only in service for a comparatively brief time, about 20 years.
[4] The Town's mains gas pipe network was taken over by Leeds Corporation in 1870. Mains electricity was not available until well into the 20th century.
[5] *Annals of Yorkshire*, John Mayhall.
[6] In the 1841 census Headingley Moor village is referred to as Moor End. Individual addresses are not shown but John Wood is listed as resident, age: 25, occupation: 'stage coach proprietor'. He is living with his wife Hannah, their three children and Katharina Wood, presumably John's mother.
[7] The name The Three Horse Shoes is taken from the blacksmith's custom of keeping horseshoes in sets of three to frustrate the devil who had cloven hooves.
[8] Leeds Intelligence 21.7.1838
[9] *Building and Estate Development in the Northern Out-Townships of Leeds 1781-1914*. Colin Treen University of Leeds 1977.
[10] Source: *Leeds Transport* by J Soper Vol 1
[11] The Otley Road route was No. 5 when route numbering began in 1926. It was renumbered route 1 in October 1929.
[12] Sanctioned by Adeline, the Dowager Countess of Cardigan.
[13] 1881 census
[14] quoted in K Tillotson's '*Novels of the Eighteen-Forties*' (1954) and again by Asa Briggs in '*Victorian Cities*' (1963)
[15] *The Leeds Police Force, 1836-1974*. Edited by Ewart W Clay.
[16] In the 1881 census Police Sergeant William Wright is living at 5 and 3 Cottage Road (Police Station) with his wife, four daughters and one son.

The Victorian Years: The Cardigan Interest

The 7th Earl and last Lord of the Manor

During August in the year Victoria became Queen of England and All Her Dominions, 1837, the 6th Earl of Cardigan died. His son and heir, James Lord Brudenell was in India at the time, having just taken command of the 11th Light Dragoons stationed at Meerut. On hearing the doubtless sad news of his landed father's death and, more to the point, his succession as the 7th Earl we are told that *'his grief was tempered by euphoria. Now he was master of Deene, a mansion in Portman Square, extensive estates in three counties* (including the manor of Headingley), *and would receive an annual income of £40,000. To celebrate, he went tiger shooting with Colonel Arnold of the 16th Lancers'*.[1]

The 7th Earl was to find universal fame fighting in the Crimea, when confused orders from Lord Raglan caused him to lead his brigade into the Russian guns (the 'Valley of Death') at Balaclava in 1854, the immensely heroic but completely suicidal Charge of the Light Brigade.

In 1837, however he could only contemplate becoming a military hero, and whilst commanding his regiment in India, he left estate matters to his land agents. During his absence, further tracts of the Far Headngley estate were sold to help defray the expenses of Lord Cardigan's military life. An auction sale of freehold plots took two days to complete in 1852.

Even after his retirement from the army, Lord Cardigan continued to live life at a pace. He married for a second time and pursued country sports from his Northampton estate at Deene. In 1868, on March 27th he fell from his horse and was killed. His young wife Adeline was to survive him for forty seven years. In 1873 she married the Portuguese Count de Lancastre ending her honeymoon with a visit to her Leeds estates.

The Earl's property was left absolutely to Lady Cardigan, who continued the cycle of land sales. On her death in 1915, the inheritance, now largely bereft of any freehold in Headingley, but including Deene Park and the Northampton estate, passed to the Brudenell family whilst the Cardigan title was merged with that of the Marquis of Aylesbury.

And so ended the Cardigan's landed interest in Leeds and Headingley, although the present Edmund Brudenell of Deene Park remains patron to a number of churches in south Leeds established during the time of his illustrious forebears.

---

[1] The Homicidal Earl by Saul David, *Little Brown & Co* 1997.

The Victorian Years:
A Rapidly Changing Landscape, the Establishment of a New Parish and more on the Becketts

The Developing Landscape

Between the 1830s, and the middle of the 19th century, the separate communities of Headingley and Headingley Moor became sub-urban in character. Land was more valuable for building than farming, and the rapid expansion of Leeds as a major manufacturing town fuelled demand for housing in the clean air of the outlying townships.

Asa Briggs notes in *Victorian Cities* that according to one G. Dodd there 'were said to be over a hundred woollen mills employing nearly ten thousand people in Leeds, in 1838'. John Marshall's Temple Mill opened in 1840, and eleven years later, was 'still one of the wonders of the age' accounting on its own for over two thousand five hundred workers. In 1841 there were thirty firms spinning flax. Pollution was so stifling that it is not surprising, Charles Dickens described the town as 'beastly and nasty' when he visited in 1847 to address the Mechanic's Institute.

The opening lines of William Osburn's 1857 poem about Leeds are worth quoting here:

> 'The AIRE below is doubly dyed and dammed;
> The AIR above, with lurid smoke is crammed.

And at the end of the working week ...

> The joyful Sabbath comes! that blessed day,
> When all seem happy, and when all seem gay!
> Then toil has ceased, and then rich and poor
> Fly off to Harrogate, or Woodhouse Moor.
> The one his villa and a carriage keeps;
> His squalid brother in a garret sleeps'.

Beyond Woodhouse Moor, to the north and west, lay the comparatively idyllic acres of Headingley with Burley – the former described in White's 1853 Directory as *'a pleasant and handsome village'*, and the latter as *'a neat rural hamlet of scattered houses and villas.'* There is no specific reference to the Headingley Moor community, although the township *'includes the large and well built village of Kirkstall, which has a good bridge over the Aire and is celebrated for the magnificent ruins of its Abbey and its ancient Forge. Between Headingley and Burley are the Leeds Botanical Gardens, now belonging to H.C. Marshall Esq and leased to Mr Clapham.'*

Piecemeal land sales for building inevitably became irresistible. We have already noted the emergence of a new monied class in Leeds and the attraction of

Headingley to build a villa 'and a carriage keep' – William Beckett, banker, at Kirkstall Grange; Henry Cowper Marshall, industrialist, at Headingley House (before moving to Weetwood Hall); Samuel Holmes, merchant, at Castle Grove; and, in 1847, John Hope Shaw, solicitor, at Shaw House, Monk Bridge Lane (later renamed Shaw Lane).

In 1852, during a two day sale at the Oak Inn, Headingley, a series of freehold plots were auctioned off by Lord Cardigan's agent, including his remaining entitlement of enclosed common land at Headingley Moor. Two new roads were planned to give access to the building plots – Claremont Road and Grove Road.

By now, the landscape around Headingley and Headingley Moor Village was fast changing to one of 'market garden land surrounded by building ground on which country villas or other good dwellings were in the course of being erected'[1]. The neighbourhood itself became home to stone masons, carpenters and other building tradesmen[2]. They were attracted to local work and the opportunity to speculate on their own account. Ann Husler, wife of the owner of the largest stone quarry in the area is recorded as owning eight desirable houses at Victoria Terrace on Headingley Moor producing between £20 and £25 income by the end of the 1850s[3].

Victoria Terrace 1971. A row of elegant houses, belonging to Ann Hustler in the 1850s facing south over formal gardens.
Photo: FHVS collection.

The diversity of housing increased, as did the diversity of property speculators. In the 1860s William Smith, a Leeds solicitor invested in eleven new houses at Torquay Terrace, and in 1868 James Wood, a builder in partnership with a local merchant, designed and built the first eight houses of Woodbine Terrace. Wood added a further five houses in 1875 and the final double fronted house ten years later. On an adjoining plot he built Oakwood House, for his own occupation in 1886[4]. Other aspiring owner-occupiers who could not afford to develop property single handed, banded together to form Building Clubs and Co-operatives. Nonetheless, most of the housing in Headingley-cum-Burley, including detached villas and respectable terraces, were let out on lease.

Inevitably, as the local population and building intensity increased, the more discerning, began to move further out of town – to Weetwood and Adel.

William Beckett and the Queen's Visit to Leeds

Surely, the most spectacular event in Leeds during the whole of the 19th century was the opening of the Town Hall in 1858. Leeds Town Hall was the most fabulous municipal public building of its time in England, and a hugely impressive symbol of civic pride and confidence.

The idea for a new public hall originated in 1850, as a memorial to Sir Robert Peel. The spur, however, to making the Leeds hall second to none, was undoubtedly the rivalry with Bradford where plans for another great building, St George's Hall, were already well advanced. Cuthbert Brodrick a Hull born rising star was only twenty nine when he won the Leeds design competition. Prior to this he had

Mr Cuthbert Brodrick, Architect 1822-1905. *From Two "Leeds Architects" by T B Wilson.* As a young man he won the design competition for Leeds Town Hall and lodged at Far Headingley during its construction.

Courtesy: Leeds City Library

been employed locally by Bradford architects Messrs Lockwood and Mawson, designers of Saltaire village and St George's Hall. Rather gallingly for them, Lockwood and Mawson came second to their own pupil in the Leeds competition.

John Hope Shaw of Headingley Moor, then Lord Mayor of Leeds, laid the foundation stone of the new hall in August 1853 and Cuthbert Brodrick, himself, moved to lodgings at Headingley Moor during the course of the building's construction.

The official opening was to be a very great occasion in the presence of Queen Victoria and Albert, the Prince Consort.

> 'The comments made at the time in the local press suggest that a mood of quite unreal romance was being cultivated in Leeds for this royal occasion. Again the Town Hall was the symbol of it, in much the same way that the Crystal Palace had been the symbol of romance for the nation in 1851'.
>
> Asa Briggs *Victorian Cities* Oldhams Press 1963

On the day, the Queen was to greet a gathering of over thirty two thousand Sunday School children at Woodhouse Moor before moving 'in gay procession' down Woodhouse Lane and through the centre of town.

One can imagine the preparations beforehand, the street decorations, the organisation of crowd control, the vying for tickets to the Town Hall, and the manoeuvring for preference within the civic reception party itself.

Where the Queen might stay was obviously an issue, and it seems that William Beckett, partner of Beckett & Co., the Old Leeds Bank, gentleman, and MP for Ripon, had high hopes of offering Kirkstall Grange as a suitable residence. For around this time he undertook a number of house alterations and refinements. The Beckett coat of arms was placed high up on the front elevation within the broken pediment of the roof gable. A series of deep bay windows was added to the south and east sides, all topped with stone balustrading, and a new stone porch was built with corinthian pillars flanking the outer doors below a ceremonial balcony. In addition, the accommodation was enlarged with a single storey extension to the west.

In the grounds on the west side of the house, a long walk was formed to a point overlooking Kirkstall Hill where a classical archway was erected commemorating the Queen's visit to Leeds.

> 'Nobody really knows the story behind the erection of this arch, but there are many theories. One is that when Queen Victoria came to the inauguration of the Town Hall she was to have had her first view of Leeds from it. Another theory suggests that an arch had been erected at the time of her visit somewhere in Leeds, and that Victoria passed through it on her way to the Town Hall, and that after the visit the arch may have been dismantled and rebuilt on the Beckett's Park site. The first theory has the strongest claim because the Beckett's were presented to the Queen at the inauguration ceremony and William Beckett commissioned the arch. It is not impossible, therefore, that William Beckett intended inviting the Queen to visit his

Kirkstall Grange. Bays and ballustrades and other embellishments date from about 1858.
From a drawing by Michael Smith.

estate and built the arch in the hope that she would. Unfortunately, all the evidence suggests that she never went.

The archway stands on a stone base, the front having four stone columns with volute capitals like those at the doorway of the Grange. The masonry above the entablature is formed of ornamental and lettered tiles which are in a perfect state of preservation. The inscription reads: To commemorate the visit of Queen Victoria for the inauguration of the Town Hall at Leeds. 7 September 1858'.

Extract taken from an undated newspaper cutting.

The woods west of the house became known as the Queenswood, and when a road was eventually built below the Queenswood, linking Kirkstall Lane with Spen Lane for new housing in the 1950s it took the name Queenswood Drive.

William was no doubt disappointed. He had gone to a lot a trouble and Kirkstall Grange was, after all, a very fine property where the Royal party would have enjoyed every comfort. According to the 1861 census, there was a household staff of six – housekeeper, housemaid, laundry maid, dressmaker and two gardeners. Somewhat less than the 'more than dozen' servants employed by John Marshall nearly sixty years earlier, but then by 1861 a great many labour saving devices had been introduced. And the house, of course, must have been particularly impressive given its magnificent parkland setting surrounded by four tenanted farms.

William Beckett may not have played host to Queen Victoria – that honour went to the incumbent Lord Mayor, Peter Fairbairn, of Woodsley House in Clarendon Road – however he did entertain in the grand style other national figures. John Mayhall's Annals of Yorkshire record that in October 1860, Lord Palmerston paid a visit to various parts of the West Riding and 'met with quite an ovation'. On the 24th 'his lordship arrived in Leeds and became the guest of Mr William Beckett at Kirkstall Grange. His official engagements concluded on the 29th at Ledsham where he was entertained to dinner by his tenantry of the village of Fairburn'.

A man of property and Member of Parliament, William Beckett had residences in Leeds, London and Brighton. He died at Brighton, after a short illness, on Monday the 26th of January 1863. He was seventy eight. His body was taken to his London home and laid in state in a room on the ground floor, which was hung with black cloth, emblazoned with the Beckett arms. The funeral service was conducted at Kensal Green Cemetery where his leaden oak coffin was placed in the catacombs below the chapel, but only temporarily, for according to his *Yorkshire Post* obituary, 'it is intended that his final resting place shall be in a new Church at Headingley'[5].

The Beckett Patronage and Foundation of St Chad's Church

This intriguing reference to a new church "at Headingley", taken from William Beckett's obituary, gives rise to the question of just who was the true patron of St Chad's Church. William Beckett's body was never removed to Headingley, although in his will he directed his trustees 'to apply at their discretion £1,000 per annum for ten years in promoting the extension of Divine worship according to the rites of the Established Church, and the endowment of the ministers'. Soon after William's death, if not before, a site was selected within the grounds of Kirkstall Grange and work began on the construction of a new church which was to cost £5,000 with a further £5,000 set aside for the endowment of the ministers – the total amount covered by the will. Yet inside St Chad's a brass plaque acknowledges Edmund Denison (William's brother)[6] as the patron who 'defrayed the cost and endowed the living'. There is no mention of William, himself.

The Beckett family were great church benefactors. They patronised Leeds Parish Church over many years and did much to establish new churches in Leeds as well as local church schools. In 1849, William's sisters Mary and Elizabeth of Meanwood Park founded and endowed Meanwood Church in memory of their brother Christopher Beckett. Christopher, a bachelor, lived with his sisters at Meanwood Hall until his death in 1847. He was an elder brother to William and his working associate at the Bank in Leeds. 'His splendid physique – tall commanding figure, and dignified bearing – was but emblematic of the qualities of his mind'[7]. He left an estate valued at £1,000,000 which passed to the next

Portrait of William Beckett (oil on canvas by Sir Francis Grant 1803-78)
Courtesy: Leeds Museums and Galleries (City Art Gallery) U.K.

elder brother, the 3rd baronet, Sir Thomas Beckett, Bart., of Somerby Park, Gainsborough. During his lifetime Christopher had been patron of Meanwood School (est 1840), and instrumental 'in securing for the district (of Meanwood) spiritual superintendence'. He also intended to erect a church 'had his life been spared'. In the event, it was left to Thomas and the two sisters to fulfil Christopher's intentions by conveying the land and providing the endowment. The church was built to designs of William Railton, renowned as the architect of Nelson's Column.

On the face of it, a similar set of circumstances seems to have surrounded the establishment of St Chad's Church. When William died, his wife Frances, was to have 'the enjoyment for life' of Kirkstall Grange. However, there is no record of her in the story of St Chad's. With William gone she probably had no desire to maintain a large home in Leeds, preferring instead the pleasanter climes and perhaps more fashionable society of the south of England. This would also account for William's tomb remaining at Kensal Green. She did donate a painted glass memorial window to the North Transept of St Stephen's Church, Kirkstall, in William's memory, shortly after his death, and in 1868 a monument sixteen feet high, was erected in Leeds Parish Church to commemorate William's charitable works, placed there by Mrs Beckett 'who bore the expense'.

Curiously there is no memorial to William in St Chad's Church, although it seems inconceivable that the new church at Kirkstall Grange was not to be the beneficiary of his will nor his intended final resting place. St Matthias, Burley was founded in 1853 and St Michael's, Headingley had been rebuilt in 1837 (and would be reconstructed again in 1886). William and Frances married in 1841 and, as part of the town's commercial elite, worshipped at Leeds Parish Church. He would, however, have anticipated (and planned for) a new church at Headingley Moor[8].

An unreliable pamphlet on the history of St Chad's printed in the 1950s tells us that 'in 1864 a small deputation of residents, said to be Messrs Ramsden, Sutcliffe and Jacob Bateson, approached Sir Edmund Beckett-Denison, to request land for the site of a Church, with a view to forming a new parish'.

If such a meeting took place, surely it was much earlier than 1864 and with William Beckett. Early consultations would have been necessary after William's death, very likely between the residents' committee and William's nephew, William Beckett Denison, an executor of the will (thereby trustee of the church endowment) and newly resident of Meanwood Hall. Sir Thomas, now eighty five and resident at Gainsborough, would have been required to sanction the conveyance. Mrs Beckett does not appear to have been involved at all. However, there was another family member taking an interest at this time, William Beckett Denison's elder brother, Edmund. This may indeed be the Edmund referred to above, not their father Edmund Denison, who did not succeed to the Baronetcy (and the title Sir) until Thomas' death in 1872.

> In Affectionate Remembrance of
> William Beckett, Esq
> Late Banker in Leeds
> Who Represented Leeds in Parliament for Many Years.
>
> He was born in the Year of Grace 1784. Fifth son of Sir John Beckett Bart., by Mary daughter of Dr Christopher Wilson, Bishop of Bristol. He married Frances Adeline, third daughter of Hugo Maynell Esq., and the Hon Elizabeth Ingram, daughter and coheiress of Viscount Irwin of Temple Newsam.
>
> He died on the 26th of January 1863 aged 78 without leaving issue. His remains are consigned to the cemetery in Kensal Green.
>
> Eminently distinguished by his unceasing readiness to promote all plans of benevolence and general utility: he also took an active part in all that concerned the welfare of Leeds.
>
> The founder of several schools, he sought to advance and extend the education of the people on Christian principles. A faithful but tolerant member of the Church of England. He gave to that Church on all occasions his substantial support, largely contributing to the repairs and construction of its sacred edifices.
>
> In business he was liberal, judicious and public-spirited. At a period of great local pressure, he merged his own interests and saved the credit of the town.
>
> In Parliament, he was amongst the foremost in supporting and carrying the measure for the shortening of the working hours for women and children.
>
> Though William Beckett has left a far nobler monument of himself in the hearts of all those who knew him, this humble record of so excellent a man, may serve to preserve his memory, when they and their children shall have followed him to the grave. It will thus fulfill the pious intention of his sorrowing widow, and extend the usefulness of
> his example to future generations.

Frances Beckett's dedication to her husband inscribed on William's memorial at Leeds Parish Church

Edmund Beckett Denison QC, the 1st Baron Grimthorpe

By any account, Edmund Beckett Denison QC was a extraordinary man, a parliamentary and ecclesiastic lawyer, amateur architect, ardent churchman and proficient clock designer. He designed the most famous clock in the land – and arguably in the world – the tower clock at Westminster Palace (chiming since 1859 on Big Ben) as well as clocks for Leeds Town Hall and Lincoln Cathedral. In 1858 he was nominally the architect of St James' Church, Doncaster, assisted by Sir George Gilbert Scott and he would later gain notoriety for the controversial restoration of St Alban's Cathedral 'according to his own ideas'. In the 1860s, Edmund Denison QC enthusiastically threw himself into the new church project on the Kirkstall Grange estate.

Quoting again from the 1950s pamphlet:

> 'Three sites for the church were discussed and the committee was told to call again in a fortnight, which they did, and the present site was chosen with its fine position off the Otley Road but very accessible, and just across the Park through a little spinney, to the Patron's residence'[9].

The services were retained of local architect William Henry Crossland, a former pupil of Sir George Gilbert Scott. Crossland drew the plans for the new church 'from designs suggested by Mr E B Denison' and superintended the work. White's directory for 1866 notes that 'a beautiful new church is now in the course of erection in the Park, formerly the residence of W. Beckett Esq. It is in the Early Decorated style, and is the gift of E B Denison Esq'. Whether Edmund's involvement was a help or a hindrance to Mr Crossland, we are not told. We do know however, that the building cost rose from an estimated £5,000 to £10,000 and the younger Edmund stood the balance. In the church today, a brass plate states that the church 'was designed by Edmund Beckett Denison Esq QC'. Mr Crossland's contribution is not acknowledged.

In Derek Linstrum's view, St Chad's 'has sometimes been considered' the work of Edmund Beckett Denison, but 'the architect was probably W H Crossland'. The Directory of Yorkshire Architects is even more direct, acknowledging Edmund's connection with St Chad's but crediting W H Crossland as 'largely responsible'. Edmund Beckett Denison was called to the Bar in 1841 'and delighted to take part in ecclesiastical controversies'. From that interest developed his passion for church architecture 'and the arrogant belief in his own omniscience'[10].

The endowment to support the incumbent minister was held in preference shares of The Great Northern Railway Company. The 1868 deed, still held by the church, declares that 'The Governors of the Bounty of Queen Anne for the augmentation of the maintenance of the Poor Clergy do accept from Edmund Denison of Doncaster a transfer of £15% irredeemable stock of and in The Great Northern Railway Company and to hold same upon trust to pay the dividend income to the incumbent for the time being of St Chad's Headingley'[11].

The Dedication of St Chad's Church

On the wintry morning of Saturday January 11th 1868, a procession left the Glebe School on the main road, where Dr Smyth, the new vicar had temporary lodgings. It made its way through deep snow to the new building led by the Bishop of Ripon who knocked on the main door with his pastoral staff and requested entrance to the church for the service of consecration. Inside the Bishop preached a sermon and celebrated holy communion. Then the congregation moved outside for the consecration of the burial ground 'a ceremony perfomed at no small amount of personal discomfort, the ground being covered some inches deep in snow which fell heavily at the time.'[12]

St Chad's Church 1868. 14th century French gothic revivalist architecture in the early decorated style. *(from St Chad's Centenary booklet.)*

Lunch was then served in the Glebe School, with the proceedings chaired by Mr Edmund Beckett Denison QC. In his speech to those gathered, including the press, Edmund oultined the 'history and origin' of St Chad's:

'Mr Denison said it had been at one time proposed by his father and another member of his family, to erect and endow a church at a cost of £5,000 each, but in consequence of some difference of opinion as to the patronage, they almost abandoned the scheme. At that juncture the father came forward and was determined to defray the whole cost, viz, £10,000, being £5,000 for the edifice and £5,000 for the endowment; knowing, however, that a suitable church could not be erected in those times for the sum proposed, he, the chairman, resolved to grant whatever additional money was required for the building. The church cost £10,000 to build'.

This is most interesting. It appears there was a rift between William and his brother Edmund. Was it a fallout over money, or the choice of architect? Was Edmund Snr pushing his son forward against William's wishes, and was he pressed to do so by his 'omniscient' son? We shall never know the true situation, but it is curious that William Beckett is not even mentioned at the dedication lunch; Frances Beckett did not attend as far as we know, (even though in the same year she presented Leeds Parish Church with a 16ft high monument in memory of her husband); it seems Edmund Snr – the accredited patron – was not at the ceremony either (although admittedly the eighty two year old may have been advised not to brave the weather nor the journey from Doncaster); and perhaps most telling of all - when the cost rose above the estimated sum, it was left to Edmund Beckett Denison QC to foot the bill. And why is all this not commented upon in the press? Could it have been a little embarrassing for the *Yorkshire Post's* new Chairman, the younger Edmund's brother, William Beckett Denison of Meanwood Hall?

Nonetheless it does seem that St Chad's owes its foundation to the one man who remains unrecognised in its history, namely William Beckett of Kirkstall Grange.

The church was dedicated in the name of St Chad. In his speech at the Glebe School lunch, Edmund (QC) explained:

'St Chad was a Yorkshireman and was the second Bishop of York 644-669, afterwards Bishop of Lichfield 669-672, and in looking for a Saint whom Dr. Atlay, the Vicar of Leeds, had not already under his care, he would bring St. Chad into the Diocese of Ripon where he hoped he would long remain. Hence the reason for the dedication to St. Chad'.

Five months later, The London Gazette contained a notification of the assignment of a separate parish to the church of St Chad, Far Headingley, under the title of consolidated chapelry, as taken from the new parish of Meanwood and the parochial chapelry of Headingley respectively.

Lord Grimthorpe 1889 by Spy (*Vanity Fair*)

The Becketts and Further Church Patronage

When the new church was dedicated on January 11th 1868, the ceremonial procession moved from the Glebe School to the church building. Dr Smyth, the first incumbent at St Chad's lodged at the school initially but arrangements were soon in hand to provide him with a vicarage. The Headingley parsonage at Holly Dene, next to the Glebe School, was still home to the Vicar of Headingley – even though now within the Far Headingley Parish boundary – a situation remedied later by the building of a new Headingley vicarage in Shire Oak Road.

Standing by the entrance to the avenue leading to the new church was the old stone farmhouse belonging to Ivy House Farm, part of the Beckett estate. It was conveyed to the Parish Church Council and became St Chad's Vicarage. Dr Smyth moved in and six subsequent vicars followed during the course of the next ninety six years before it was replaced by a new parish hall, the Parish Centre, in the 1960s.

There was no desire to maintain two church schools and the Glebe School was allowed to close. The little school at Hollin Lane, however, transferred to the new Parish and plans were soon put in hand to enlarge the building by adding a new schoolroom, the cost being 'mainly defrayed' by the Beckett family.

St Chad's Vicarage demolished in 1964.   *St Chad's Centenary Brochure*

In 1872 Edmund (QC) was again in Leeds supervising the installation of a new clock he had designed for St Chad's churchtower. It was set going on November 27th 1872 and was the only time-keeper in Leeds with the full Westminster chimes — appropriate enough from the designer of the clock which chimes on Big Ben. The clock at St Chad's has an external diameter of six and a half feet.

During the same year, 1872, Sir Thomas Beckett died, aged ninety four. Edmund Beckett Denison Snr, himself eighty six years old, became the third brother to succeed their father's title, but only briefly. He died eighteen months later in 1874 and the line of succession, including title to the Kirkstall Grange estate, passed to Edmund (QC), now Sir Edmund Beckett Denison QC and who in 1886 would be decorated by the Crown in his own right as the first Baron Grimthorpe[13]. Edmund himself lived until 1905, his ninetieth year, and left a huge personal fortune valued then at two million pounds.

Beckett family connections after William

William's estate, like his brother Christopher's, was substantial. It was valued at £700,000 and again, like Christopher's, devolved upon Sir Thomas, for although J Sprittles notes that William and Frances had a daughter, William's biographer in *Memoirs of Eminent Men* records that Frances survived her husband 'without children.' One reason for Frances' apparent withdrawal from Kirkstall Grange may have been to allow another branch of the family to take up residence, possibly her husband's nephew, William Beckett Denison, the youngest son of William's elder brother Edmund. On the demise of Christopher Beckett in 1847, young William had been 'summoned' from Trinity College, Cambridge, to join his Uncle at the Bank. He might have considered a career in Railways, for his father was Chairman of The Great Northern Railway at Doncaster, but William's future lay in the family Bank. During his uncle's retirement years, the nephew took over the reigns of management and when Elizabeth Beckett (of Meanwood) died in 1864, he moved his family into Meanwood Hall — not Kirkstall Grange.

The occupancy of the Grange after William's demise is not clear. We know that his nephew's eldest son, Ernest, was in residence by the 1880s. Before that, the property was probably offered on lease. In 1871 a stained glass window was placed in the south aisle of St Chad's Church to the memory of 'the late lamented John Metcalfe Smith Esq., of Kirkstall Grange, whose remains are resting within a few hundred yards of it.'

At the Bank, William Beckett Denison was a highly successful and demanding manager. In 1866, shortly after taking over executive control from his late Uncle William, he arranged a merger with the old established banking firm of Cooke & Co., of Doncaster and a few years later, the East Riding bank, Bower Hall and Co., was also taken over by Becketts. He was described as a 'stern but benevolent dictator'. An entry in his personal staff register, dated May 3rd 1875 is revealing in character. It appears that a certain clerk at the Bank ...

> "... *refused to give up an incipient moustache.* (William) *Had reminded him some days before that it was against the rules to wear a moustache and he must remove them* (sic). *Observing that he had not done it, spoke to him again, when he argued about it, and finally had to tell him that he must make his own decision between this and tomorrow whether he cut off his moustache or left the Bank'.*[14]

The Clerk in question at first chose the latter alternative, but when he was refused a quarter's salary in lieu of notice he *'offered to cut his moustache and stay on'*. *'Which I agreed to allow'* is William's final comment.[14]

Edmund Beckett Denison (QC) played no active part in the affairs of the Bank, although a replica of the Big Ben clock was to stand in the Manager's room at the Park Row premises, in later years, as a reminder of the family connection.

William had three sons Ernest, Gervase and Rupert. All three had illustrious careers at the Bank, with Rupert, the youngest, becoming the first Chairman of the Westminster Bank after the merger with the London and Westminster Bank in 1921. The merger was probably precipitated by the elder brother's (Ernest's) death in 1917.

Ernest Beckett

Ernest (William) Beckett was born in 1856 at Roundhay and in 1864 his father moved the family to Meanwood Hall. As a young man he entered the family firm and became part of the Leeds business elite. He was also MP for Whitby. In 1883 he married an American, Lucy Tracy Lee from New York, and settled at Kirkstall Grange. He travelled the world extensively and after Lucy's tragic death in childbirth, he made two particularly intrepid voyages. In 1891 he visited South America and 'went up the great rivers of the interior'. He also travelled to China and Japan and rode along the North-west frontier of India in 1895. In *Contemporary Biographies* his

Ernest Beckett   (*Contemporary Biographies*)

addresses are given as Kirkstall Grange, Leeds; Wood Lee, Virginia Water; and 17 Stratton Street, Piccadilly. He was clearly affluent and influential. Like his Uncle, he was also fond of entertaining celebrated guests at Kirkstall Grange ...

> Mr Ernest Beckett, now Lord Grimthorpe, a lover of all superiorities, who has known the ablest men of the time, takes pleasure in telling a story which shows Oscar Wilde's influence over men who were anything but literary in their tastes. Mr Beckett had a party of Yorkshire squires, chiefly fox-hunters and lovers of an outdoor life, at Kirkstall Grange, when he heard that Oscar Wilde was in the nieghbouring town of Leeds. Immediately he asked him to lunch at the Grange, chuckling to himself beforehand at the sensational novelty of the experiment. Next day 'Mr Oscar Wilde' was announced and as he came into the room the sportsmen forthwith began hiding themselves behind newspapers or moving together in groups in order to avoid seeing or being introduced to the notorious writer. Oscar shook hands with his host as if he had noticed nothing, and began to talk.
>
> 'In five minutes,' Grimthorpe declares, 'all the papers were put down and everyone had gathered round him to listen and laugh.'
>
> At the end of the meal one Yorkshireman after another begged the host to follow the lunch with a dinner and invite them to meet the wonder again. When the party had broken up in the small hours they all went away delighted with Oscar, vowing that no man ever talked more brilliantly. Grimthorpe cannot remember a single word Oscar said: It was all delightful,' he declares, 'a play of genial humour over every topic that came up, like sunshine dancing on waves.'[15]
>
> From *Oscar Wilde* by Frank Harris, 1916

Ernest did not succeed to the title Lord Grimthorpe until 1905. This story from Frank Harris is undated but almost certainly goes back to the 1880s, possibly during Oscar Wilde's 1883 lecture tour of the English provinces. His repertoire on this tour consisted of three talks: The House Beautiful, The Value of Art in Modern Life, and Personal Impressions of America. Two years earlier Wilde had toured America lecturing on the Aesthetic movement for Richard D'Oyly Carte, as a herald to Gilbert & Sullivan's latest 'aesthetic' opera, *Patience*.

Sir Arthur Sullivan probably visited Kirkstall Grange, himself, in 1895 when his friend the Prince of Wales (the future King Edward VII) and entourage were Ernest Beckett's house guests whilst attending the Leeds Music Festival. Sir Arthur was the triennial Festival's musical director and conductor.

Triumph and Tragedy

Ernest was undoubtedly a genial host to the rich and famous. He was also part of the social network surrounding the Court of St James. When the Prince of Wales came to Kirkstall Grange it must have been like Hollywood coming to Far Headingley. But tragedy, as well as triumph marked Ernest's life. By the time of the Prince's visit, two blows had fallen upon Ernest Beckett in successive years, leaving him in grief and shock. The first occurred in December 1890 when his father, William, was violently killed in a bizarre and horrific accident:

AWFUL DEATH OF MR BECKETT MP

CUT TO PIECES ON THE RAILWAY

'The Press Association's Wimborne correspondent, telegraphs that a gentleman, supposed to be Mr W Beckett MP has been killed on the London and South-Western Railway at Wimborne.

Yesterday he arrived at Wimborne by the 2pm train from London, and went out of the station. Shortly afterwards he was seen in the drive which leads to Canford Manor, the residence of Lord Wimborne.

The drive passes under the railway, and between there and the station is an iron girder bridge spanning the river Stour. The gentleman appears to have turned from the drive and

GOT ON THE LINE

to walk back to the station.

He was observed on the bridge by a signalman just as the 3.50 train from Bournemouth came up. The engine passed him, but the wind which was blowing strongly at the time, increased by the rush of the train, seems to have drawn him under the third carriage.

He was carried for about 20 yards and

CUT TO PIECES

The remains were carried to the Railway Hotel, where the police inspected them. The deceased was dressed in a brown waterproof coat *(which seems to have got caught by the train)* and a dark undercoat, on the collar of which was the name 'W. Beckett Esq., MP'.

The Yorkshire Post

Ernest, abroad in Algiers at the time, now became heir presumptive to his uncle's title. He was thirty four and well established at Kirkstall Grange with Lucy and their two daughters Lucille and Mabel. Whilst grieving for his father, Ernest was at least able to look forward to a happy family event. Lucy was pregnant. The second tragedy, however, was looming.

On Sunday May 3rd 1891, their only son Ralph was born. At first all seemed well and there were general celebrations at the Grange and within the wider community. But, within a few days there was concern for the mother's condition. She became weaker and weaker. On the Wednesday 'a change for the worse took place, and she gradually sank' passing away 'peacefully' on Saturday afternoon (May 9th). Lucy Beckett, the young mistress of Kirkstall Grange, was buried at Adel Church 'amidst every sign of grief and sympathy on the part of the large assembly present'[16]. She was twenty seven years old.

In his sermon on Sunday 10th, Rev Hoyle the Vicar of St Chad's remarked that 'less than a week ago the joy-bells were rung in honour of the birth of her first son; and today the muffled peal that calls us to Church announces that she has passed away'[16].

Ernest was devastated, for as Vicar Hoyle noted in his funeral oration to Lucy 'two sorrows – the heaviest that can befall a man – have fallen upon her husband within half a year.'[16]

Lucy Beckett and the Founding of the St Chad's Home for Waifs and Strays

American socialite, Lucy Tracy Lee had married Ernest Beckett in 1883 and during her time of comparative luxury at Kirkstall Grange she dedicated herself to the local interests of a national charity, The Church of England Society for the Providing of Homes for Waifs and Strays, founded in London in 1881. Over thirty childrens' homes opened during the 1880s and in 1889 Lucy was present for the opening of the Society's twenty ninth home at Glebe House in Hollin Lane near the little church school. Glebe House accommodated about thirty girls who were employed machine-knitting stockings and doing laundry-work in order to produce an income for the home. The vicar was chaplain to the house which was known as St Chad's Home for Waifs and Strays. Lucy was very much involved and paid towards the upkeep of a parish nurse. Glebe House soon proved too small and plans were already well advanced for a new and larger children's home when Lucy died.

In her memory, Ernest donated £3,000 towards the new building which opened in Hollin Road three years later. Only months before Lucy had been pleased to learn that her father-in-law had left £10,000 to be distributed to various charities including the appeal fund for St Chad's Home for Waifs and Strays, which Lucy herself had so ably championed.

St Chad's Home for Waifs and Strays, Hollin Road, opened by Ernest Beckett in 1894. The Beckett Coat of Arms is featured in a stone panel above the main entrance.   *Courtesy: Ian Ballantine.*

On November 6th 1893 there was a foundation laying ceremony to mark the start of building works on a site in Hollin Road opposite the tram stables. Each of Lucy's children, including two-year-old Ralph (no doubt assisted by his father Ernest), laid a stone carved with their initials in the presence of various dignitaries, the architect Mr W A Hobson, matron, and the girls of Glebe House. Building work continued for over a year, and on December 1st 1894 Hollin Hall was officially opened.

> 'A large procession was formed after a service at the church, which walked down to the home ... Everyone crowded round the front of the new building to watch the opening and dedication of the new home by the Bishop of Richmond. He led the ceremony to the front door. There Lucille Beckett, eldest daughter of Mr Ernest Beckett MP stepped forward with a brand new key and opened the front door'.
>
> St Chad's Parish Magazine 1893

Above the front door, a stone tablet, carved with the Beckett family crest, signified the contribution made by Ernest Beckett and his late wife Lucy, in whose name the building was dedicated.

The new building accommodated sixty girls plus the workrooms. Outside was a playground with slides, swings and a pond. In 1896 a laundry was added, and in addition to making stockings and socks for sale, the girls did the laundry for most of the large houses in the area. They also attended St Chad's School which had itself just been relocated to its new premises in Otley Road.

St Chad's School

In 1869 the little school at Hollin Lane transferred into the care of Dr Smyth and the Churchwardens of St Chads. The Beckett family continued in their local patronage (notwithstanding the gap in the family's occupation of Kirkstall Grange) and in 1870, a 'handsome room, thirty two feet by eighteen', added to the little Hollin Lane school house, was opened at Easter, the cost having been 'mainly defrayed by contributions from E Denison, the patron of the living, and E B Denison, and Sir Thomas Beckett the owner of Kirkstall Grange'[17].

The enrolment numbers of the little church school are interesting in that it is another indicator of a growing community. By 1872, one hundred pupils were enrolled, although the 'average attendance' was sixty. Within twenty years the attendance figures more than doubled, first under the Schoolmistress Miss Burton, and then under the first appointed Headmaster, Mr Sugden. By the late 1880s, it was clear much larger premises would be required. A piece from St Chad's Magazine gives a brief portrait of the progress from a simple schoolroom to 'a very handsome and commodious' new building:

> 'The old school in Hollin Lane was erected in 1839, and consisted then of one large room with mistress' house attached. In 1872, just after the formation of the Parish, the large class-room next to Weetwood Lane, was added; and in 1883 the mistress' house was converted into upper and lower classrooms, the porch at the back of the

building was added, the two large rooms were wainscotted, and other minor improvements were made. So matters remained until a few years ago, when the conclusion was forced upon the then Vicar and Managers that the school accommodation was both insufficient and unsatisfactory. Two schemes were set forward: the one for enlarging the old Schools, the other for building a new one; and happily the bolder scheme was adopted. Lord Grimthorpe generously gave the site, on the Otley Road just above the Vicarage; Messrs Perkin and Bulmer, of Leeds, were appointed architects; and the foundation stone was laid by Mr E.W. Beckett MP on November 12th 1891'.

St Chad's Magazine, Dec. 1892

Mr E W Beckett, is Ernest Beckett of Kirkstall Grange, and Lord Grimthorpe is his uncle Sir Edmund Beckett Denison QC, enobled as a hereditary peer in 1886.

In 1895 the Church Magazine reported the sale of the old school buildings to Mr C.G. Oates of Meanwoodside, which is really quite neat, since it was, by all accounts, the Oates family who had donated the land in the first place.

Moor Road Chapel — the Wesleyan Mission

The Methodist connection with the little school at Hollin Lane is interesting. Although the church school records before 1869 are lost, it is known that the building was used by the Methodists for the 'improvement' of young men. Tommy Waite, a shuttle and bobbin maker on the Otley Road and local Methodist leader, took the classes.

The Wesleyan Mission Chapel opened in Moor Road in 1860. *Mike Peace 1974.*

Headingley Methodist Church opened in 1845. In his History of Headingley Methodism, J Stanley Mathers notes that 'by 1851 the population of the area had grown to around six thousand and was still increasing. Indeed in the early days of the new Church there was such pressure on the premises that the Vicar (of Headingley) allowed the use of the Infants School at the top of Hollin Lane. But when St Chad's was opened and the school was needed, the Far Headingley Chapel was built'. This implies a very amicable arrangement and would indicate that the small chapel in Moor Road dates from 1868.

However, the archives of Headingley Methodist Church[18] reveal that in 1858, the schoolroom was being used for preaching. Perhaps these 'improvement' classes were getting too close to the poaching of Anglican souls, for in the following year it appears that Reverend Williamson, the Vicar of Headingley, asked for the use of the school 'to be returned to him'. The Methodist Church Leaders 'refused until another room had been obtained', indicating a formal arrangement of some kind had been entered into with the Vicar. During 1859 a site was found and the decision was taken to build a new room in Far Headingley. The new chapel opened in Moor Road on Sunday March 18th 1860 at 2.30pm. The Minister, Reverend J V B Shrewsbury officiated. It seated 124 people, 'all free – no pew rents'[19]. On the Monday evening there was a Public Tea Meeting followed by a week of services.

Did this event press upon the local Anglicans that Headingley Moor (Far Headingley) needed its own parish church? Certainly by the time of his death in 1863 William Beckett had decided to endow a new Anglican church in the neighbourhood.

Now commercial business premises, the old Moor Road chapel still looks modestly ecclesiastical, with its simple lancet windows and pointed arched doorway.

St Oswald's Anglican Mission Chapel at Highbury

In the 1880s, to meet the demand for low cost housing, streets were laid out on the slopes, south east of Headingley Moor, above Samuel Smith's Highbury Works Meanwood Tannery. They were soon filled with back to back, and through terraced, brick houses for mill workers and the 'labouring' classes. In 1887 the tannery (built 1856) was described as one of the largest in the country and 'the chief support of the inhabitants of Meanwood'.

Rev Smyth, the vicar of St Chad's, had always been 'much disquieted' by 'the scanty attendance of working men at our public worship'[20] and with a growing population of poor and needy parishioners at Highbury he set about establishing a small mission room in the midst of that community.

On July 10th 1889 a plot of land in Highbury Mount was conveyed to the Reverend Thomas Smyth, vicar, George Clemens, drysalter, and John Atkinson, solicitor, for £150. The following year the Ripon Diocesan Calendar recorded:

A RAPIDLY CHANGING LANDSCAPE

St Oswald's Church. Drawn by W J Varker for the Centenary brochure in 1989.
Courtesy: W J Varker

The only known photograph of Highbury Working Men's Club, taken in 1905.
St Oswald's Church, Highbury Centenary Brochure

> 'Far Headingley. St Oswald's Mission Chapel in the new district of Highbury was opened for Divine Service on February 1st 1890. The Mission room will seat 100, and can be screened off from the chancel for the purpose of meetings and lectures. Underneath the chancel are the vestry and heating chamber. The whole is a commodious structure of red brick and has been erected according to the plans of Messrs Smith and Tweedale, architects, at a total cost, including the amount paid for the site, of £745, the whole of which sum has been defrayed'.

Fred Casperson, author of the centenary history of St Oswald's admits that church records do not show who contributed to the building fund, but on this occasion it appears that the Becketts, in particular Ernest Beckett at Kirkstall Grange, were not the principal patrons.

In 1891 Rev Smyth was succeeded at St Chad's by Rev Joshua Hoyle, and in 1896 Vicar Hoyle was succeeded by the Rev Howard Stables. During that time, a sizeable congregation had built up at Highbury. In January 1896, Rev Stables was already writing of 'the pressing need' to enlarge the building:

> 'The Mission Room, which is a very suitable and pretty little building, holds 100 when full. I am sure 200 would often be found in it if there were seats for them'[20].

The following year St Oswald's was extended to the west by two bays and an aisle added to the north side. The total cost was £664, almost as much as the original building. When it re-opened on December 15th 1900 'the Mission was full and, despite the provision of extra seats, a number of people had to be turned away'.

The church also became involved in the building of a Working Mens Club on land adjoining the Mission Room, bought for this purpose by Rev Stables. In his research, Fred Casperson finds Howard Stables curiously secretive about the main benefactor, and concludes it was probably the Vicar himself. In November 1902, Rev Stables wrote:

> 'The Lord Mayor came with the Lady Mayoress on Saturday 27th September to open the Working Men's Club at Highbury. To greet him, Highbury Terrace was profusely decorated with bunting, flags, streamers etc ... my anonomous friend, the donor of the building, was present ...'[20]

The Working Men's Club thrived until after the second world war. In its heyday there were two billiard tables, weekly women's whist drives and domino leagues, but changing patterns of recreation and shifts in the local population caused the membership to decline. It closed in 1956 and was sold for use as temporary school premises – the proceeds being used to buy a curate's house for the parish. The old club building was eventually demolished in 1965 after eleven years of neglect and dilapidation made restoration unviable.

The Mission church itself, although never consecrated as a church, has continued to serve a small but loyal congregation throughout the latter half of the 20th century. Thanks for that are in no small measure due to the dedication of its present churchwarden, Alfred Johnson[21].

Recalling St Chad's in the 1880s

Before closing this particular chapter let me return to the mid 1880s, when the parish church of St Chad was still a teenager. St Oswald's Highbury is not yet built nor is Glebe House children's home. Ernest and Lucy Beckett have not long settled down to married life at Kirkstall Grange. Dr William Spark, organist of Leeds Town Hall and organiser of the triennial Leeds Festival of Music, attends a Sunday Service in the church and later recollects ...

> 'The sweet music of the bells chiming the people to prayer; the bright sunshine and the keen northern air; the happy cawing of the jackdaws about the tower; the procession as I entered the edifice, of the priests and white-robed choir; and the deep, rich, solemn tones of the beautiful organ – each and all made an impression on my mind which will not be easily lost or unremembered'.

Musical Reminiscences Dr W Spark published 1892

Notes

[1] *Leeds Mercury* 10 March 1855.
[2] By the mid 1860s a whole host of occupations were represented in Far Headingley. Kelly's Trade Directory for 1866 lists four farmers, two surgeons, several shopkeepers, a cowkeeper, hat manufacturer, tailor, draper, tanner, brewer, accountant, mariner, artist, shoemaker, merchants, joiner, bleacher, wheelwright, printer, painter, stonemason, stone merchant and plasterer.
[3] Hustler's Row in Meanwood, a terrace of twenty cottages, was built by John Husler in 1847 as another speculation, and probably to provide employment for his quarrymen. Curiously, and no doubt accidentally, over a period of years the name changed to Hustler with a 't'. Arthur Hopwood.
In the 1841 census, we find John Husler, thirty five years old, stone merchant, living at Oates Farm House, Headingley Moor End. Ann Husler, his wife is also thirty five. They have eight children.
[4] Eveleigh Bradford has extensively researched the history of Woodbine Terrace, fourteen elegant family houses for middle income businessmen. The frontages face onto large garden areas, originally designed to be enjoyed by the occupants communally, with shared paths and seating areas. Beyond were the woods and fields of Meanwood Ridge – semi rural views and spacious gardens - it was a welcome retreat from the city grime. James Wood, himself, undertook all the development roles. He was a land speculator, property designer, builder, landlord and on-going owner. Extraordinarily, the whole terrace remained in the family's ownership until the 1970s.
 Woodland Terrace in Stainbeck Lane is also attributed to James Wood who clearly liked to find a name for his properties which combined his own family name. A discreet signature and a subtle reminder of his connection.
[5] The obituary continues, 'to which Mr Beckett has been a very liberal contributor but which has yet to be erected.'
[6] Edmund Beckett took the name Denison (or Beckett-Denison) in 1816. Sir Thomas Denison was a distinguished lawyer, and High Court judge of the King's Bench. When he died, his estates passed to his widow, and then to Dame Denison's great grand-niece, Maria Beverley, of Beverley. Edmund married Maria in 1814, and on succeeding to Sir Thomas' fortune assumed the name Denison by Royal Licence in 1816. This coupling of family names was not uncommon, particularly when great inheritances were involved.
[7] Obituary notice from the *Yorkshire Post*.
[8] New church building had become a sign of Anglican revivalism since the Vicarage Act had gone through Parliament in 1844 'authorising the division of the Parish and Vicarage of Leeds into several parishes and vicarages'.
[9] A clear reference to William Beckett. After William's death the house was let. It was never to be the home of Edmund or his sons. Edmund's grandson Ernest was the next Beckett to take up residence and then not until the 1880s.

[10] From '*Lord Grimthorpe*' by Peter Ferriday, published by John Murray 1957.
[11] Edmund (Beckett) Denison Snr was Chairman of the Great Northern Railway Company for twenty years and established the company's plant works at Doncaster.
[12] *Yorkshire Post* and *St Chad's Centenary Booklet*.
[13] The Manor of Grimthorpe, near Pocklington, in the East Riding of Yorkshire was part of his mother's inheritance from Lady Ann Denison.
[14] from '*The Westminster Bank in Leeds*' 1966.
[15] A wry anecdote about Wilde, who famously wrote of 'English country gentlemen galloping after a fox – the unspeakable in full pursuit of the uneatable.' *A Woman of No Importance* 1893
[16] St Chad's Parish Magazine 1891
[17] Rev R V Taylor, *The Ecclasie Leodienses*, 1875
[18] Minutes of Leaders Meetings, Headingley Methodist Church 1858/59/60
[19] Kelly's directory of 1881 refers to the "Wesleyan Mission" in Moor Road with 150 sittings.
[20] *St Oswald's Church Highbury. The Centenary Book*. Fred Casperson.
[21] More of whom on page 163.

The heart of the old common. A view taken from Cottage Road in 1971.

FHVS collection

The Victorian Years:
Umbrageous Foliage and Rich Gardens.

Victorian Far Headingley, particularly Headingley Moor Village, embraced an extraordinarily diverse community. Some of the wealthiest families in Leeds were residents and some of the poorest – many of the poorest having to be thankful to the richest for their subsistence. Sustaining the large households 'upstairs', required many low-paid hands 'downstairs'. Financial ease and financial hardship were neighbours. It was accepted. But there were also the middle classes taking up residence in lines of smart new terraces. Victorian Far Headingley held an amazingly diverse mix of people and bound a strong community.

In this section, we take a stroll past some notable properties in the area. Kirkstall Grange is not included having been regularly referred to elsewhere in the book.

Castle Grove, Headingley Moor

Samuel Holmes, a Park Lane linen merchant was one of the first and one of the biggest investors in Headingley Moor when land was first released for sale following the 1829 Inclosure Act. Between 1831 and 1834 he built Castle Grove, a pleasant plain fronted gentlemen's residence within a large garden plot. Thirty years later, he was still living there with his much younger second wife, Mary. A gate house had been built at the bottom of the drive and another house, **West Grove**, was now standing on the west field plot, also within his ownership. When Samuel died in 1865, Mary Holmes moved to West Grove and sold Castle Grove to Joseph Conyers, a leather factor.

Richard Vaughan's history of Castle Grove, tells us that the large family of Joseph Conyers 'realistically permits the assumption of the first major (building) extension being made by him'[1]. Both wings of the house were enlarged, substantially increasing the accommodation, the front facade was remodelled by adding two front bay windows plus a portico entrance. A new stable block was erected with space for carriages and extensive greenhouses were built.

Mr and Mrs William Joy briefly followed the Conyers as occupiers in the 1890s and in 1894 Castle Grove was again sold, this time to John Kirk for the sum of £8,000.

John Kirk was a highly respected Leeds businessman and philanthropist. He was Chairman of the family firm, Samuel Kirk & Sons Ltd (Dyers and Finishers), a Trustee of Leeds and Skyrack Savings Bank, and Chairman of the Board of Guardians.

When John Kirk bought Castle Grove he saw the opportunity of transforming an already impressive villa into a small but quite opulent mansion house and appointed local architect, Thomas Butler Wilson, to produce some lavish designs[2].

John Kirk JP 1835-1908.
From "Contemporary Biographies".

The alterations to Castle Grove were complete by 1896 when a series of contemporary photographs and illustrations were published in 'The Architect'. It had been a major rebuilding exercise, leaving little of the original house but the two front rooms on ground and upper floors. Behind these now modest offices there stood a magnificent salon:

'This salon, with the remaining apartments grouped round and opening from it, is the principal and most spacious apartment of the house, and forms the common room of the household, fulfilling the several functions of lounge, writing and reading room, music and ballroom. The apartment rises to a height of twenty eight feet. Its columns are of marble, with their capitals and bases in ormolu. The floor is of oak parquetry, inlaid with broad lines of walnut, whilst richly-figured Italian walnut is used for the whole of the remaining woodwork, the Atlantes to the mantel being gilded. The walls are hung with tapestry. Fibrous plaster forms the ceiling and upper entablature, from which are suspended ormolu lanterns'[3].

The marble columns support an arcaded gallery, approached from the grand staircase, and present day visitors to Castle Grove Masonic Hall easily sense the social statement John Kirk was making to his business connections and the wider community at the time.

Off the salon were other 'apartments' including a new split level billiard room and dining room. Italian and French influences predominated and some Jacobean English oak pannelling, reputed to have originated from Wade Hall, a 16th century house in Wade Lane, can still be seen in the Oak Bedroom having been first installed in neighbouring Moor House.

John Kirk died in 1908 and was buried at St Chad's Church. Inside the church a stained glass window on the south aisle is dedicated to him by his son, Reginald. The adjacent window commemorates Hannah, his wife, who died in August 1899. A plaque in the Clarendon Wing of Leeds General Infirmary records a bed endowed by John Kirk in his wife's memory and in Leeds Art

A view of the salon at Castle Grove in 1896 from a print which appeared in *The Architect* July 10th 1896. *Courtesy: Leeds City Library.*

Castle Grove

1834 for Samuel Holmes

c 1870 for Joseph Conyers

1895 for John Kirk

Castle Grove. From Georgian house to late Victorian mansion.
From *A History of Castle Grove* by E Richard Vaughan 1996.

Gallery hangs Atkinson Grimshaw's painting 'Westminster Embankment' having been donated by 'John Kirk of Castle Grove'.

According to his obituary 'he was a generous giver to persons in want or difficulty; but he never liked publicity in his giving'[4].

The story of Castle Grove in the twentieth century continues on page 185.

Moor Road and Cottage Road corner in 1906. The gates and lodge (gatehouse) to Castle Grove are seen on the right (demolished 1935)   *Courtesy: Ian Ballantine.*

Moor House (demolished)

Another substantial villa, built soon after the enclosure awards, on a large plot of land east of Castle Grove was **Moor House**. According to Colin Treen's researches, Moor House was built for Mr C Kirkby. It stood at the top of the ridge overlooking Meanwood Valley with a long south facing aspect onto formal gardens and an impressive carriage drive down to Moor Road. It was demolished in the early part of the 20th century for building land – the Moor Park estate.

Thanks to Ann Alexander of Moor Park Mount, we have a copy of the 1899 auction particulars and a site plan, but sadly no floor plan or photograph have come to light during the preparation of this book.

In an attempt to fill part of the gap, using the ten year censuses to track some of the occupiers of Moor House, a little more is revealed. In the 1841 and 1851 censuses, individual properties are difficult to identify with certainty so we must move directly to the 1861 census Moor House is not named but there is reference to a Highfield House standing next to Castle Grove. It is the home of

Francis Tetley (of the brewing family)[5], his wife Isabella, and their nine children. Francis and Isabella move to Weetwood in about 1863 after completion of their new villa Fox Hill, and it appears that Highfield House (or Moor House) is then let to tenants.

In 1871 Mary Jackson is at Moor House. She is a young widow, twenty seven years old with five children between the ages of ten (Arthur) and two months (baby Wilfred). In the census record she is described as 'head' of the house. An aunt, Ann Hutton (62) is living with the bereaved family, and William J Brien a Roman Catholic Priest is listed as 'visitor'. Among the household staff there is a nurse, nursemaid, butler, housemaid and cook. We get no more of a glimpse than that.

In 1881, John Pearson is resident. He is a fifty eight year old agricultural chemist living with Eliza, his forty two year old wife, their son Robert (8) and step-son Harry (22). In the house are four domestic servants – governess, cook, housemaid and butler. In the coach house resides Samuel Gaunt, the 'domestic' coachman, his wife Sarah and their three sons – John the domestic groom (19), James a grocer's errand boy (15), and Henry a schoolboy (13). Maria Gaunt (68), an aunt, is also living at the coach house.

Moving on to 1891 we find Frances Tetley and Ellen Tetley, at Moor House. They are the surviving daughters of Joshua Tetley the Leeds brewer. Now aged seventy eight and seventy six years old respectively the sisters are shown as 'living on own means'. The butler has gone and the resident domestic staff are now cook, housemaid, waiting maid and coachman. William Plant (48) is the coachman, living in the coach house with his wife Mary (51), Elizabeth their daughter, a dressmaker (22), and John their son, a twelve year old schoolboy.

On June 15th 1899 Messrs Oliver and Appleton hold an auction and Moor House is sold on behalf of Charles Francis Tetley Esq of Leeds and Thomas Holtby of Driffield. Charles Tetley is the eldest son of Francis and Isabella and inherited his father's property in 1883. In 1902 he became Chairman of the brewery. Frances and Ellen Tetley, already elderly spinster aunts in 1891, left the house during the 1890s and Charles took the decision to sell. It was demolished and plans were set in train to develop the Moor Park estate.

Curiously, the front boundary wall was taken down and reconstructed further back, markedly increasing the width of Moor Road which was clearly intended to become a major thoroughfare between Meanwood and Weetwood. Fortunately the road widening was never completed beyond the Cottage Road junction[6].

This description of the property is taken from the auctioneers particulars of sale:

> 'The RESIDENCE is substantially built of stone, and occupies a choice site in the most attractive residential suburb of Headingley. The grounds are well arranged, and the house is approached by a capital carriage drive from Moor Road, which is well timbered on both sides.

The internal accommodation presents:

On the Ground Floor – a large entrance hall, reception room or vestibule, an excellent drawing-room, dining-room, a library (finely panelled in old carved oak)[7], servants' hall, cooking kitchen, scullery, butler's pantry, store rooms and larder;

On the First Floor – which is approached by a substantial pitch pine staircase, there are 10 bed and dressing-rooms, bath-room, box-room, lavatory and w.c.;

In the Basement – two store cellars, larder, wine cellar and coal cellar;

The Outbuildings include – two stone-built lodges for gardener and coachman, one three-stall stable with hay loft over, two loose boxes, coach-house, saddle-room and carriage washing shed;

A Conservatory and Vinery adjoins the Residence, and in addition to Pleasure Grounds there is an extensive Kitchen Garden, Orchard, a Paddock and a Close of Pasture Land.

All that Messuage called MOOR HOUSE containing in the whole 5 acres, 3 roods, 27 perches, more or less, lately in the occupation of Miss Ellen Tetley.'

The present day footpath from Moor Road to Meanwood Ridge steps marks the old eastern boundary of Moor House. In 1899 it was known as High Close Road and separated Moor House from the adjoining, undeveloped plot, owned by Samuel Smith Esq. The gardener's lodge stood at the Moor Road gates and the coachman's lodge was located inside the grounds at the top of High Close Road on the site of what is now No 2 Moor Park Mount. The latter is no longer distinguishable as the coachman's lodge and may have been fully or partly demolished using salvaged stone to construct two semi-detached houses on the site.

Mr Samuel Smith's Vacant Moor Road Plot and his Patriotic Neighbour, Mr Ramsden of Albert House, Monk Bridge Road

To the east of Moor House was a vacant field which remained undeveloped until construction of the Moor Park estate began in the 1920s. It is shown as belonging to Samuel Smith on the 1899 sale particulars of Moor House. Samuel Smith Snr built Meanwood Tannery in 1857[8] and may well have intended to commission a large villa at Far Headingley for himself and his family. It was not to be.

Samuel's son, also named Samuel, inherited his father's Highbury tannery *and* his uncle's Tadcaster brewery. He worked at the tannery for a short while but in 1886 made the decision to move to Tadcaster in order to run the brewery[9]. The Moor Road site, meanwhile, lay fallow.

Adjoining Mr Smith's plot was land acquired from the Cardigan estate in 1851 by Mr Henry Ramsden who appears to have commissioned the building of **Albert House**. The Prince Consort had masterminded The Great Exhibition in 1851 and unwittingly gave his name to the house which was probably not constructed for another four years according to the researches of John Spencer. It is a classic Jacobean styled stone villa with later billiard room addition, standing behind a raised terrace looking towards Monk Bridge Road across wooded gardens and a circular carriage drive. At the back of the house are the usual outbuildings including the coachhouse and stable now converted to a garage.

Between 1867 and 1894 it was the home of the Rev J E Briggs. He was succeeded as owner by Mr T Hilton who added the billiard room to the west side. Mr and Mrs James Spencer bought the house in 1951 and, at the close of the century, still live there with their son John, a specialist in feudal law.

Moorfield Lodge and Moor Grange

Opposite Moor House stood, and still stand, **Moorfield Lodge** and **Moor Grange**. Both houses were built on land awarded to George Bischoff, a Leeds cloth merchant, and Christopher Beckett under the 1829 Headingley Moor Inclosure Act. The first mention of a dwelling on the site seems to have been in 1840 when Benjamin Smith, to whom George Bischoff sold his land in 1837, died and his trustees put his estate on the market together with a dwelling house 'lately erected on the same allotment by Benjamin Smith'.[10]

In 1867 Moorfield Lodge was inherited, from his wife (née Margaret Turner), by James Walker Oxley, of the banking firm William Williams, Brown and Co. He owned it for about ten years before moving to his newly commissioned house, Spenfield at Weetwood.

University records show that Moor Grange (formerly known as Moor Ham) was owned by William Hall. In 1895 he sold the house to Arthur Mayo-Robson, Professor of Surgery at the Yorkshire College (the forerunner to Leeds University). The Professor died in 1899 and in 1902 both properties came into the possession of the Middleton family (Leeds solicitors). The situation apparently remained unchanged until 1950 when Leeds University acquired the estate from the executors of Mrs Jessie Middleton for £10,000. Under University ownership the properties were combined and named Tetley Hall in recognition of the long-standing association between the Tetley family of Leeds brewers and the University - in particular, Colonel Charles Harold Tetley, University Pro-Chancellor for twenty years from 1926, University benefactor and Chairman of Joshua Tetley & Sons between 1934 and 1953.

New purpose built additions opened in 1962 designed by Dennis Mason Jones, better known as the architect of Bodington Hall.

Burton Crescent

In April 1874, glebe land[11] attached to the former Headingley parsonage, Holly Dene, was sold at auction to Thomas Simpson[12], and Burton Crescent was laid out for villa development. A deed of 1874 states that Thomas Simpson's land was to be divided into building plots facing a new road, constructed fifty seven feet wide, to be called Burton Crescent.

UMBRAGEOUS FOLIAGE AND RICH GARDENS   87

Burton Crescent.   *Courtesy: Ian Ballantine.*

The Simpson family, strong Methodists, had a close friendship with another Methodist family, the Burtons. Thomas' brother William Simpson, himself a Methodist Minister and Missionary had married Mary Burton while out in India in 1857. Is Burton Crescent named in honour of the Burton family and, in particular, Thomas' sister-in-law? It seems highly likely.

There are further Methodist connections with Burton Crescent. In 1878, one of the building plots was purchased for the Headingley Methodist Minister's house ('The Manse' at 9 Burton Crescent). The Minister at the time was the Reverend Alfred H Vine who wrote the hymn 'O breath of God, breathe on us now'[13]. It's a nice twist given that the land had for years been Church of England property.

Two neighbouring houses in Burton Crescent, which also later passed to the University for incorporation into the Tetley Hall campus, are of special interest – **Burton Grange** and Oak Lea (renamed **Burton Lea**). They were built in 1874 to designs by William Hill, a renowned Leeds architect whose practice was responsible for Bolton Town Hall (1865), Yeadon Town Hall (1879) and Portsmouth Town Hall (1884). William Hill was a former assistant to Cuthbert Brodrick and was strongly influenced by him. Bolton Town Hall in particular is a clear tribute to Brodrick's achievement at Leeds. The University acquired Burton Grange in 1952 and Burton Lea in 1955.

Two other interesting houses in Burton Crescent are **Fairfield** (1875) built on the site of the old Glebe School, and **Parkhurst** (1881) constructed just across the road from Fairfield for a Leeds iron founder – ornate ironwork crowns the roof.

In a separate transaction, Thomas Simpson bought the old Glebe School from the Rev Henry Tuckwell, Vicar of Headingley in July 1874 shortly after having acquired the larger neighbouring acreage[14] He may have cleared the old school away altogether but since Fairfield was built on the same site, parts of the school foundation walls are likely to have been incorporated into the new house. The distinctive round headed, stone mullioned windows which may have been a feature of the old school (see illustration on page 50) are also a feature of Fairfield (and incidentally Victoria Terrace which faces Fairfield on the north side), but there the resemblance ends. Although Fairfield stands quite close to the Otley Road it had substantial grounds to the rear, bounded by a long, high stone wall on Burton Crescent. At the far end was the drive to the coachhouse and stables[15].

Thomas Simpson was clearly a major property investor/speculator in Far Headingley. The deeds of the New Inn are revealing in that (for a conveyance of 1893) they indicate more of Simpson's acquisitiveness:

> 'The inn is on land ... bounded on or towards the south by property formerly belonging to Mrs E Livesey but then to Thomas Simpson; on or towards the east by the devisees of James Rider but now of Thomas Simpson; and on or towards the west by the Leeds and Otley Turnpike Road'[16].

Fairfield remained a single residence until it was divided into flats (and the coach house separately sold) in 1939.

Grove Lane – Oakfield Terrace Building Club and Early Building Societies

A further disposal of land belonging to the Headingley Glebe Estate (the Church of England) was made in April 1874. Ten acres south of Monk Bridge Road were sold to speculators for £2,400. Within six months, two and a half acres (of the original ten acres) were acquired by a Leeds estate agent, Benjamin Richardson, for £1,210 – a 100% gain in value. On the same day, Richardson conveyed his interest to the **Oakfield Terrace** Building Club Trustees for £2100 – a further virtual 100% gain. The Church must have been left questioning the original deal.

Not only did Benjamin Richardson net nearly £900 from the transaction but he retained a share in the Building Club. During the preceding months he had brought together a consortium of seventeen individuals, each wanting to

UMBRAGEOUS FOLIAGE AND RICH GARDENS

An early poscard view of Oakfield Terrace, Grove Lane. *Courtesy: Ian Ballantine.*

Grove Lane 1923. At the time of formally laying out and widening the "muddy and deeply rutted" lane. Grove Gardens is the terrace of houses on the left, built at a time when houses would naturally back onto, and not front, the unmade lane. Oakfield Terrace is further down on the left. *Courtesy: Leeds City Library.*

invest in a fashionable house in Headingley. By setting up the Building Club it was possible to finance construction of an eighteen villa terrace without borrowing heavily from a Bank, if at all. It was a form of 'terminating' Building Society. On completion of the building work, each shareholder was free to occupy or sell his house. The Club was then effectively dissolved.

The Building Society movement developed from small co-operative, terminating building clubs like the Oakfield Terrace Building Club to non-terminating building societies offering 'mutual' shareholders a return on their capital through general mortgage lending business. Leeds 'Permanent' Building Society was an early example, its own origins pre-dating the Oakfield Terrace Club.

To make the project succeed well, Benjamin Richardson recognised that he needed the services of a top designer. Very adroitly he drew in the services of nationally renowned Leeds architect, William Hill, by inviting Hill to become a shareholder and, ultimately, a householder. His business partner, T H Watson, also took a share in the Club. On May 23rd 1874, the *Leeds Mercury* carried the following advertisement:

> RICHARDSON and WATSON are forming a Club for the Erection of Terrace Houses, with eight rooms each and large gardens at Headingley, to be called Oakfield Terrace. The position is the best in the district, having a southerly aspect, and within five minutes walk of the tram. For full particulars apply at the offices, 13 Park Row.

William Hill produced designs for a handsome line of high Victorian houses and the remaining shares were quickly snapped up to allow construction to start late in 1874. When finished, Benjamin Richardson moved into the end house adjacent to Meanwood beck (plot 18), his partner took plot 14, and William Hill had plot 2 at the Headingley end.

> 'For the first decades of its life, the terrace stood alone, except for a few larger detached stone houses in the neighbourhood. Along the ends of the front gardens ran a carriage-road with a turning circle by numbers 16, 17 and 18. This road was bounded by a stone wall, which separated it from a muddy, deeply rutted lane curving away under the Ridge towards Meanwood Road. In 1921, **Grove Lane**[17] was laid: the gardens were lengthened and the present stone wall was erected in place of iron railings. The allotments opposite (until the first world war the site of a cricket pitch) disappeared as did the open fields at the back of the houses, but the terrace has contrived to retain something of its original rural character'.
>
> from *Oakfield Terrace 1874 to 1974, A Short History*, by Colin Treen 1975

Hollin Lane

One or two local architects speculated in property development themselves. George Corson, a Far Headingley resident and renowned architect bought land at Headingley in the late 1860s which he laid out as **Shire Oak Road**, selling plots to buyers willing to build houses to his design. Similarly, Sir John

Hollin Lane, seen from Manklin's (or Snow's) Farm in 1915. Leeds architect, Thomas Ambler formally laid out the road and contributed the first pair of villa houses in 1874. Prince Alamayou died at 1 Glebe Villas Hollin Lane in 1879. *Courtesy: Ian Ballantine*

Barran's architect, Thomas Ambler bought land in Far Headingley in 1874 and proceeded to lay out Hollin Lane[18]. **Clifton Villas**, one of two pairs of semi-detached houses built on high ground which banks steeply down to Hollin Lane are attributed to Thomas Ambler and date from 1877. Other houses in Hollin Lane and the adjacent **Glebe Terrace** are of similar style and period 'and may also have been designed by Ambler' according to C J Higenbottam in his survey of Ambler's work. Generally, however, this was not a hugely successful venture for the architect who found it difficult attracting customers.

Hollin House stands on the west side of Meanwood Beck at Meanwoodside. Originally Manklins (subsequently Snow's) Farm, the landholding between the beck, Hollin Lane, Weetwood Lane and Weetwood Mill Lane was acquired by Joseph Oates, of Weetwood Hall, in 1796. His son Edward inherited the property in 1824 and may have built Hollin House before acquiring the Meanwoodside acres in 1834. The property and farm remained part of the Oates estate and in 1883, Bryan William Grace Oates, younger brother of Captain Lawrence Oates (and Edward's grandchild) was born there. Margaret Ratcliffe, writing in *Ransome At Home*, notes that more recently Arthur Ransome, lodged at Hollin House for a time when it was the home of Mrs Bruce[19].

Shaw Lane 1904. *Courtesy: Ian Ballantine.*

Shaw Lane 1917. *Courtesy: Ian Ballantine,*

Shaw Lane

In 1847 John Hope Shaw, a prominent Leeds solicitor began acquiring Headingley Moor inclosure allotments on the south side of the old common with frontages to Monk Bridge Lane. He commissioned, **Shaw House**, which at one point nestled in over five acres of private grounds. When John Shaw died in 1864, the house 'with vinery, hothouse, fernery' and 1.5 acres, was sold independently of the remaining four acres which became divided into five further plots for villa development.

John Shaw was Mayor of Leeds and laid the foundation stone of Leeds Town Hall during his mayoral year, 1853. The Town Hall's young architect, Hull born Cuthbert Brodrick, lodged at Headingley Moor during the five year construction period but exactly where he lodged is unknown and remains an intriguing question. Could it have been at Shaw House? If not it was clearly closeby. Brodrick was a member of The Leeds Club where accommodation was also available, but the Club's records have failed to reveal his Headingley Moor address.

Today, Shaw House fronts Shaw Lane, re-named in memory of John Hope Shaw. In the early 1930s, Dr Fred Whalley moved his general practice to Shaw House from North Lane and it has remained a doctor's surgery since that time.

In July 1865 John Dresser, a corn factor, bought the middle plot from John Shaw's executors. The Jacobean style house now known as **Shaw Grange** (19 Shaw Lane) was built c1870 and given the name The Laurels. It was renamed Scarcroft Lodge from 1908 and briefly became a hotel, The Abbey Twilight Hotel in the 1960s. Thereafter it came into the ownership of the eminent surgeon Mr Geoffrey Wooler who returned it to a dwelling house.

John Dresser also bought the plot immediately adjoining Shaw House from Mr Shaw's executors. This conveyance is dated February 1866. Three villa residences were in the course of erection in 1874 at the time of a mortgage deed to Joshua Ikin (surgeon), the Reverend Thomas Wilson and Henry Nelson (gentleman). By 1891 the property was known collectively as **Oak Bank**. After the Second World War Oakbank was converted to flats with a ground floor restaurant. For a number of years the restaurant traded as Oakbank Restaurant. It then became L'escargot and more recently the Sala Thai. Today, there are eighteen flats above the restaurant.

The third conveyance from John Shaw's executors, and the fifth plot, was probably the large block of land to the west and north of Wesley Terrace with frontages to Shaw Lane and Moor Road. The 1890 Ordnance Survey shows **Springville** standing on this site. However, all trace of this villa sadly disappeared when it was demolished in the 1960s and replaced with modern apartment blocks, **Masham Court**.

Some Weetwood Houses:

Oxley Hall and Spenfield

Other individuals contributing impressive houses to the Far Headingley area looked to the Weetwood countryside for suitable sites, included Henry Oxley, who lived at Weetwood Villa (now **Oxley Hall**) in Weetwood Lane, and his son James Walker Oxley who commissioned Spenfield on the Otley Road.

Henry Oxley's interest in the locality began in 1858 when he bought seven acres of the former Englefield Estate from land speculator John Naylor, a Leeds stuff merchant by trade. Henry Oxley was a wealthy banker, a partner in the firm of William Williams, Brown & Co. He retained John Simpson, a local architect (former assistant to Cuthbert Broderick and Thomas Simpson's cousin) to design him a suitably imposing house on the Weetwood acres. The result was Weetwood Villa, a neo-Gothic mansion, built c1861. Henry lived there for almost thirty years. After his death in 1890 the property passed to James Oxley and the house was leased to Arthur J Tannett Walker. In 1920 James gifted Weetwood Villa (subsequently renamed The Elms) to the University of Leeds and it became Oxley Hall, a University Hall of Residence.

Weetwood Villa, The Elms, and since 1920, Oxley Hall. This photograph is dated 1916.

Courtesy: Ian Ballantine.

When a young man, James Walker Oxley followed his father into the Bank. He married Margaret Turner in 1867 and inherited, through her, Moorfield Lodge in Moor Road. Within a few years he too began to look forward to an even more handsome lifestyle, on the family acreage at Weetwood. He retained the most eminent architect of the day, George Corson, who designed **Spenfield** for him.

Built between 1875 and 1877, Spenfield was, by any account, a remarkable house:

> 'The severe and somewhat muscular Gothic exterior of Spenfield belied a luxuriously rich Aesthetic interior, particularly in the extensions and alterations carried out by George Armitage (a nationally renowned interior designer) and Corson, beginning with the dining room in 1888, followed by the new wing containing that essential Victorian mark of prosperity, the billiards room, in 1890. The eclectic mix of interior decorative styles, ranging from Corson's Gothic trefoils and Saracenic fretwork and ceilings – several rooms had walls modelled on those of the Alhambra – to the rather more idiosyncratic style of Armitage with its Aesthetic Movement peacock motifs and Renaissance-inspired panelling, must have provided a glittering backdrop to his (James Oxley's private art) collection'
>
> Matthew Winterbottom (with James Lomax)
> Leeds Art Calendar No 113, 1994

Spenfield, an early sketch   *Courtesy: Huan Mallalieu*

Spenfield from the south east c1890 after the addition of the billiards room, to the left of the entrance front.
Courtesy: Huan Mallalieu

James Walker Oxley photographed at Spenfield in the 1920s. *Courtesy: Huan Mallalieu*

Mr George Corson, Architect and himself a Far Headingley resident. 1829-1910. From *Two Leeds Architects* by T B Wilson.
Courtesy: Leeds City Library

James Oxley became senior partner of the Bank upon his father's death in 1890 when James was fifty six years of age. He retired nine years later when the bank merged with Lloyds and seems to have thrown himself (and his considerable fortune) into collecting works of art. He died in 1928. Twenty years later his 'reclusive' son Henry Oxley bequeathed the collection to the City. Ernest Musgrave, Director of Leeds City Art Gallery describes his first impression:

> 'Treasures from almost every country in Europe and from the Orient were there (at Spenfield) in profusion. Heavily carved ivories in the form of gargantuan tankards from central Europe; the beautiful but gruesome executioner's swords and sheaths from Japan, and more delicately cut ivories from China. Here in a specially designed case, the finally wrought metal and enamelled mace by a German master craftsman, once the property of some Netherlandish Burgomaster. In another case, vessels of gilded bronze encrusted with mother of pearl, colossal bronze vases and temple ornaments from the Far East, silver and silver mounted vessels from all over Europe. An embossed silver gilt cup and cover made in Augsburg keeping company with a silver mounted cup and cover made in Elizabethan England and bearing the Norwich hallmark; an elaborately modelled silver hunting horn given by H I H Fredericus Carolus of Cassel to his secretary in 1634; dishes, cups and vases of beautifully engraved rock crystal set in metal frames generously embellished with gemstones and enamels in the manner of Benvunto Cellini, together with vases of agate, mamchite and lapis lazuli'
>
> from The Leeds Art Calendar No 113. 1994

Spenfield became the offices for Leeds Waterworks, and subsequently Yorkshire Water. It was sold in 1997 to Greenalls plc and incorporated into the Village Hotel and Leisure complex after a new hotel building had been constructed in the grounds.

Bardon Grange, The Hollies and Fox Hill

The principal purchaser of land from the Englefield Estate during 1858 was William Brown, a Bradford cloth merchant and manufacturer. He acquired ninety three acres on both sides of Weetwood Lane and commissioned **Bardon Grange** and its lodge c1860. Both properties are attributed to Cuthbert Broderick. The house remained in the Brown family until at least 1920 when it was acquired by the University of Leeds – the same year the University acquired Weetwood Villa (Oxley Hall)[20].

George William Brown (William Brown's son) followed his father into the family business of Stansfield Brown and by the 1870s had taken up residence at **The Hollies**, an impressive villa and gatehouse constructed c1860 beside the Weetwood stone quarry, just on the other side of Weetwood Lane to the family house of Bardon Grange.

The irresistible attraction to George of The Hollies was the extensive landscaped grounds abundant with rhododendrons leading to private woodland

The Hollies, Weetwood c. 1920s.   *Courtesy: Ian Ballantine.*

walks meandering down to Adel Beck and Meanwoodside. His son, Harold Brown was born at The Hollies in 1879 and, when still a young man entered the family firm before going off to fight in the Great War. Tragically he was killed in action towards the end of the war in 1918 and in 1921 the bereaved George Brown donated the house and grounds to the City Corporation in his son's memory.

The grounds became Hollies Park and the house a sanatorium for children suffering from tuberculosis.

> 'Visitors to the grounds which were open to the public were able to see these children playing on the lawn in front of the house. Later The Hollies became one of the many Leeds City Council residences for the elderly'.

Leeds Tercentenary Handbook

In August 1921 George William Brown bought **Rye Cottage** in Moor Road and the adjoining cottages known as **Ellis Terrace** to accommodate various family retainers formerly resident at the Weetwood houses. Miss Boyd, personal companion to George William's late sister at Bardon Grange came to live at Rye Cottage.

William Francis Tetley will have noted work progressing on the building of The Hollies as he rode out from his Moor Road villa to view his own Weetwood realm which formed the continuation of the valley side. On this woodland site rose **Fox Hill** in 1863 to the designs of George Corson, an opulent mansion complete with spire (now demolished) and garden terrace offering sweeping views of the valley forest and giving access to:

'walks that passed by great tumbled boulders and ferny hollows, while rustic staircases descended deep into the wood'.

George Sheeran *Brass Castles* 1993

Fox Hill is now better known as Moorlands School. Mrs Paula Woolnough, Director of Marketing for the school writes:

> Stone for Foxhill was taken from a quarry directly adjacent to the construction site in order to comply with building regulations at the time which aimed to provide work for local men. Many of the master craftsmen left their mark and we have many engravings, particularly in the roof area with some risque 19th century comments as well!
>
> Foxhill had a large complement of full-time staff, and in order not to offend the family whilst they ate, a special underground servants' tunnel with turret steps was built so that the servants could enter the building without seeing the family or being seen. In addition, a high level window was made in order to block the view of the servants' heads as they passed by the dining room to ensure complete privacy.
>
> In the servants' quarters there is a room with more highly decorated stone than most in that wing. This was the nursery where the lady of the house would attend her children. Mr and Mrs Tetley had a large family of fourteen children.
>
> We still have the original plans of the building indicating where the servants worked and a potted history of many of the individuals too. An additional wing was built on so Francis Tetley could conduct his business at home as well as in Leeds. For added privacy, there are no front windows from Mr Tetley's library office.
>
> Francis Tetley found the Yorkshire winters too cold and he would head off to warmer climes abroad each winter leaving his children in Leeds. They stayed at home to read the sobering Victorian inscriptions which enrich the main gallery: Night is the Mother of councils; Our little life is rounded with sleep, etc.
>
> After the Great War, many households had to change their ways. Large retinues of staff were not available and Foxhill was put up for sale. In subsequent years, this great house became a retirement home for lawyers and judges, a country club with restaurant and gaming room, and in 1968, a school. Moorlands Preparatory School for Boys had been established at St Chad's Villas, (Arthur Ransome's former address) from 1898. In 1968 the school governors decided to make the move to Foxhill.

Paula Woolnough, June 30th 1999

Bardon Hill and Joseph Pickersgill

Thomas Simpson, the Leeds solicitor, also bought Englefield land in 1858 but it was several years before he retained his cousin, John Simpson, to design **Bardon Hill** – impressed no doubt by John's work for Henry Oxley at Weetwood Villa. Bardon Hill, a magnificent Gothic villa, was built between 1873 and 1875. Given the obvious expense involved in constructing Bardon Hill it is a measure of Thomas Simpson's means to note that in 1874 he was also buying up glebeland, including the old Glebe School, and laying out Burton Crescent for development.

Thomas Simpson died in 1898. The house, clearly too much for his widow to manage, was offered for sale by auction in May 1899 and acquired by Joseph Pickersgill, a self made millionaire. Mrs Simpson died in 1901.

Bardon Hill, Bishop's House, Our Lady's Primary School and latterly St Urban's School. Taken from the 1999 sales particulars.

Courtesy: The Catholic Diocese of Leeds. & Weatherall Green & Smith.

The 1899 sale particulars, prepared by Newsam & Gott of Leeds describe a lavish house with extensive servants' quarters and include a plan of the ground floor arrangements (see page 102). Note the centrepiece of the Hall – a fully installed organ 'with stool, hydraulic apparatus, bellows and fixings in the cellar'.

In 1899, the property also came with a 'Cow House for three; Provender Chambers; Range of Piggeries; Fowlery and Turnip House' and separate KITCHEN GARDEN, whilst 'opposite the two principal fronts of the Residence are the tastefully disposed PLEASURE GROUNDS and LARGE TENNIS LAWN'.

Joseph Pickersgill had made his fortune as a racehorse owner and turf commission agent, keeping a book for King Edward when Prince of Wales. He was also a successful property speculator and the financial partner of Mr Robert Chorley in the Leeds printing firm of Chorley and Pickersgill. He stabled prize horses at Bardon Hill and built for the purpose a magnificent stable block at the rear of the house. He died in 1920 at which time Bardon Hill was re-auctioned and became Bishops House, the formal residence of the Roman Catholic Bishops of Leeds.[21]

Between 1951 and 1956 Bishop John Heenan lived at Bardon Hill. When he left Leeds for Liverpool, the decision was taken to convert Bishops House to a school. Our Lady's Primary School opened in 1956 and remained at Bardon Hill for the next forty years changing its name latterly to St Urban's School. In 1996 the school relocated to a new site and three years later the house, grounds and outbuildings were sold to a housing developer. John Heenan became **Cardinal Heenan**, Archbishop of Westminster in 1963. He died in 1975.

However, it is **Joseph Pickersgill** who remains the chief character most closely associated with Bardon Hill.

> 'Endless stories are told of the late Mr Joseph Pickersgill, the Leeds turf commission agent. The late Colonel North paid Mr Pickersgill a small fortune by backing heavily ten of the biggest 'outsiders' in the Grand National in the year when it was won by the favourite Ilex. On the other hand 'Boss' Crocker, the American, received from Mr Pickersgill, a cheque representing a fortune when his horse, Orby, won the Derby in 1907.
>
> No bet was too big for him to take and it has always been understood that such commissions as were placed on behalf of King Edward – both as Prince of Wales and subsequently as reigning monarch – were dealt with in Mr Pickersgill's book. He was an aristocrat of the 'ring'.
>
> In the late 1880s, Mr Pickersgill ventured into racehorse ownership and had for several years a very useful string of horses in training at Watson's Richmond stables. The best remembered of his horses was Bobbie Burns. A mounted hoof of the horse was a prized treasure at Bardon Hill.
>
> In Leeds, Mr Pickersgill has long been spoken of as a millionaire. The popular belief as to his great wealth was supported by his very extensive speculations in property. He bought largely of business premises and land sites when the property market was languishing. Today the Pickersgill estates in Leeds are both numerous and valuable'.
>
> *Yorkshire Post* Obituary column 24.8.1920

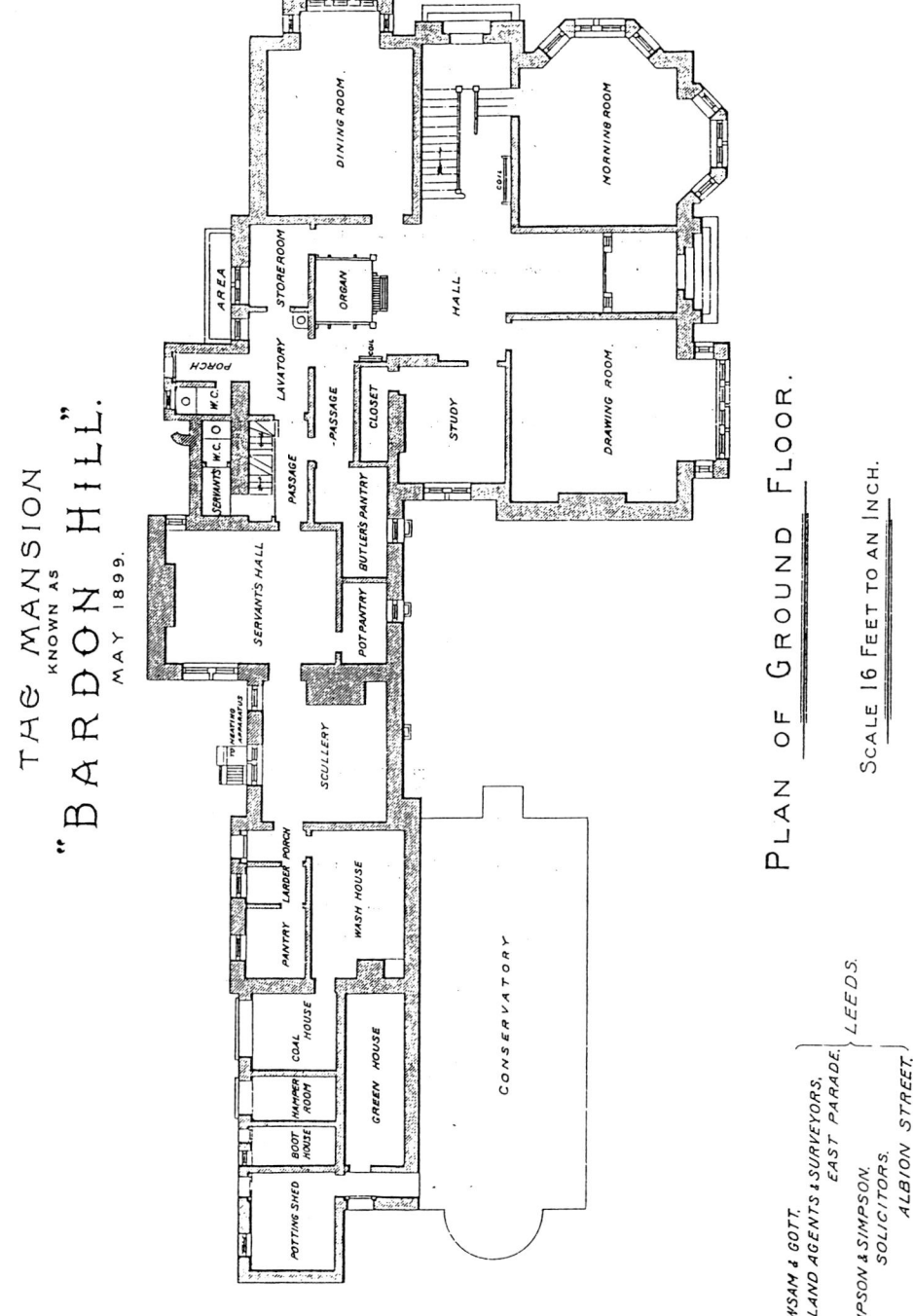

UMBRAGEOUS FOLIAGE AND RICH GARDENS

Still a familiar view. Bardon Hill Lodge, Weetwood Lane before 1920. *Courtesy: Ian Ballantine.*

Joseph Pickersgill began life as a butcher's boy and, when only a teenager, ran his own butcher's shop in a shabby district of Leeds known as the Shambles, just off Briggate – rebuilt in 1901 – now the Victorian Quarter. It was an area of Leeds where the 'race-card was called and betting was openly conducted'. In later years when his horse, Robbie Burns was entered for the St Ledger he promised every butcher's boy in Leeds a new suit of clothes if he won. Sadly for every butcher's boy in Leeds, Robbie Burns 'broke down' in training and was withdrawn from the race.

Joseph Pickersgill died 'suddenly of a heart attack' at Bardon Hill in August 1920. He was seventy one. The funeral service was conducted by Canon Marshall at St Chad's Church before the burial at Woodhouse cemetery.

The most potent memorial to Joseph Pickersgill, inevitably remains the stable building at Bardon Hill which he built, sparing no expense, making Far Headingley – unlikely though this may seem – home to one of the most opulent structures of its kind in the Country. A fine stone building with lavish interior wall tiling, cast iron stall dividers and stained glass windows. It was later converted into a large Assembly-Dining Room for the school and it now stands derelict awaiting another conversion, this time into a series of mews houses. But in 1920 the auctioneers were in no doubt about its reputation and wrote that Joseph Pickersgill's STABLES:

> 'believed to be second to none in the Kingdom, were erected at enormous cost and are now in splendid order grouped on three sides of a paved yard. The buildings are

South elevation

Two views of Weetwood Hall in 1927.
Courtesy: Ian Ballantine.

West elevation

of stone in the half timbered style, with high pitched roofs covered with red tiles, and surmounted by a tower cased in copper and containing a clock which chimes the quarters on four bells, strikes the hours, and has four illuminated dials, and which forms such a well known feature of the district. The major portion of the exposed woodwork is of teak put together exclusively by wooden pins or screws. Central heating is installed and the lighting is by electricity.

The STABLES have tiled walls throughout and a fireproof ceiling, and are divided into five stalls and four loose boxes, the fittings being electroplated; the windows, which have leaded lights, are of teak and so are the doors; over all is a corn chamber, battery store, and workshop with concrete floor, and two cranes are fixed. The SADDLE ROOM has a panelled teak ceiling, teak harness cupboards on two sides with plate-glass doors, bit cupboard with three glass doors, stone fireplace and grate and concrete floor. The CARRIAGE HOUSE is lofty and open to the roof. A narrow glass and ornamental iron verandah runs on two sides of the yard, and in the centre is a broad covered space to correspond, the yard being enclosed by stone walling with iron railings and a pair of teak gates attached to imposing dress stone pillars'.

Extract from the 1920 sales particulars. *Courtesy: Leeds Diocesan Archives.*

Weetwood Hall

As we have seen Sir Henry Englefield Bart purchased a not insignificant part of Daniel Foxcroft's Weetwood estate during the mid 1700s. The Hall, its grounds and 249 acres of farmland, however, came into the ownership of Lady Anne Denison (the last owner occupier). When Lady Denison died in 1785 aged seventy two, the estate was administered by her trustees until it passed to Edmund Beckett on his marriage to the Denison heiress Maria Beverley in 1814.

In 1821, Edmund and Maria sold Weetwood Hall to Edmund's brother, Christopher Beckett (of Meanwood Hall from 1824) and it remained with Christopher and his successors in title until the conveyance to Leeds University in 1919[22]. From the demise of Lady Denison the Hall became home to three noted tenants.

Joseph Oates was in residence by the 1790s and died at the Hall in 1824, in his eighty-first year. He was an important landowner in his own right and left Manklins farm (formerly also part of the Foxcroft estate) to his son Edward, enabling Edward and Susan Oates to endow land for Hollin Lane school in 1839[23]. Following Joseph Oates came two emminent Victorians – Henry Cowper Marshall and Alf Cooke.

Henry Cowper Marshall was the fourth son of John Marshall, the famous Leeds industrialist (Marshall Mills). He was born in 1808 at Kirkstall Grange (then New Grange) where he lived until John and Jane Marshall took their family to the Lake District in 1815 retaining Headingley House off Kirkstall Lane, as their Leeds home. By the late 1830s, we find from directories of the time, that Henry, was living at Weetwood Hall. He was an Alderman of Leeds, Mayor in 1843, and owner of the Leeds Zoological & Botanical Gardens site[24].

Alf Cooke 1842-1902.
From *Contemporary Biographies*.

Exclusive Weetwood Lane in 1907. A cyclist walks his bike past the lodge to Weetwood Hall. Opposite is the lodge to Quarry Dene a Jacobean Manor styled villa built for Leeds solicitor John Rawlinson Ford in 1885. The house, set in the former open sided quarry on George William Brown's estate had 'well elevated' views across the valley. The architect was Wm H. Thorpe. Beyond this scene the road bends round to the right passing Foxhill.

Courtesy: Ian Ballantine.

He married Catherine, the daughter of **Thomas Spring-Rice**, Chancellor of the Exchequer in Lord Melbourne's 1835 government and father of the penny postage scheme. Interestingly, Thomas Spring-Rice, himself married into Henry's family, taking his eldest sister, Marianne, as his second wife in 1841, thereby becoming both father-in-law and brother-in-law to Henry.

Henry Marshall was still living at Weetwood Hall at the time of his death in 1884. His family remained in residence at the Hall until 1889 when the tenancy of the property was acquired by Mr Alfred Cooke of Moor Cottage in Moor Road[25]. The following year Alf Cooke was elected Mayor of Leeds. The lodges to the Hall were built at this time.

Alf Cooke was a pioneer of colour printing in England and owned Crown Point Printing Works in Hunslet Road, claimed to be the largest in the world. He died in 1902 aged sixty and is buried at St Chad's, having served there for many years as Churchwarden. His wife Anne died in 1914 aged sixty two and is also buried at St Chad's. Alf Cooke was an industrious, innovative and successful man who made his fortune and was well able to take up the lease on Weetwood Hall. The family grave, however, reveals personal tragedy:

Mabel Cooke:	died July 1878 aged 5 weeks
Alf Battye Cooke:	died April 1879 aged 6 years
Fred Cooke:	died Dec 1886 aged 29 days
Nellie, daughter:	died June 1916 aged 41 years

In 1919 Weetwood Hall was acquired by the University of Leeds from Sir Henry Hickman Beckett Bacon and became a residence for women students, bringing to an end the Beckett family's long term association with Weetwood.

. . . and Meanwoodside (demolished)

Meanwoodside, since the 17th century, home to various Thomas Whalleys, ultimately passed to the last of the family line, Francis Whalley, and on his death in 1784, to absentee family beneficiaries, the Rinder family in Lincolnshire.

Adjoining the Rinder estate on the Far Headingley side of Meanwood beck was Snow's Farm, (previously Manklin's Farm), the property of Joseph Oates of Weetwood Hall. Snow's Farm was inherited by Edward Oates from his father (Joseph) in 1824 and gave Edward an interest in expanding the landholding. He attempted to buy part of the Headingley Moor common land, after its enclosure in 1829 but was put off by the inflated prices and turned his attention to the Rinder estate, part of which he managed to acquire in 1834, including Thomas Whalley's now dilapidated Yeoman's house[26].

Through this purchase Edward's landholding was greatly extended. At forty two years of age he had great plans for landscaping the grounds and building a fine house. He was also embarking on married life. In 1836 he wed Susan Grace, the daughter of a rich Leeds merchant.

Meanwoodside in Meanwood Parish – as built by Edward Oates in 1838 with the old Whalley house on the right.   *Courtesy: Mrs Denvas Chitty (Mary Kitson Clark) once of Meanwoodside.*

According to the researches of Colin Treen, Edward devoted himself to transforming Meanwoodside while living at his widowed father-in-law's home, 'a seven servant establishment situated on thirteen acres', St Anne's Hill, on the Burley side of William Beckett's Kirkstall Grange estate.

> 'Edward's diaries suggest that he was at Meanwoodside almost every day when in Leeds but the occasions upon which his wife and children dined or stayed there were occasions to warrant a diary entry. The two residences were a brisk thirty minutes walk apart, with a possible short cut through Beckett's Kirkstall Grange estate. This proved hazardous on one occasion when he lost his way in thick fog and almost fell in his own beck'.[27]

His ambition was to create a fine house within its own park, the centrepiece of which was to be an American garden. He set about building 'a great pond' to the west of Thomas Whalley's dilapidated farmhouse and constructed 'a series of small weirs and dams in the beck course, to counteract the visual disadvantages of intermittent flow'. To many it must have seemed a doubtful project given the industrial waste deposited into Adel beck from several mills and tanneries.

> 'His longer term strategy was to open up additional sources by boring and clearing out springs on his own and his neighbours' land, to renew field drains and divert their flow. Diary entries record the hunt for suitable springs; in 1841 eleven water sources were recorded; in 1844 Oates was checking on the performance of twenty separate springs'.[27]

The fine stone bridge which crosses the beck near Hustlers Row cottages is referred to by Colin Treen as 'The American Garden Bridge'. Close-by, the goit and damstones weir still show how Edward divided the beck to form cascading streams which filled a whole series of ponds stocked with perch and trout amid lawned grounds and garden beds filled with rhododendrons, azaleas and a whole host of American plants 'as bear our climate'.

Edward Oates physically toiled away at the garden for thirty years. He died in 1865, by which time Meanwoodside was a horticultural wonderland.

In addition to the garden, Edward renovated the old farmhouse adding a new and imposing structure 'a well proportioned building in fine ashlar with a deeply eaved roof of green slate'[28]. In 1870, or thereabouts, it was substantially remodelled by Edward's widow, Susan. The 'old' part was pulled down and a matching extension added.

Edward and Susan had four sons and a daughter. Their two middle sons Francis (Frank) and William became noted naturalists. Both were fellows of the Royal Geographical Society and enthusiastic big game hunters – and in the 1870s nobody would have seen a contradiction in that. Frank was born in 1840. After graduating from Oxford he travelled to South America were he made a collection of birds and insects. He became one of the first European explorers to see the Victoria Falls from the Zambesi but, whilst there (in 1874) he contracted a mortal fever and died. In 1881 his journals were published by his younger brother, Charles, under the title *Matabele Land and the Victoria Falls: A Naturalist's Wandering in the Interior of South Africa*.

William Oates married Caroline Buckton of Meanwood and moved to London. Their son Lawrence Edward Grace Oates was born at Putney, in 1880, and his brother Bryan was born at Hollin House, Far Headingley in 1883. The family made frequent visits to Meanwoodside to see relatives. Lawrence's second birthday 'spent in Leeds, brought a firelit birthday tea, and some marvellous presents'[29]. He grew up to become the national hero **Captain Oates**, who joined Scott's fatal 1912 expedition to the South Pole. The Pole was reached, but on the return journey the weather closed in and Lawrence became severely lamed by frostbite. He realised that he would not make it home. Anxious to avoid slowing his comrades down and risking their survival, he resigned himself to a snowy grave, leaving the safety of the tent with the legendary words 'I am just going outside and I may be some time'. It was his thirty second birthday.

There is a memorial tablet to Lawrence Oates on the stonework at the entrance to Memorial Drive leading to Meanwood Church.

William's younger brother Charles Oates, became a barrister in Leeds and continued to live at Meanwoodside until his death, as a bachelor, in 1902. He was fifty eight. The property was left in Trust to his nephews Lawrence and Bryan Oates.

In 1904 Lt Col Edwin Kitson Clark took a lease on the property, eventually buying the freehold in 1917. With some foresight, and noble intention, Lawrence had willed his share of the Meanwoodside estate to Bryan as early as 1906, leaving

Bryan sole beneficiary after his brother's death – that heroic event being recorded on the Abstract of Title simply as 'died in the Antarctic Regions'. At the end of the First World War Bryan cut his ties and sold the Meanwood property.

The house and grounds were home to the Kitson Clarks for fifty years. The Colonel died in 1942 and was survived by his widow, Georgina and daughter Mary. On the death of Mrs Kitson Clark, in 1954, the property was put up for sale and acquired by Leeds Corporation for the purpose of creating a public park. There were plans to turn the house into a natural history museum with a Polar room to commemorate Captain Oates, but the cost was considered prohibitive and, there being no desire to retain the building as a house, it was demolished. The former outbuildings remain, opposite the park swings, but with no obvious traces left of the old house which once adjoined. As for Edward Oates' spectacular gardens, the rhododendron walks and the stone bridges over the beck, are now the only poignant reminders of a horticultural showpiece.

Notes

[1] E Richard Vaughan, *A History of Castle Grove* 1996.

[2] Thomas Wilson specialised in interior design and would publish *Modern House Interiors* in 1897, having gained his experience and a national reputation through commissions from affluent Leeds businessmen like John Kirk. By the turn of the century he had offices in Leeds, Harrogate and London. Towards the end of his life, he wrote an appreciation of Cuthbert Brodrick and George Corson under the title *Two Leeds Architects*, published in 1937.

[3] *The Architect* 1896.

[4] *The Yorkshire Post*.

[5] Francis Tetley was the 'son' in Joshua Tetley & Son. Joshua and Hannah Tetley had eight children, seven daughters and one son.

[6] An undoubted enhancement for the future, and a useful traffic calming measure would be to re-form Moor Road to its original 30ft width, extend the shallow gardens of the present houses which front onto the road, and recreate the 'well timbered' aspect by planting an avenue of trees. Alternatively, the existing pavement could be widened and trees planted.

[7] It is assumed the old oak pannelling was bought by John Kirk at that time and refitted in Castle Grove.

[8] Meanwoood Tannery, also known as Highbury Works was built on the site of Wood Mills. Samuel Smith purchased the old mill premises from the Martin family in 1856.

[9] John Smith, the brother of Samuel Smith Snr, set up as a brewer in Tadcaster Main Street in 1847. When John Smith died, a bachelor in 1879, he left the brewery premises to his nephew, Samuel Jnr. The business was continued by William Smith (another brother of John) but knowing that he did not own the premises, he moved out and built the present John Smith's brewery in 1883 leaving the Main Street premises empty. In 1886, Samuel Smith, the nephew, re-opened the old brewery and, after a few years gave up the Meanwood Tannery inherited from his father in order to concentrate solely on brewing. Arthur Hopwood.

[10] Benjamin Smith bought 17 Cottage Road in 1838. He was clearly interested in property investment in this area. Donald Hood.

[11] 'glebe' - a portion of land going with a clergyman's benefice.

[12] Thomas Simpson of Bardon Hill, Weetwood Lane, Leeds solicitor and founder of the law firm until recently known as Simpson Curtis. See the Simpson Family Tree on page 217.

[13] *A History of Headingley Methodism*, J Stanley Mathers MA 1970.

[14] The proceeds (£862) were set against the new Parochial Church Institute building in Bennett Road designed by George Corson.

[15] The Weetwood banker, J W Oxley, owned land behind the coach house. He sold a small parcel to Thomas Simpson in 1880 for the building of the coachman's house to Fairfield and more would be sold in the 1890s

for the laying out of **Heathfield Terrace** and the construction of houses 10 to 34. My thanks to Clare Richardson of the (Fairfield) coach house for sharing the results of her own research into the history of the Glebe School, and Fairfield.

[16] Source: Whitbread property records.

[17] The origins of Grove Lane are not clear. It was a well defined track long before being formally laid out in 1921, the upper part (Shaw Lane end) being known as Mill Lane. At the Meanwood end, just beyond Meanwood Beck it passed Rowley's 19th century Ganister Quarry, at one time of great importance to the iron making industry in Leeds. For the previous two hundred years quarry workers extracted minerals from the ground by cutting out grooves and were known as 'groovers'. Dr A J Moyes speculates that this could have given rise to the name.

Alternatively, the lane may have been known for passing through particular groves of trees. Or then again, near the point where Grove Lane passes over Meanwood Beck, a mill race was cut to Groves Mill.

[18] Hollin – derived probably from Holly, which grows abundantly in Meanwoodside, or Hollow.

[19] Ransome At Home by C E Alexander, *Amazon Publications* 1996 with an additional chapter on the Ransome family homes in Leeds by Margaret Ratcliffe.

[20] "William Brown was a stuff merchant with premises in Bradford and linked to the business of Thomas Stansfield of Weetwood Grove (Stansfield Brown). The banking firm of William (Williams) Brown & Co had premises in Commercial Street and, later, Park Row in Leeds; the Oxley family of Spenfield and Weetwood Villa (The Elms) were close neighbours of William Brown and were partners in the banking firm. Presumably the same William Brown". Dept of National Heritage, Schedule of Listed Buildings (revised 1996).

[21] The Royal Commission on the Historic Monuments of England, historic building report on Bardon Hill (Nov 1995) notes that after 1920, the house became the residence of the Chancellor of the University of Leeds and then the Palace of the Roman Catholic Diocese of Leeds.

[22] Researched by Arthur Hopwood, who also notes that in 1919 'a small strip of land on the west side of, and adjacent to, the Hall was sold to Leeds Corporation', no doubt for the duelling of Otley Road and extension of the tram rails to the 'new' Lawnswood terminus.

'The Headingley Tithe Award of 1848 confirms that Christopher Beckett was the owner of the Weetwood Estate and that the occupier of Weetwood Hall and forty four acres or so was Henry C Marshall. The other main tenant was Joseph Smith who had the house on the left hand side of Weetwood Lane near its present junction with the Ring Road together with about 179 acres (Tether Farm)'. Arthur Hopwood – unpublished notes 1993. Christopher Beckett, Banker and Railway Entrepeneur, was clearly also a major landowner in late Georgian/early Victorian Leeds.

[23] Another branch of the Oates family owned Carr House, later rebuilt as Carr Manor.

[24] Leeds Zoo opened in 1840. It never became really successful and never boasted much of a collection of animals. In 1848, Henry Marshall leased the site to Thomas Clapham and it survived a further two years before being closed. The land was sold as building ground in 1858 and Cardigan Road was laid out. The last remaining vestige is the castellated bear pit which stands on Cardigan Road.

Thomas Clapham also ran Leeds Royal Park near Woodhouse Moor where a large platform for dancing measuring above 17,000 sq.ft. 'is beautifully lighted up with thousands of gas lights on Music and Gala evenings'. Charlton and Anderson's Directory 1862.

[25] Also listed in some directories as Rose Cottage. Confusion here because 46 Cottage Road has also been known in the past as Moor Cottage.

[26] Not entirely "put off". In researching the deeds to 27 Moor Road, Jim Dryhurst discovered that the site had formed part of Lot 30 in the post inclosure landsales of 1831, for which Robert Moxon successfully bid on behalf of himself and Edward Oates. The plot was divided and Nos 25 and 27 Moor Road subsequently built. 'According to our former neighbour, John Wilson, No 25 used to be known as Oates Cottage'. The Moxon family retained No 27 until 1890.

[27] Colin Tree, *Edward Oates and the Making of the Lost American Garden at Meanwoodside'* Thoresby Society 1995.

[28] Frederic Casperson, local historian.

[29] Sue Limb and Patrick Cottingley, *Captain Oates – Soldier and Explorer'* B T Batsford Ltd

The Victorian years:
Peg-it-up Baths and a Yard for the Duck

George Merry Reminisces

Samuel George Merry was a small boy growing up in Far Headingley in the 1880s. Born in Carlisle in 1879 his family moved to Leeds when George was still very young. They lived in Hollin Place, behind the tram depot. Mr Merry Snr. was a tramdriver employed by the Leeds Tramways Company. There were twelve children, all somehow accommodated in a small terraced house with two bedrooms on the first floor and two attic rooms. There was no luxury living here, but George remembers his childhood years in late Victorian Far Headingley with affection and enthusiasm. In 1972, then aged ninety three he recorded an interview with his son Robert. This is an extract from the transcript:

Robert: You lived at Hollin Place. I've seen it. It wasn't a mansion was it?

George: No, not really. There were fourteen of us, including my Mother and Father. We had two actual bedrooms and two attics. No electric light. We used to have gas, but took candles upstairs to go to bed. There was no bathroom. We had a 'peg-it-up'. I used to get in and have a nice little bath. Once my Mother washed my Dad's overalls in my bath water before I got in. I was black when I got out. After that it was always clean water. In the backyard, we kept a lovely big Belgian hare called Benny, and we also had a duck called Packy. I lived there, just beyond the Three Horse Shoes for twenty three years.

Robert: You went to St Chad's School and sang in the church choir didn't you?

George: I sang solos in St Chad's church choir when I was eight or nine years old. I remember a choir trip to Scarborough, just with lads, you know. I had ninepence to spend. Chuck Winterburn had most. He had one and threepence. All I had was ninepence. Before I went into 'train I put a penny in the slot and got a packet of slim jims – coconut spice, five bits as big as your fingers. When we got to Scarborough, I was surprised. I'd never seen the sea. So I went onto 'front. There were some tricycles for hire. So me and Jonnie Magge and Billy Stokoe had a go. That cost me tuppence. Church paid for 'meal. Then we had an hour on a fishing smack. Then Percy Richardson says, 'Now you lads, you can do what you like this afternoon and come back here at five o'clock for tea'. So I set off on me own. I went on 'quay. There were fish hanging up, herring, six on a string for a penny. Then I went on 'front and saw a shop, a fancy shop. I saw some earrings in the window. Whitby jet, tuppence a pair, for me Mother. Then I went a bit further. There was a confectioner. I bought a big mint humbug for a penny for my father. Then I went to a newspaper shop. I bought Chips and Comic Cuts.

Robert: Fish and chips?

George: No, that was the name of the paper, Chips and Comic Cuts. That was a penny.

Robert: Tell us more about your singing. I believe on occasions you went to some of the local big houses didn't you?

George: Oh well, this is a long time ago. I'd be perhaps eleven or twelve. One Christmas morning I sang the solo of Shepherds Abiding in the Field and Alf Cooke, he was a church warden, came round to the back of the church to visit his son's grave. He was with his two daughters, Miss Maggie and Miss Nellie and Master Jack. We were all coming out of the back of the church and I heard Alf Cooke ask some of the lads, 'which was the boy who sang solo this morning?'. 'That's im at back wi' bungie on. George Merry they call im'.

Robert: What's a bungie?

George: Oh, an ordinary straw hat.

Robert: In the winter?

George: Oh yes, yes. Well he came up to me and gave me a present. It was a sovereign. Good Lord, a sovereign! Then the eldest daughter, who was about twenty asked 'was I doing anything tomorrow', which was Boxing Day. 'No'. Well, would I go up to the Hall to sing for them. 'bring some music with you, especially the one you sang this morning'.

Robert: That would be Weetwood Hall. Was she going to play the piano?

George: Exactly, yes. So I went back into the vestry and told Percy Richardson, the organist and choirmaster, and he said 'well take what you want'.

Robert: What happened after you'd sung for them?

George: Well I was taken into a room and they fitted me with one of Jack's overcoats. I suppose the one I had on must have been shabby.

Robert: Let's talk a little more about your early days in Far Headingley. Obviously you must have had ways and means of earning an honest copper, by doing odd jobs and making a bit of pocket money?

George: Yes, well there was one way. I used to go to Ernest Petty and borrow his barrow and collect horse muck. There was plenty of that about in those days. I used to get a barrow load and take it to Mrs Bolton's in Cottage Road, and she used to give us tuppence a load. She would sprinkle it under the trunk of a big pear tree.

Robert: What about holding horses then?

George: Well we used to do pretty well when the Otley show was on. When they were coming back of course, a good many of them used to stay at the Three Horse Shoes and call in and have a pint. 'Hold your horse, sir?' 'All right lad'. And they'd be in for perhaps ten minutes and give you a penny or tuppence. I remember once a chap gave me a threepenny bit. God, a millionaire. I went straight over the road to Dunwell's which was a bakery. I remember I bought a penny rice bun and I still had tuppence left.

Robert: You also had a job wheeling an invalid lady about, didn't you?

George: Yes, Professor Bodington's daughter. She was a proper cripple. I used to be always taking her on a fine day.

Robert: What, in a bath chair?

George: Oh yes. And I used to get sixpence a session, perhaps an hour, an hour and a half, perhaps two hours. Well Arthur Loveridge had it before me and Arthur Loveridge went to live away from Leeds, so of course, the job was vacant. Any amount of lads applied for it, but I got it. I used to do about two session a week and get a bob.

Robert: Tell me about the Three Horse Shoes. I believe in your time all the beer was brewed by the landlord, wasn't it?

George: It was. There was The Woodman, The New Inn and The Three Horse Shoes. They all used to brew their own beer. I think most of the pubs in Leeds did that. Well on brewing days, believe me, the smell of hops round Headingley was lovely.

Robert: And you used to go with a jug sometimes didn't you?

George: I used to go with a big jug and a penny from my father, and I would say 'a gill of beer Mr Askey' and he used to give me what they called a long pull. He'd fill it for a penny, and I'd say 'can I have a clay pipe for my father?' 'Ah, get away, you had one last week'. 'Well I broke it Mr Askey'.

Robert: He knew your father didn't smoke. What did you want with a clay pipe?

George: I would blow bubbles with it. As kids we used to smoke anything – a bit of string pulled to pieces – and have a puff.

Robert: Is that why you're still smoking today? You must have got the taste.

George: I'm not smoking so much today.

Robert: No, well you're certainly not smoking string. At Christmastime didn't breweries deliver beer to your own cellar. That must have been cheap beer.

George: Oh, Lord help me yes. Tetleys would go round from door to door about a month or so before Christmas. We used to get a nine gallon barrel of beer for seven and six. They'd deliver it and put it wherever you wanted. They'd tap it for you, and when you'd finished it you sent them a postcard and they'd come and collect it.

Robert: And what about bread. I suppose your Mother had baking days did she?

George: She'd have two baking days a week. I'd go down to the Co-op in Headingley for seven pounds (I used to say half a stone) of flour and a penny worth of yeast and my Mother would bake bread and oven cakes. The smell in our house was lovely.

Robert: Tell me about Beckett's Park. I don't suppose it was a public place in those days?

George: Oh no, it wasn't a public place, but there was a right of way from Otley Road through to Headingley Station. But it wasn't a park where people could roam about and do what they liked you know, because they had a ranger who went around with a dog. But St Chad's had a cricket club in the park, by the side of the church and the club was in the local cricket league.

Robert: Have you ever seen performing bears in Leeds?

George: Yes. A man used to come round the streets with one on a rope. It would get up on its back legs and dance around while the man sang. He had a pole in his hand which the bear would catch. Then the man would go knocking at the doors for a meg, a penny. I remember the circuses at Cardigan Fields too. Bill Cody. Buffalo Bill. They did all sorts, but the star turn was a race every day between Indians, Mexicans and cowboys. About two of each. And it was a serious affair. Then there was a menagerie came to Leeds, in City Square before the GPO was built. This was before City Square as we know it. It was just a big wide derelict space. Wombwell's Menagerie. There was lions, tigers and elephants. The lot. They used to parade around Boar Lane before they had the show.

Robert: Can you tell us something about prices in the early 1900s?

George: In Duncan Street, there was the Bombay Tea Stores and about every six months or perhaps every year, they used to make a speciality of a sovereign's worth for a man. This is what you could get for a sovereign: a good hardwearing three piece suit, a pair of hobnailed boots, a pair of socks, a shirt, a pair of braces, a collar and tie, a handkerchief, a cap and a pound of tea. It sounds unbelievable but it's absolutely true.

Robert: There's another interesting thing, I think, about Jacksons the Hatters and the sandwich men.

George: Jacksons used to make a speciality of a three-and-ninepenny hat. Their slogan was: 'If in life you wish to shine, wear one of Jacksons three-and-nine'. Well, Dunns, a London firm came and opened a shop in Boar Lane and they made a three-and-ninepenny hat in competition with Jacksons. So they got about half a dozen sandwich men to walk down Boar Lane, up Briggate, up Upper Headrow and down Park Row – round and round – in the gutter. Not to be outdone, Jacksons did the same and they followed round and round. So Dunns added more to their numbers and, of course the procession got bigger and bigger.

Robert: How many do you think there were eventually?

George: Well, if I was guessing I should say about thirty. Anyway the police stepped in and stopped it because they were going round behind each other.

Robert: They'd be bumping into horses and carts and things like that, wouldn't they?

George: No, they were kept in the gutter.

Robert: Sam Jackson, he was the owner of the shop?

George: Aye, that was 'im.

Note: In 1895 the annual St Chad's choir outing was to Scarborough. Possibly not the trip remembered by George Merry but the same arrangements seem to have applied. The August church magazine reported that more than forty in all went on the trip ...

> 'After an excellent dinner at the Albermarle Rooms the party separated to enjoy themselves in several ways; some by sailing, others by rowing, and others again by taking a hand in the different distractions provided ashore. To those on land the day appeared exquisite in its summer brightness, but we heard whispers that some of the more adventurous sailors did not escape without paying the usual landsman's tribute to the sea. All, however, were ready to enjoy a hearty tea, and the journey home was begun soon after 8 o'clock. A block on the line unfortunately delayed the train, and Leeds was not reached till nearly midnight'.
>
> St Chad's Church Magazine August 1895

... And 100 years later?

George Merry would be aghast. At the close of the twentieth century, a pint of beer at the newly refurbished Three Horse Shoes is £1.55, Haddock and chips at Bryan's is £2.85 and a bag of chips 95p, an ounce of tobacco from George Corker at Far Headingley Post Office is £4.30, and a single bus fare to Leeds now costs 85p in peak times.

Oh, and the church choir outings have changed a bit too:

> 'Most years, members of St Chad's Choir go away for a week-end to sing in a Cathedral. We've been to Portsmouth Cathedral and St Asaph's in Wales, travelling by coach and staying in nice hotels. We usually stop at a museum on the way and arrive at our destination in high spirits. We sing on the Saturday evening and again during two services on the Sunday. We always have a great time. Last year we sang at Liverpool Cathedral but that was a day trip'.
>
> Alison Overend 17, Head Chorister 1999

The Victorian Years: The Prince and the Professor

The Prince …
The Extraordinary Story of Prince Alamayou 1861-1879

In the nave of St George's Chapel at Windsor Castle is a brass tablet, erected by Queen Victoria, to the memory of Prince Alamayou, the son of King Theodore of Abyssinia. The inscription reads 'I was a stranger and ye took me in'. Prince Alamayou died at Far Headingley on November 14th 1879. This is his story.

In 1855, Emperor John II of Abyssinia (modern Ethiopia) was overthrown in a civil war. A minor tribal chief, who took the name Theodore, became king and assumed his divine right to rule as a despot, much as he suspected Queen Victoria ruled over the British Empire. He admired Great Britain and it was natural to him to seek greater ties.

According to Lord Amulree, who first put this story into print, sometime in the early 1860s Theodore wrote to Queen Victoria proposing the establishment of an Abyssinian Embassy in both London and Paris. He received no reply, his letter, it appears 'having been unfortunately filed away in the Foreign Office', possibly for want of an interpreter to translate Amharic. Deeply insulted Theodore 'threw' the British Consul to Abyssinia, Captain Cameron, and several other British subjects into prison causing a diplomatic storm. An envoy was sent to negotiate their release, but 'on a sudden whim Theodore threw him and sixty other Europeans into prison and had them chained in iron anklets and fetters'.

A regiment of British troops was mobilised on the Indian sub-continent under the command of Sir Robert Napier, which took nearly a year to reach Magdala, the Abyssinian capital – it being necessary to build a railway inland from the African coast to transport equipment and provisions. Napier stormed Magdala in April 1868 and to avoid capture Theodore committed suicide by shooting himself.

During his incarceration, the British envoy described meeting 'Dayaz Alameeo, the prince imperial and real heir to the throne – a nice youth about eight years of age'. With the country now in turmoil, and Theodore dead, it was decided to evacuate the Prince to England under the care of Captain J C Speedy, a member of Napier's staff and an Amharic speaker. His mother, Queen Terunish, was to accompany him but fell mortally ill before reaching the African coast. As she lay dying she asked Captain Speedy to be a father to her son, and we can imagine a very poignant scene as the young, earnest captain promised his faithful protection.

From this moment an extraordinary relationship was to develop between the English soldier and the frightened African child prince. As Captain Speedy later wrote:

'the distressing alarm that then seized him rendered him so timid that for the following three months no persuasion could induce him to sleep out of my arms, and so great was his terror that if he happened to wake and find me asleep although still in my arms, he would wake me and earnestly beg me to remain awake until he should fall asleep; and it is only by continued care and tenderness that he is gradually losing his timidity'.

They arrived in England in July 1868 and went directly to Captain Speedy's home at Freshwater on the Isle of Wight, not far from Queen Victoria's summer residence at Osborne. Captivated by the story of the Captain and the unhappy Prince, the Queen summoned them both to Osborne House and immediately took a very affectionate interest in the welfare of the young boy:

'Prince Alamayou must, on no account, be removed from the kind, judicious and almost maternal care of Captain Speedy. The poor child cannot bear him for a moment out of sight; Captain Speedy is very gentle in his Christianity. The child is extremely nervous and his reason even might be endangered if the poor little helpless orphan were removed from the *one* person to whom he seems to cling most tenderly'.

Other diary entries made by the Queen note that on July 17th Captain Speedy brought the boy again to Osborne ... 'he was so nice and gentle', and on July 25th ... 'just after luncheon saw the little Alamayou in his picturesque Abyssinian dress, gave the dear little boy a watch and chain'.

In this idyllic environment, Alamayou soon recovered his confidence. 'His disposition is excellent', wrote Captain Speedy in October 1868, 'and his former shyness is replaced by a most winning manner. He is remarkably intelligent for his age and makes quick progress in English'.

In December the Captain married his fiancee, Miss Cottam, and life began to settle down for Alamayou. When Captain Speedy resumed his career the following year, as District Commissioner of Police at Seetapoor, India, Alamayou went too – with the sanction of the British Government, which considered that Alamayou should stay with Captain and Mrs Speedy for the following two years, after which the situation would be reviewed.

Alamayou was ten years old in April 1871, 4ft 6ins in height and 'growing a fine lad' according to his adopted parent, Captain Speedy. 'I cannot get him to care for his books but otherwise he is the best boy in the Universe'. Gladstone's government, however, estimated that it was time for Prince Alamayou to return to England and begin his more formal education in spite of the pain of separation this would undoubtably cause both Alamayou and Captain Speedy.

When the Captain was appointed a colonial magistrate in Penang, Alamayou was brought back to England and enrolled at Cheltenham College under the headship of Rev Jex-Blake. He remained at Cheltenham until 1875 spending some holidays with Mrs Speedy and some with Sir Thomas Biddulph, Keeper of the Privy Purse in the Queen's Household. At first Alamayou felt repressed and lost within his new regime, but in 1873 Rev Jex-Blake was able to report that 'he now reads for his own amusement, he is always cheerful, and I have never seen him out of temper'. In April of that year Sir Thomas Biddulph wrote that 'the poor boy is staying with me here for part of his holidays, and is as gentle a child as is possible to see and appears to have little trace of his savage origin'. He was back with the Biddulphs in September, for the Queen mentions in her diary that 'Mary Biddulph brought little Alamayou, who is a dear boy' and again in January, 'took tea with Mary Biddulph at Osborne, where we found little Alamayou.'

In 1875, Rev Jex-Blake was appointed a master at Rugby. Alamayou moved with the Jex-Blake household and began his schooling at Rugby where he became attached to one of his tutors, Cyril Ransome. There was concern in government circles that Alamayou could one day make his claim to the throne of Abyssinia. As late as 1878 General Gordon wrote to the Queen's private secretary expressing alarm at 'Captain Speedy's doings, as he is supporting the chiefs to proclaim Alamayou.' Nothing however, it seems could have been further from the young man's own mind, but it does indicate the political sensitivity of the times.

When Cyril Ransome became Professor of History and Modern Literature at the Yorkshire College in Leeds (later the University of Leeds), he moved to lodgings at Hollin Lane, Far Headingley. Once again Alamayou felt lost and visited Professor Ransome in Leeds whenever possible. During the summer of 1878 Cyril Ransome took his pupil to Paris to see the International Exhibition, and later that year Alamayou, now seventeen, left Rugby to be enrolled at the Royal Military College at Sandhurst as a cadet.

Sandhurst did not suit Alamayou. Sir Stafford Northcote, then Chancellor of the Exchequer, soon learnt that he was not doing well and was unhappy. What to do with Alamayou was becoming a problem for the government. 'He has a hankering after his own country where he said he had two aunts and a half brother living. I told him that his going to Abyssinia was out of the question, and he then said there was no one in England who had ever done him so much good as Mr Ransome and that he would like to go to him', Northcote wrote.

An extract from a Government paper held with Cyril Ransome's archive letters at the Brotherton Library in Leeds University, records officially that:

> 'Prince Alamayou had been for the previous year in the Royal Military College at Sandhurst and it had been considered advisable that he should accept an invitation from Lord Napier (of the earlier Abyssinian adventure) to proceed to Gibraltar in order that, under his lordship's observation, his fitness for a military life might be judged of. Prince Alamayou, himself however, was anxious to pursue his studies for some time longer in this country, and expressed a strong preference for doing so under the care of Mr Ransome, who had been his private tutor (for two years) at Rugby, and whom Mr Jex-Blake strongly recommended, when bringing his own charge of the Prince to an end, as the latters guardian and instructor'.

Cyril Ransome agreed to this proposal. The Government and Queen Victoria acceded and according to Treasury Papers of the time, Cyril Ransome took

Prince Alamayou 1861-1879. *Courtesy: Brotherton Library, University of Leeds.*

charge of Prince Alamayou on October 1st 1879 'for six months at least' at two hundred and fifty pounds with fifty pounds put at Alamayou's own disposal. At last, Alamayou's future looked more settled. He was released from the rigours of military training and allowed the freedom of semi-obscurity in Leeds with his friend and tutor. Sadly, it was not to be. Months of anxiety and stress had taken their toll. Within days Alamayou had caught a chill which his body hadn't the strength to throw off. It was the ultimate tragedy. In an extraordinary twist of fate, he simply caught cold and died.

In his unpublished autobiography, Cyril Ransome explains:

> 'Prince Alamayou came to live with me and Rev Annesley-Powys, now Vicar of Meanwood at 1 Hollin Lane, Far Headingley[1]. Unfortunately, by a foolish act, he caught a violent cold which developed into pneumonia. Though he was attended from the very first by Dr Clifford Allbutt, he died in the presence of Mrs Jex-Blake, a nurse and myself on November 14th 1879. I accompanied the body to Windsor where it was buried on November 22nd in St George's Chapel.'

And the foolish act? It seems he fell asleep in the outside WC in the middle of a cold night.

The Treasury papers record that 'a week after his arrival at Leeds, he was seized with a severe cold and was found to be suffering from a slight attack of pleurisy with pneumonia.'

Telegrams were received and sent daily between the Queen's private secretary, Sir Stafford Northcote's office and the Post Office in Far Headingley. There was great concern and consternation during the whole six weeks of Alamayou's steadily deteriorating condition:

> 'I feel I ought to let you know how dangerously ill he is,' Northcote wrote, in a letter to Lady Biddulph. 'The last accounts are rather better, and there seems to be fair grounds for hope; but he is still in a critical state. He is suffering from an attack of pleurisy and has been twice tapped in the chest. His illness has been aggravated and his strength sadly reduced by an extraordinary fancy that he had been poisoned, which let him for some time refuse all food and medicines. He has now become more reasonable as to taking what is ordered.'

The celebrated Leeds doctor, Clifford Allbutt, attended Alamayou and there were visits from a number of distinguished consultant doctors. Lady Biddulph came to see him at the express wish of the Queen who also wrote to him. When the Queen's letter arrived 'he was quite conscious and was much pleased to hear who it was from. He opened it easily and read a few lines, but the exertion pained him.' He asked that the letter be put where he could see it and there it remained until the end.

Cyril Ransome and Mrs Jex-Blake were with him during his illness. He died holding their hands at 9.15am on November 14th 1879. The Queen was telegraphed at once. Later that day she wrote in her diary:

> 'Was very grieved and shocked to hear by telegram that good Alamayou had passed away this morning. It is all too sad. All alone in a strange country, without seeing a person or relative belonging to him, so young and so good, but for *him* one cannot repine. His was no happy life, full of difficulties of every kind, and he was so sensitive, thinking that people stared at him because of his colour, that I fear he would never have been happy. Everyone is very sorry.'

That evening a Court Circular was published: 'The Queen has received today, with much concern, the news of the death of the young Abyssinian, Prince Alamayou. Her Majesty sent Sir John Camell twice to see him and received constant telegrams as to his state during his illness, and the Queen has always taken a warm interest in this young prince who endeared himself to all who knew him, by his amiable and charming character.'

The Queen asked that Alamayou be buried at Windsor. From a report in the *Yorkshire Post*, we know that the body was placed in an airtight shell with glass over the face, and this was enclosed in a polished oak coffin. It was removed from Hollin Lane on November 20th and taken on a funeral carriage, covered by a pall, to Leeds station. From there it was transferred onto a train and made the long journey to Windsor via Crewe, Rugby and Willesdon Junction, accompanied by Cyril Ransome.

The train arrived at Windsor in the evening of the 20th and was met by a hearse with four horses and one of the Queen's carriages for the Professor. The funeral took place at St George's Chapel, Windsor Castle, the following day at noon, whilst snow gently fell outside 'whitening the roofs of the chapel and castle towers.' The chief mourners in attendance included the Chancellor of the Exchequer Sir Stafford Northcote, Cyril Ransome, General Napier, Dr Jex-Blake, Mr Victor Biddulph and Captain Speedy. One can only guess at the Captain's heartfelt reflections that day. The Queen sent a wreath for the Prince's coffin which was laid to rest in a brick vault, outside the Chapel.[2]

The following week, Punch published this poem:

Prince Alamayou

Son of Theodore, King of Abyssinia; taken at Magdala, April 13 1868.
Died at Leeds (Ward of the Queen, the Chancellor of the Exchequer, and the people of England), Nov 14 1879. Buried, by the Queen's desire, at Windsor, Nov 21.

POOR RASSELAS! Short thy life, but not unloved,
And not so sad, let England hope and trust;
A kind Queen's mother's heart for thee was moved,
And near her kin finds room for thy dark dust.

From THEODORUS – God of battle's gift,
To faithful hands the childhood's care we gave;
Love by thy death-bed heard thy simple shrift:
And thou cam'st nearest kingship in thy grave.

Alamayou was eighteen years old.

Notes

[1] 1 Hollin Lane is 1 Glebe Villas, now 2 Hollin Lane.
[2] Sources: Prince Alamayou of Ethiopia by Lord Amulree, reproduced in the Ethiopia Observer, the journal of Independent Opinion, Economics, History and the Arts, Vol 8 No 1 1970, Hotspur Press Manchester; Local press cuttings; Archive papers of Cyril Ransome, the Brotherton Library, Leeds University.

... And the Professor

His famous son, another Princely tale and Early Literary Clubs.

After the trauma of the death of Prince Alamayou, Professor Cyril Ransome resumed his career as Professor of History and Modern Literature at the Yorkshire College. He married Edith Boulton and moved to 6 Ash Grove in the Hyde Park area of Headingley in 1882. Two years later his son, Arthur, the future novelist, was born. The family moved back to Far Headingley in 1890. Between 1890 and 1893 they lived at No 2 Balmoral Terrace, just off Shaw Lane, and then at 126 Otley Road (known as 3 St Chad's Villas) – opposite St Chad's vicarage.

> 'I was born on January 18th, 1884, in Leeds, where my father was Professor of History. Long afterwards my mother showed me the house in which I was born, a mean, ugly little building, one of a row, not far from Woodhouse Moor. The first house I remember living in must, I think, have been pulled down to make room for the growth of what was then the Yorkshire College and subsequently became Leeds University. I remember little of it but hearing Silvie and Bruno read aloud, and that winter peephole through the frost on the nursery window. From there we moved to a house half way between the Skyrack Inn and the Three Horse Shoes on the outskirts of Leeds. I remember that house by a bush of white guelder roses and my own small garden of pansies with a border of Virginia stock. But I well remember the Shire Oak, the ruin of which remains enclosed in an iron paling, and the old horse-drawn omnibus that used to start from the Skyrack and had straw on the floor to keep the passengers' feet warm. For a long time it kept up its hopeless competition with the horse drawn trams, in which, sometimes, I used to go to Leeds with my Mother. The trams started from their stables by the Three Horseshoes, and they were valued neighbours when we moved to our last Leeds house, 3 St Chad's Villas, opposite St Chad's church and the vicarage where the Hoyles (very distant connections of ours) kept sand-lizards in a glass vivarium. The horse trams did not hurry, and a small boy could keep pace, trotting level with them along the pavement. My mother used to tell of her shame when she had set out for Leeds leaving me, not ready, at home and, sitting in the tram, looked back and saw me running steadily down the hill from the Horseshoes a very long way behind'.
>
> <div align="right">Arthur Ransome, <i>The Autobiography</i>, Jonathan Cape</div>

In 1897 Cyril Ransome gave up his chair at Leeds and returned to Rugby to teach sixth form students and to give himself the opportunity of going into Parliament. A few years earlier, however, he had badly injured himself. Whilst at the family's favourite Lake District holiday retreat, Nibthwaite, he went fishing for sea-trout one night and fell over an old grindstone. His leg became infected and was amputated. The surgery, however, was not successful. 'For some years after the accident Father refused to be defeated' according to Arthur in the autobiography. Cyril never properly recovered. He died soon after his return to Rugby in 1897 aged forty seven.

Interestingly, it seems Prince Alamayou was not the only 'royal' pupil of Cyril Ransome. Government diplomats had clearly taken note of the Professor's reliability and discretion, as well as his skill as a personal tutor and guardian. In the autobiography, Arthur refers to his father's pupil Tsau-Chee, nephew to Theebaw, King of Burma:

> 'Tsau-Chee had been at the dinner when Theebaw the King of Burma suspected a plot, offered his plate to a dog, and, the dog dropping to the ground, took pistols and shot one after another thirteen (I am not sure of the number) of his relations who were dining with him, leaving alive Tsau-Chee alone. I remember Tsau-Chee for his extreme skill in making paper boats and for his horror when at night he found one of my furry fox-moth caterpillars crawling across his cheek'.

Arthur Ransome, The Autobiography, Jonathan Cape

Tsau-Chee visited the family at Nibthwaite and at Far Headingley (Balmoral Terrace). In a letter from London, to 'Mr Ransome', dated July 8th 1882, Tsaw-Chee writes:

> 'I am very sorry that I missed seeing you when I was in Leeds. The fact is that I was told that all of you were away. I did not receive your letter until I returned home. I am greatly disappointed at not having seen all of you, as this was the only opportunity I shall have of visiting Leeds before my return to Burma. I start for the continent on August 3rd, and embark for Rangoon from Marseilles on the 27th. I must therefore wish all of you goodbye by letter. With kind regards to all. Trusting that you will have a very jolly vacation, I am, dear Mr Ransome yours very sincerely, Tsaw-Chee'.[1]

He wrote to Mrs Ransome on July 15th, responding to one from her and telling her he was looking forward to seeing his father and mother 'and all of my people in the Shan States'. He also mentions his last minute shopping – two guns, two rifles, one revolver and a camera 'which is three times as large as my old one'.

There is a small epitaph to this story. It comes from Mr Frank Atlay, the son of a Vicar of Leeds and, himself, manager of the ruby mines in Burma:

> 'I was sitting on the verandah of my house with a young Indian Prince who had been having lunch with me. We had spoken of many things, he having just returned from England. I asked him what he had liked best there. He was silent for a little while, and then said 'Leeds Parish Church'. I almost jumped out of my chair, as he added 'oh, how that choir sings'. He had lived for three months in Leeds with a Professor of the Yorkshire College, and attended the Parish Church Sunday Evening Service'.

Recollections: 60 years ago and onwards H & J & B M Walker 1934[2]

Dr Atlay was Vicar of Leeds at the time of the consecration of St Chad's church in 1868.

Arthur Michell Ransome grew up to become a journalist and popular writer of children's books. His classic children's novel *Swallows and Amazons* was written

Edith Ransome

Cyril Ransome

Arthur Ransome

Courtesy: Leeds University Brotherton Library Special Collection.

in 1930 and drawn directly from his own childhood recollections of school holidays at Nibthwaite. After his schooling at Windermere and Rugby he became a reporter on the *Daily News*, and then the *Manchester Guardian*. He learnt Russian and was sent to cover the 1918 Moscow Revolution as a journalist. In 1924 he divorced his first wife and married Trotsky's secretary Eugenia Shelepin. They fled Russia and settled in the English Lake District. He died in 1967.

During his lifetime Arthur Ransome kept in touch with Far Headingley through visits to his mother, Edith. She returned to Leeds in 1912. His autobiography gives other snippets from his early days and introduces more characters:

> 'I enjoyed a succession of educators whom I shared with the son of one of my father's friends. This was Ric, (*Eric Rucker Eddison*). His father was Octavius Eddison, a Leeds solicitor, whose saddle-horse I have seen, in those liesurely days, tied up outside his office in the middle of Leeds. His uncle, Dr John Eddison was a friend of Andrew Langs. Both lived at Adel. We shared a governess, a kindly comfortable Miss Glendenning, who lived by the Shire Oak. The Eddison's dog-cart used to take her to Adel, picking me up on the way'.

Eric Eddison also became a writer. His best known book 'The Worm Ouroborus' is a fore-runner of the works of J R R Tolkien, although Tolkien denied he had been influenced by it. In fact Arthur Ransome wrote to Tolkien after The Hobbitt appeared describing himself as 'a humble hobbit fancier'. Tolkien himself spent time in Leeds, living at Far Headingley, Woodhouse and West Park, whilst working at Leeds University. But to return to Ransome ...

> 'My first school was a day school, half way between Headingley and what was then the Yorkshire College. I reached it by tram. I was not at that school for long (for) my father sent me to boarding school at Windermere'.

During the winter of 1913/14, aged twenty nine, he writes:

> 'That winter I worked hard. I wrote two children's books. I stayed with my mother at Headingley, *(his mother was now living at 28 Grove Road)*, dined with an uncle in The Curfew Club to which my father belonged, saw a pantomime in the same theatre in which, so long ago, I had seen my first'.

Arthur refers here to dining with an uncle in The Curfew Club. I think he must mean that he dined *at home* with an uncle *who belonged to* The Curfew Club. The Curfew Club was the name given to a conversation club founded in March 1886 and restricted to only twelve members. Its object: 'to promote social and intellectual intercourse among its members'. Subjects excluded 'any involving points of theology; and any within the range of party or municipal politics'. No doubt the conversational business of the club was principally centred round a good dinner.

Cyril Ransome was a founder member. He was living at 4 De Grey Rd[3] at the time. Arthur was four years old. Octavius Eddison was also a member as was a Mr Smithells[4] and a Mr Tillard, both from St Chad's Gardens. Meetings were held monthy, each member hosting one meeting every year. Hence twelve members. The club was still going strong in 1936.

A more formal, and distinctly more serious club was founded by Cyril Ransome himself in 1889. The Ransome Literary Club also had a membership restricted to twelve people. Its object: 'the reading and conversational discussion of such works as may be agreed upon'.

They evidently did not limit themselves to twelve meetings a year, nor their own homes. The club's records indicate, for example, that the 320th meeting was held on March 6th 1906 in the University Refectory. In the formal notice to this meeting is a list of books read since the Club's foundation. The choice was not always light and racy:

'Book	Author	Time Occupied
Essays, Civic and Moral	Bacon	1 year 10.5 months
Tempest	Shakespeare	1 month'

The 890th meeting was held on January 26th 1934 at 28 Grove Road (Edith Ransome's house). Temperley's *'Europe in the 19th and 20th Centuries'* was continued to page 571, after which the next meeting was fixed for February 9th 1934 at Mr J R Whiting's house.

Edith Ransome left Grove Road in 1938. But she was back in Far Headingley in 1939 to attend the 979th meeting of The Ransome Literary Club held on April 1st at Castle Grove, which had become in 1934, Castle Grove Masonic Hall.

Cyril Ransome belonged to yet another club The Conversation Club, also restricted to twelve members and a monthly cycle of meetings at the homes of each member. The club was already established before Cyril arrived in Leeds. Dr John Eddison, for example, had been elected a member in July 1871. Cyril joined in 1890 and Octavius Eddison 'of St Helen's Adel', the following year.

Entertaining and social, or worthy and stuffy – who knows, but these clubs certainly endured during a time of rapid change, improving education and no television!

Among members of The Conversation Club was **Nathan Bodington** 'elected 29th September 1885'. Nathan Bodington MA, an Oxford graduate, had moved to Leeds from Mason College in Birmingham to take up a post at the Yorkshire College in 1882. He became a colleague of Cyril Ransome and lived at 3 St Chad's Villas (126 Otley Road), opposite St Chad's Church.

In 1894, now Principal of the College and Professor of Classics and Philosophy, he took a house in Shire Oak Road in Headingley, vacating 3 St Chad's Villas for his friends Cyril and Edith Ransome, who moved from Balmoral Terrrace with young Arthur[5].

In 1904, Sir Nathan Bodington became Vice Chancellor of the newly chartered University. As a personality he was described as 'formal and somewhat academic' but 'patient, courteous and impartial'. He died in 1911 aged sixty three and is buried in St Chad's Church grounds, near the tower entrance.

The Bodington Hall complex at Lawnswood, a University Hall of Residence and University playing fields, are named in his memory.

Notes

[1] Reproduced by kind permission of the Brotherton Library, Leeds. King Theebaw (or Thibaw) of Burma 1858-1916, was deposed by the British in 1885. The British subsequently governed Burma until its independence in 1948.
[2] I am grateful to Margaret Ratcliffe, a local Ransome scholar for drawing my attention to these references.
[3] De Grey Rd was on the site of the present day University Parkinson Building.
[4] Arthur Smithells B.Sc F.R.S. later moved to 29 Moor Road.
[5] In 1898 St Chad's Villas became Moorlands School. It is now a Hotel.

Into the Twentieth Century:
The Beginning of a New Age and the end of an Old Order

At the turn of the century, Ernest William Beckett was still living at Kirkstall Grange, Alf Cooke – churchwarden at St Chad's – was resident at Weetwood Hall with his wife and daughter, James Oxley had recently retired and was building his exotic art collection at Spenfield, John Kirk was at Castle Grove (now impressively enlarged), Charles Oates was living at Meanwoodside set in the grounds of his father's extraordinary garden and young George Merry, the tram driver's son, now twenty one was embarking on a working life which would soon take him to Brighton.

The Ransomes had left Far Headingley for the Lake District, St Chad's School had left its Hollin Lane site and moved to new premises in Otley Road and St Chad's Home for Waifs and Strays was well established at Hollin Hall turning out knitted stockings to distant customers:

Harriet Heaton was fifty one and living in London in 1903 with her husband the Revd William Heaton. Her diary for that year is still kept by her great grand daughter Margaret Bonsall who now lives in Weetwood Lane. In 1903 Harriet noted:

> 'Stockings footed by Mrs Pollard, Rotherham, by machinery 9d per pair. Also at St Chad's Home, Far Headingley, Leeds, one of the Homes for Church of England Waifs and Strays for delicate crippled girls'.

Meanwhile the modern world was in its infancy. New mass industries were developing. The horseless carriage was the wonder of the age and the telephone would soon be commonplace. In 1901 The National Telephone Company Exchange Ltd began to operate a telephone exchange from 30 Moor Road, while John Kirk, a keen early motorist, adapted premises in Cottage Road as a garage – premises which would later be converted into a cinema, heralding a new age in public entertainment.

Queen Victoria died in January 1901 and the Prince of Wales (Bertie) succeeded to the throne as Edward VII, at the age of sixty one. It was a time when Britain's confidence and influence in the world was at its zenith. Power and privilege belonged to business barons and the landed gentry. Social position depended on wealth and connections.

Ernest Beckett and the King's mistress

In Leeds, one of the most dashing figures on the social scene was undoubtedly the very wealthy Ernest Beckett of Kirkstall Grange. After the death of his wife

Lucy in 1891 he travelled widely and entertained impressively. The Prince of Wales had been his guest at Kirkstall Grange in 1895 for the Leeds Music Festival and week-end parties for politicians, aristocrats and celebrities were a regular feature of his Leeds calendar. We can only imagine the hustle and bustle around the Grange and within Far Headingley caused by the need to make preparations – carriages up and down the coach-drive, gardeners tending the grounds and kitchen gardens, maids changing linen upstairs and setting tables downstairs, local tradesmen calling, deliveries made – it must have been a constant whirl.

Ernest clearly revelled in high society and, besides Kirkstall Grange, maintained two London addresses – at Stratton Street near St James' Palace, and at Virginia Water, a carriage drive from Windsor across Windsor Great Park.

At some point he became intimate with Mrs Alice Keppel, wife of the Hon George Keppel, a lieutenant with the Gordon Highlanders whom she had married in 1891 when she was twenty-two. The Keppels were part of the smart Belgravia set where 'life's principal domain was social' but George did not have the income nor perhaps the charisma to satisfy his wife. She was soon turning to Ernest Beckett for amusement and the liaison allegedly produced a love-child.

> Mrs Keppel was ambitious and her nose for profit shrewd. She wanted more than George could give. 'Throughout her life' her daughter Sonia wrote of her, 'mama was irresistably attractive to bank managers'. The attraction worked both ways. Violet was born on the 6th of June 1894, three years into the marriage. By the time of her birth the Keppels had moved from Wilton Street to a larger 18th century house at 30 Portman Square. Violet's father was said to be (Ernest) William Beckett, senior partner in the family bank, Beckett and Company of Leeds, member of parliament for Whitby, owner of a large villa in Ravello and heir to the Grimthorpe title. Mrs Keppel viewed adultery as sound business practice, a woman's work[1].

Was the move to Portman Street financed through a Beckett Bank draft and was he truly Violet's father?

The story becomes all the more interesting because within a few years Alice Keppel would become mistress to the Prince of Wales himself, an open relationship that continued throughout his reign as Edward VII, and Violet – Violet Beckett – it would seem, would marry Major Denys Trefusis, become a writer and the secret lesbian lover of novelist Vita Sackville West.

> Vita Sackville-West told Violet's first biographer, Philippe Julian, that (Ernest) William Beckett was probably Violet's father. And (Ernest) William Beckett's grandson said Violet 'undoubtedly had the Beckett nose'.
>
> Violet was never altogether clear whose nose she had. Beckett's American wife died in 1891, the year of Alice's marriage, leaving him with three small children. Perhaps Alice consoled him in his plight. 'My mother,' as Violet was to write, 'not only had the gift of happiness, she excelled in making others happy.'
>
> Violet did not know who her father was, though she was sure he was not her mother's husband George. In adult life she claimed to be the daughter of Edward VII, but she did not confront her mother on the subject – *toute verite n'est pas bonne a dire*[1].

In 1903, Ernest decided to emigrate to Ravello in Italy, where he built his Villa Cimbrone overlooking the Bay of Salerno. He was forty six. Whether he emigrated because he was tired of his business life or because of his potential for embarrassment to the Court of St James is a matter for speculation. In any event he remained in touch with Alice Keppel.

> In May (1913), Violet and her mother stayed in Ravello at the villa of Lord Grimthorpe – the banker reputed to be Violet's father. Vita stayed too, to vex Rosamund (Grosvenor) who was having a romance with a sailor[1].

In 1905 he succeeded to his uncle's title and became the 2nd Baron Grimthorpe. He died in 1917 and is thought to have been buried in the pseudo-classical temple of Bacchus on one of the terraces of his Mediterranean Villa.

Gervase Beckett – the last Beckett at Kirkstall Grange

Ernest's early 'retirement' to Italy enabled his brother Gervase, to take possession of Kirkstall Grange with his wife Mabel and their growing family. Two children, Marian and Cynthia, had already been born to them at their former home in Gledhow, Leeds, and two more, Beatrice and Prunella, would be born at Kirkstall Grange:

> 'All his (Gervase's) children were born in Leeds, the late Dr Octavious Croft, the Leeds surgeon and gynaecologist, being in attendance upon Mrs Beckett. Dr Croft often recalled the journeys to the Grange and in particular those during the night, when the carriage was sent to his home, the hoofs of the horses and the rumbling of the wheels breaking the silence of the night, especially in the drive through the Park from Otley Road to the house, when all nature was still, and he the lonely passenger in the coach'.
>
> '*New Grange, Kirkstall*' J Sprittles,
Thoresby Society Miscellany Vol 13 Pt 1. 1959

In 1923, nineteen-year-old Beatrice Beckett married the second son of Sir William Eden, Robert Anthony Eden. The marriage faltered after the wartime death of their son, Simon, and they separated in 1946. In 1950 Anthony Eden became Foreign Secretary in Churchill's government and two years later, married Churchills's niece, Clarissa. He became Prime Minister in 1955 and was eventually enobled as Lord Avon.

But all this still lay ahead in an unknown future when Winston Churchill arrived with his secretary Edward Marsh at Kirkstall Grange and signed the visitors book on February 7th 1907 – three year old Beatrice, no doubt excitedly watching the comings and goings from the nursery windows.

Fourteen months earlier, another eminent Parliamentarian had been a weekend guest at Kirkstall Grange. This was Arthur Balfour, Prime Minister from 1902 to 1905. His visit on December 18th 1905 was not only recorded in the visitors book, but also on camera. In the photogragh, Arthur Balfour stands on the steps of the Grange. His thirty nine year old host, Gervase Beckett, is standing to his right and other members of the group include Lady Balfour, Mabel Beckett, and Arthur Balfour's brother Gerald.

In 1905, Gervase had been elected MP for Whitby, a seat previously held by his brother Ernest and in 1921 he became Sir William Gervase Beckett having been created a Baronet.

Another photograph taken at this time and also reproduced here by kind permission of Sir Martyn Beckett (Gervase's son from his later second marriage), shows Marian Beckett sitting in a carriage at the front of Kirkstall Grange with an unknown companion.

The last entry in the visitors book is dated January 1908, for in that New Year, the family moved to Kirkdale Manor near Helmsley in North Yorkshire very much more convenient to Gervase's Scarborough and Whitby constituency, although paradoxically, he would become MP for Leeds North in 1921.

Kirkstall Grange is sold and a College Established

Gervase's younger brother, Rupert, who was to forge his own brilliant career in Leeds becoming treasurer of Leeds University, Chairman of the Westminster Bank and Chairman of the Yorkshire Post, might well have considered making Kirkstall Grange his home in 1907. However, this was not to be. Instead the family, (or strictly speaking, Ernest Beckett in Italy, now the 2nd Lord Grimthorpe) agreed to sell the Grange and thirty five acres of land to Leeds Corporation for the purpose of establishing a teacher training college. At the same time a further nineteen acres, known as Churchwood, was freely donated to the college.

A magnificent group of college buildings and seven residential halls designed in a 'Wrennaissance' revival style by G W Atkinson was opened in 1913 as Beckett Park Teacher Training College. The Grange, itself, was integrated into the development dominated by the college scheme. No longer the private residence of the Beckett Banking dynasty but still retained as an impressive annex to the new college.

The Great War

In 1914 came the Great War in Europe. Soon casualties from the front line were returning home and within a year Beckett Park college was taken over as a military hospital. St Chad's school became a First Aid Post and across the Otley road, the children of St Chad's Home for Waifs and Strays were making their own contribution to the war effort. In 1914 they made 13,611 pairs of socks for the British troops.

On the steps of Kirkstall Grange in December 1905. Left to right: Lady Betty Balfour, Mabel Beckett, Gervase Beckett, Arthur Balfour, Gerald Balfour, Mr Saunders and Mrs Oliver Howard.
Courtesy: Sir Martyn Beckett.

Marion Beckett and unknown companion in a carriage outside Kirkstall Grange c1905.
Courtesy: Sir Martyn Beckett

Aerial view of G W Atkinson's Beckett's Park Training College campus c1950. The gable frontage to Kirkstall Grange can be seen in the foreground on the left hand side of the college green. During the two world wars the buildings served as a military hospital.

Courtesy: Leeds City Library.

Fanny Dykes was a young girl at the time, living with her parents at Cardigan Cottage just opposite St Chad's Church[2]. The cottage garden fronted onto the Otley Road and from there she watched a constant stream of wounded soldiers being transported up to the temporary military hospital, having been brought to Leeds station from the war front by train. In an age before television it brought the tragedy, not the glory, of war home and left a deep impression on Fanny Dykes. It was a vivid memory which she passed on to her son Alfred Johnson and which he still reflects upon over eighty years after the war ended.

Seventy six Far Headingley men died in the Great War. Their names are recorded on a bronze, oval tablet fixed to a stone pier forming part of St Chad's war memorial. Designed by J Harold Gibbons the memorial was erected at the end of the church drive, and later re-positioned in a formal memorial garden facing Otley Road. It consists of a cross of Guiseley stone backed by a semi-circular wall ending in two stone piers. As if anticipating World War Two, the second pier would eventually carry its own roll call of honour.

After the war the new Beckett Park college buildings reverted to teacher training, (but not until 1926) and in 1933 a sports faculty was added, the Carnegie Physical Training College.

The Children's Home

The Childrens Home, at Hollin Hall continued to house, educate and employ orphaned, poor and needy children until the Second World War, when the building was commandeered as an Air Raid and Ambulance Station. After the war, the Hall was bought by the Yorkshire College of Housecraft which later merged with Leeds Polytechnic paradoxically bringing two buildings bearing the Beckett Coat of Arms – Hollin Hall and Kirkstall Grange – into single ownership (the College) for the first time. Weetwood Junior school occupied the former ambulance depot which had been erected in the grounds of the Hall during the war. In 1995 Leeds Education Authority acquired the Hall itself, demolished the old ambulance depot and reopened the Hall and grounds in 1997 as an enlarged Weetwood Primary School after major renovation and alteration work.

The Second World War air raid and ambulance station which became the buildings of Weetwood Primary School until 1995 when the school was relocated into the adjacent Hollin Hall.
Photo: David Hall.

Schools in the 20th Century

Three private fee-paying schools have flourished in Far Headingley through the twentieth century. On April 4th 1898, a small school for boys opened at St Chad's Villas, Otley Road (next door to Arthur Ransome's old address). This was **Moorlands School** established by Mr Raundrup with just one pupil. From this unpromising start, numbers grew and the school developed, eventually expanding into the adjoining property. It was to remain at the Otley Road site until 1968, decamping to Grasmere only briefly during the war when the school building was taken over by the Ministry of Defence. In 1968 the governors sanctioned the acquisition of Mr Tetley's former Weetwood mansion house at Fox Hill and the school moved. The Otley Road premises became an hotel.

> The school has many interesting associations. Graham Hill visited to show the boys his formula-one racing car, and Sir Alan Ayckbourn, when a school parent, wrote a play especially for the pupils to perfom (at Fox Hill). One member of staff joined the French Resistance during the Second World War and returned to the school with his French fiancee. The school itself, evacuated to Grasmere when St Chad's Villas were requisitioned by the Defence Department. Stories abound of icy swims and bracing walks in the Lake District.
>
> Mrs Paula Woolnough

Moorlands School at St Chad's Villas Otley Road. The school was founded in 1898 in the house on the left. Arthur Ransome lived in the house on the right as a young boy between 1893 and 1897.

Courtesy: Ian Ballantine

The School became co-educational in 1981.

In 1935, Beryl Davies established a private school at 170 Otley Road. She named it **Richmond House School** and took twenty four five-year-olds at three guineas a term. As numbers increased 172 and 168 Otley Road were acquired. In 1954 the assembly hall extension was built and a first floor dining hall added three years later. During the second world war the children were evacuated to Windermere and soldiers were billeted in the school.

Miss Davies retired in 1979 and the school was taken over by a Council of Management, which became a Board of Governors in 1989 when the school was purchased from Miss Davies. The school has continued to expand in the 1990s, acquiring its playing fields in Glen Road and adding a sports pavilion.

In 1999, the school had an enrolment of 240 pupils and a teaching staff of 22. Today, it is still known by many as Miss Davies' School.

The smallest private preparatory school in Far Headingley is **St Agnes' School** in Burton Crescent. In 1898 Miss Rose Harland and her sister Miss Ethel Harland set up the school in their home at St Agnes' Villa just off Shaw Lane. Rose Harland was reputed to have been a formidable character demanding obedience and punctilious manners in her pupils. The school was acquired in 1925 by Elisabeth Philips, who retreated to a nunnery nine years later, disposing of the school and the property to another pair of sisters, Cynthia and Maud Harvey. With the Misses Harvey the school became a PNEU (Parents National Educational Union) School.

After the brief wartime evacuation in 1939, the school resumed at Burton Crescent early in 1940. Miss Maud Harvey died in 1956 and Cynthia retired in 1960 but continued to live at the property. Subsequent headmistresses have been Miss Hughes (1960-1978), Mrs Pamela Corfield (1978-1995), Mrs Burrows (1995-1998) and Mrs McMeeking (from 1998).

Today the school takes 56 two to seven year-olds, compared in 1900 to its enrolment of 38 up to age fourteen-year-olds.

The 1990s have also seen major changes in state supported school provision. Middle schools, a feature of the English comprehensive system since the 1970s, were closed and primary schools enlarged. **St Chad's Primary School** could not accommodate its new numbers and a new building was constructed on a playing field site at West Park, beginning a new era for the school.

Fears that the old school would be demolished were averted when the one hundred year old buildings were bought for a private nursery school and handsomely renovated and restored.

Similarly, **Weetwood Primary School** could no longer function from the former ambulance station behind Hollin Hall, hence the decision in 1995 to acquire the Hall from Leeds Metropolitan University (successors to Leeds Polytechnic) and relocate the school. The building was converted and reopened as Weetwood Primary School in 1997.

Today, children run in and out of the main entrance, still crowned in stone with the Beckett's family crest, and play near the foundation stones laid by Lucy Beckett's own little infants in 1893, Lucille, Muriel and two-year-old Ralph. Hollin Hall was intended as a building for children and it is very fitting that it should revert to a building for children. That would appeal to Lucy Beckett and the generations of children who grew up there as waifs and strays.

Two schools founded in the centre of Leeds by the Leeds Educational and Literary Institute, later known as the 'Mechanics' Institute, are also of interest. The Mathematics and Commercial School for boys opened in 1845 and the Ladies Educational Institution in 1854. Both schools were originally located in South Parade and later moved to purpose built premises adjacent to the new Mechanics Institute building (the Civic Theatre) in Cookridge Street. The Albert Hall, as it was known, was designed by Cuthbert Brodrick and opened in 1868.

In 1885 the boys school became Leeds Boys Modern School. The girls school became Leeds Girls School in 1868 and then Leeds Girls Modern School in 1893. Leeds Corporation Education Authority took over financial control of both schools in 1906 and transferred the girls school to a larger building in the city the following year.

Otley Road, West Park in 1941. The Leeds Modern School (opened 1930) is on the left and the dualled section of main road has the tram cable posts in the central reservation. The tram terminus is now at Lawnswood. The message to drivers heading north is "DRIVE SLOWLY", although the solitary motorist heading towards Leeds has the road entirely to himself. On the right is the coach house to another Victorian gothic villa, Weetwood House c1880.

Courtesy: Ian Ballantine.

After the First World War there was a wave of house building as new suburbs were created and city centre slums cleared. Rising school numbers and housing displacement precipitated the need for new buildings on the outskirts of the city and in the mid 1920s a site was acquired at West Park on the new Ring Road. In 1931 the two schools were relocated into magnificent new buildings designed in a neo Georgian style by the Education Department's architect Fred Broadbent and costing £120,000. Both schools had accommodation for 600 pupils each, expansive shared playing fields on the south side and a central swimming pool. The boys retained the name Leeds Modern School and the girls became Lawnswood High School. Forty years later, in 1972, the schools amalgamated fully as Lawnswood School.

These fine buildings came under threat of demolition in 2000 following claims that they could not be adapted to the modern combined school's requirement and must make way for a contemporary building. If they are destroyed it will be a sad loss.

Past Times and Pastimes

Cricket

Nationally, the name Headingley is synonymous with Yorkshire Cricket and Test Matches. From the founding of the game, wherever stumps could be pitched, cricket has been an English summer passion, and that is no less true in Yorkshire than any other English county. Idyllically, it is played on a village green or church meadow, notwithstanding the lure of big matches played at the county grounds. In Far Headingley, St Chad's Cricket Club dates its foundation from the early 1880s.

In fact the Club did not establish itself in front of the church until 1922. Before that the club played in the grounds of Kirkstall Grange, and later moved to the Weetwood Hall estate, subsequently Bodington Hall playing fields.

Writing in 1960, R W Boning records:

> 'Those with long memories recall matches played at Harewood and Hunsingore, when the team and supporters travelled in horse drawn wagonettes. In the two years after World War One some very hard work was put into levelling off allotments formed during the war (in front of St Chad's), and during those years, on dark September or October evenings, dimmed figures armed with picks, shovels and wheelbarrows, worked on the ground by the light of storm lanterns, digging, laying ashes, forming the 'square' and generally levelling the outfield. In 1922 home matches were played for the first time'[3].

Canon Charles Marshall, Vicar of St Chad's from 1907 and 1947 played for the Club during the whole of his forty years as incumbent of the parish:

> It was said that if a parishioner wished to get married at 3 o'clock on a summer Saturday afternoon, Canon Marshall would do his best to persuade the happy couple

to hold the ceremony at 2 o'clock, so that he could lead the eleven on to the field at the start of a match'[3]

Today, St Chad's Broomfield Cricket Club Far Headingley has three senior teams and two junior teams competing in the Wetherby League.

Golf

It is an anomaly to many people that Headingley Golf Club is located at Adel. In fact the club might be more properly titled Far Headingley Golf Club, for it was established in the Far Headingley Parish in 1892.

Forty acres of Moor Grange Farm, between Butcher Hill, Spen Lane and the present line of the Ring Road, toward the northerly extremity of the former Cardigan estate, were laid out with nine holes 'being about a mile around'. The farmhouse itself became the clubhouse. It was part of the late 19th century boom in golf course development and Leeds was as hooked on the game as any other part of the country. During the following years golf clubs would open at Leeds and Rawdon (1896), Woodhall and Otley (1906), Horsforth (1907), Alwoodley (1908) and Moortown (1909).

'Far' Headingley golfing pioneers at the Spen Lane clubhouse 1898.

Courtesy: Headingley Golf Club.

'It is recorded that when golf was played for the first time on the links at Far Headingley, in spite of unfavourable weather – a high wind blowing and rain falling most of the afternooon – so great was the number of players that the links had upon them them from an early hour in the afternoon until dusk, almost as many players as could follow the sport with pleasure to themselves, and without inconvenience to others'[4].

A number of prominent figures attended the opening day on Saturday October 29th, including the Leeds bankers, and local residents, Ernest Beckett MP of Kirkstall Grange, and James W Oxley of Spenfield. Players were dressed in knickerbocker suits or jacket, tweed trousers and bowler hats. They were attended by boys as caddies and 'in each hole stood a flag as a guide'.

'Judging from the number of players on Headingley's opening day – including several ladies – it was felt it would not be long before the area at the disposal of members would be increased'.

The nine hole golf club thrived and within a few years attempts were being made to buy land on the opposite side of Spen Lane in order to increase the course to a full eighteen holes. Negotiations with the Beckett and Cardigan estates however were not concluded, possibly because there were already prospects of higher land values for house building – residential development here would soon form the new suburb of West Park.

At the turn of the century there were over two hundred members. The club's popularity even resulted in the re-routing of the Corporation's ten seater horse buses from the Three Horse Shoes to the golf ground, two journeys being made daily and five on Saturday. In 1905 the horse drawn trams were replaced by a motor bus.

When the membership topped three hundred it became more urgent to enlarge the existing course or move to a new location. The Club was turned into a limited company in 1905 and £3,000 was raised from debenture shares taken up by its members. In 1906 the club moved to its present site just north of Adel church, having leased about fifty acres of rolling farmland. To serve the new course at Adel, the Corporation ran a motor bus service for the first time into Leeds from Adel.

Notes

[1] *Mrs Keppel and her Daughter* by Diana Soutami Harper Collins 1996.
[2] Cardigan Cottage was one of a group of stone houses standing on the north side of St Chad's Road. St Chad's Parade now occupies the site of the Otley Road garden from where Fanny watched the passing soldiers and the enlarged bus depot took the remaining land until it too was demolished in the early 1990s. A photograph of Cardigan Cottage appears on page 33.
[3] St Chad's Christian Fellowship brochure 1960
[4] *1892-1992 Headingley Golf Club Centenary Brochure*. Written and compiled by Ray Oddy.

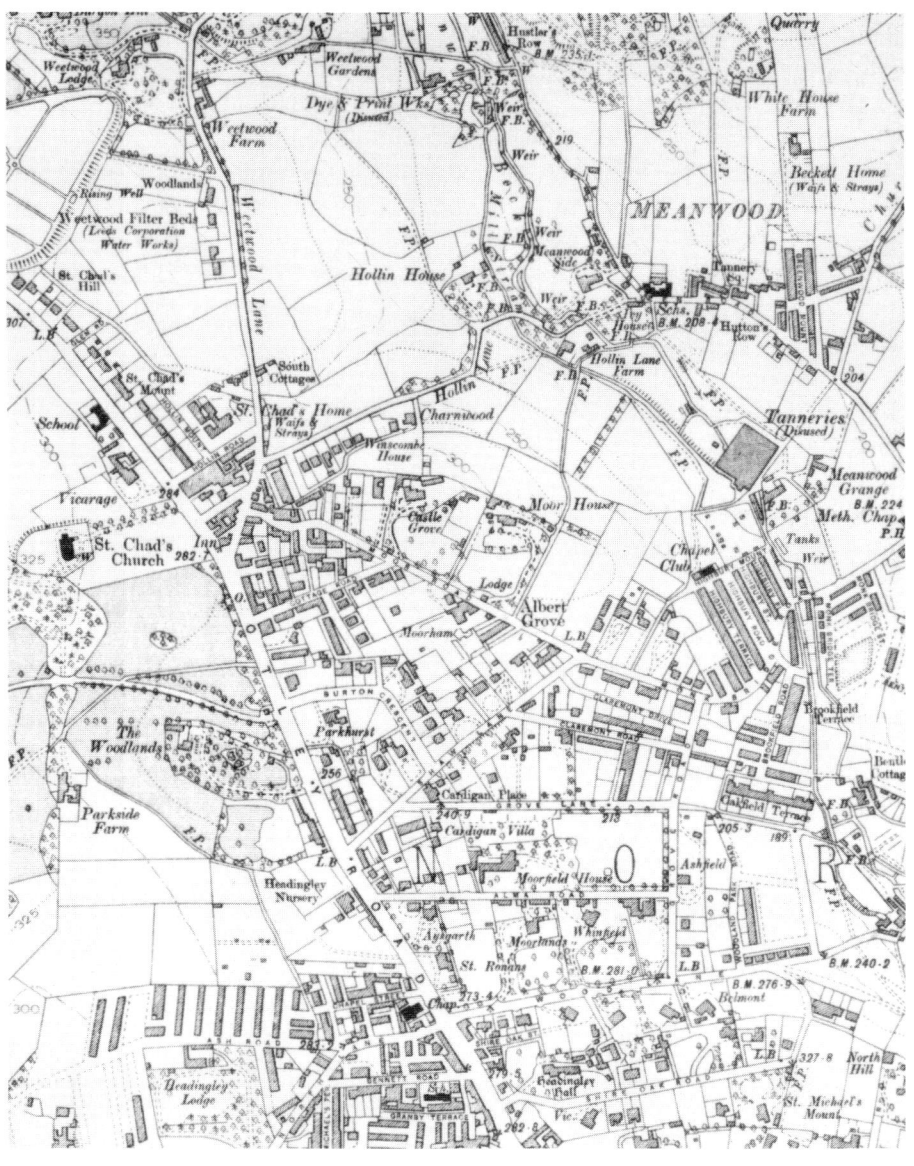

An extract from the Ordnance Survey, 1909 edition. The Conservation Area as we know it is fully developed. Ambushed by 20th century suburbia, John Marshall's Headingley House and Headingley Lodge are just surviving as the Grimthorpe and Escourt terrace houses get constructed. Fine villa houses in large formal gardens occupy much of the east side of Otley Road into Headingley and the Beckett estate fills the west side with the exception of the vicarage and church, plus the row of stone houses just above Headingley Nursery. The Woodlands was a large brickbuilt house built sometime in the mid to late 1800s and demolished in the early 1930s. The gate posts to the drive are still visible on Otley Road but nothing remains of the house and gardens save for a large copper beech tree integrated into the Beckett's Park housing. Known as the Red House, because of the colour of the brickwork, the cleared site became a playground for local children until the late 1930s when new houses were constructed. Parkside Farmhouse remained until the 1950s when it too was demolished for housebuilding, the last occupier being Mr William Lye. *Reproduced from the 1909 Ordnance Survey Map.*

The Twentieth Century: Enlarging the Parish Church

The Vicar of St Chad's from 1896 to 1936 was the Rev Walter Howard Stables, a popular and generous man with eminent local family connections – the Stables of Horsforth. It was Walter Stables who oversaw the enlargement of St Oswald's Mission Church at Highbury in 1899 and who is acknowledged as the main benefactor of the Working Mens Club which was built on a site next to the Mission church in 1902.

He was, himself, an accomplished musician and regretted that St Chad's church had been built with an architecturally delightful, but musically constraining, semi-circular apse, which restricted the size of the choir and organ. He very much wanted to enlarge both which could only be done by removing the apse and rebuilding the whole east end. When we look at old photographs of the church now (page 64), the apse seems a most attractive and pleasing architectural feature:

> 'The original church of St Chad had an apsidal east end with an ambulatory behind the holy table. A pulpit of stone richly ornamented with shafts of Devonshire marble occupied the space where now stands the lectern, whilst the present lectern stood near the chancel step on the south side. A stone screen arcaded and richly curved, divided the chancel from the ambulatory, whilst the ambulatory was separated by a

St Chad's Church in 1936.　　　　　　　　　　　　　　*Courtesy: Leeds City Library.*

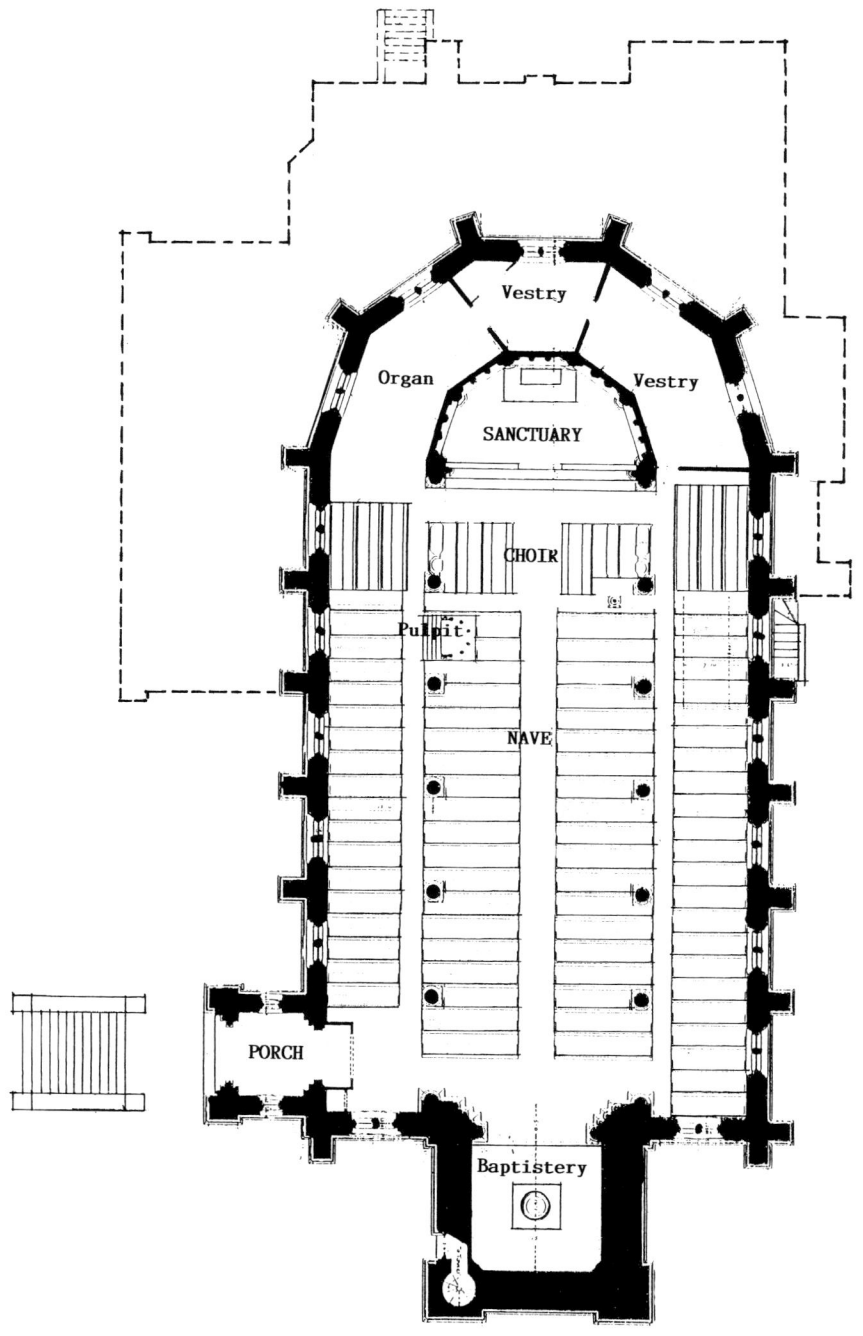

St Chad's Church floor plan 1869-1909 showing the east end after 1909 in outline.
Courtesy: Charles Sewell.

screen of wood to provide a choir vestry and organ chamber which stood on the north side. The choir stalls had seating for about ten boys and eight men'.

J Sprittles. *St Chad's, the First Hundred Years* 1968

When Howard Stables died in 1906, his family considered that a fitting memorial would be a completely new chancel which would accommodate more choristers and a much larger organ. They sponsored plans to take down the original chancel, vestries and organ chamber:

> 'Between 1909 and 1911 the attractive pentagonal apsidal end was demolished, and the present chancel built', which gave adequate provision for an organ chamber with vestries for both clergy and choir. The Side Chapel was also built. The magnificent organ, built by Harrison and Harrison of Durham, is considered to be one of the finest in the North of England and was given as a memorial to the Rev W Howard Stables by his family. It was dedicated on 8th April, 1911. The cost of building the new east end was about £6,000'.

J Sprittles. *St Chad's, the First Hundred Years* 1968

Reference to the 'east' end is worth noting, for in fact St Chad's is not built to an east west orientation as is the general custom. It stands parallel to the Otley Road to give it a more commanding presence. The 'east' end faces south.

A consequence of a south facing 'east' end is the impact of sunlight streaming through the chancel clerestory windows as well as the great 'east' window during sunny Sunday morning services. Margaret Rope appreciated this fact and used it to dramatic effect when designing the pictorial great east window – a tableau of The Creation represented in five, stained glass, lead set panels. It was painted and fired in Margaret Rope's Chelsea studio before being transported to Headingley and installed at the end of the First World War.

And what of the people who filled the church?

> 'As to the congregation, the social revolution which followed the first world war had clearly not been without its effect. No longer was it a church of the Edwardian type where the families attended in the morning and the servants in the evening. The families still came – some of them even twice – but the domestics had disappeared, and in their place the expansion of housing and the newly established training college brought an accession of democracy hitherto foreign to a wealthy parish. Over it all presided the benign figure of Canon Marshall'

W A Wightman, *St Chad's Centenary Brochure*, 1968

In 1931 a public appeal went out for funds to purchase the cricket ground (then leased to the church) plus the old allotments on the Otley Road frontage – a total of 21,046 square yards – from Lord Grimthorpe. £3,500 was raised which secured the future of the cricket club and protected the view of the church from Otley Road. The frontage land was due to be sold for shop sites. Instead this portion of ground was laid out as a peace garden and vested in Leeds Corporation to tend and maintain for the future. The war memorial was moved subsequently from the church drive entrance to become the focal point

The Otley Road frontage to St Chad's Church in 1926. Note the war memorial standing on its original site at the entrance to the church avenue. It was not relocated to the new memorial garden until after the Second World War. *Courtesy: Leeds City Library.*

of the garden. In 1933 the churchyard to the rear and north of the church building was extended.

During the Second World War, the church bells were silent (by law), all the choirboys were evacuated 'at a stroke' and winter services had to be held in the afternoons, because the windows could not be properly blacked-out.

Such was the concern to avoid any possible war damage to Margaret Rope's east window, that it is said it was removed for a time and safely buried near the church, although I have not had this corroborated. Alfred Johnson, recalling the war more than fifty years later, remembers, as a young man, fire watching with others (including the vicar) on the steps of St Chad's and hearing German planes overhead on a bombing raid of Leeds. The following morning bomb craters were found in the grounds of Becketts Park but the church was unharmed. There was only one significant bombing raid on Leeds during the 2nd World War and that took place on the night of March 14th 1941.

Before the war, Canon Marshall 'envisaged a church hall and school to be built on the land below the present (new) vicarage but all unnecessary building was denied, so a new church hall had to wait.'[2]. It was not until 1961 that plans were made to demolish the old vicarage and build a new house for the vicar at the top of the church avenue. On the site of the old vicarage a parish hall was

The stone screen from St Chad's original chancel "arcaded and richly curved", rescued after demolition and reconstructed as a garden retreat at Meanwooside by Edwin Kitson Clark. Mary Kitson Clark (right) sits with her cousin Christine Kitson.

Courtesy: Mrs Derwas Chitty (Mary Kitson Clark)

built costing £35,000. It was opened on April 24th 1966 and is better known today as St Chad's Parish Centre.

The church building itself was re-roofed and redecorated in 1980 at a cost of £53,000. The roofers were William Procter & Sons of Sheffield who laid 74,450 Rosemary tiles on 1,241 square metres of roof. For the first time in decades the bright red hue of the new tiles brought colour back to the blackened stone edifice, and on a bright day, whether by design or by accident, the distinct image of a Roman Cross can be easily discerned, in deeper textured tiles, right in the middle of the east facing roof slope.

In 1986/7, the Harrison organ was rebuilt by Messrs Jacksons, Organ Builders of Ilkley at a cost of over £36,000 and in 1992 the Church was completely rewired for the third time[3]. These late 20th century expenses put into perspective our inflationary times when compared with the original building cost of £10,000 and even the 1909 cost of rebuilding the 'east' end (£6,000).

Two thousand years after the birth of Christ, St Chad's Church reaches its own 132nd anniversary. It remains a focal point in the built landscape of Far Headingley. It stands, appropriately, on ancient Abbey land and is a monument to the people who endowed, designed, built and subsequently maintained her; to all who have worshipped there; and to those from the local community who are buried there. On December 31st 1999, the tower bells rang in the new Millennium as Edmund Beckett's clock struck midnight and the Christian mission of St Chad's moved into a new century of change and spiritual challenge.

Vicars of St Chad's Church:

The Rev Thomas Cartwright Smyth	1868-1890
The Rev Joshua Fielding Hoyle	1891-1896
The Rev Walter Howard Stables	1896-1906
The Rev Canon Charles Marshall	1907-1947
The Rev John Wylie	1948-1960
The Rev Kenneth Blackburn	1960-1970
The Rev Canon Roger Robinson	1970-1982
The Rev Brian Abel	1982-1986
The Rev Barry Overend	From 1987

Notes

[1] Stone from the apse at St Chad's went to Meanwoodside where it was used to form a semi circular garden enclosure. It disappeared with the demolition and clearance of Edward Oates' house at Meanwoodside in the 1950s. The new east end of the church was designed by J. Harold Gibbons. Impressively lofty and spacious from the inside it was none the less a massive intrusion which greatly upset the balance and rhythm of the original form. The scheme included a new side chapel. The war memorial was also designed by J. Harold Gibbons.

[2] St Chad's Centenary Brochure (1968)

[3] The church was rewired in 1909 and 1946. A sound system was installed in 1983.

Postscript: Headingley Crusaders and Leeds Reformed Baptist Church

Vacant land behind Heathfield Terrace was purchased anonymously before the war and given to Headingley Crusaders, an interdenominational Christian organisation founded to teach the Christian faith to boys and girls. Plans were drawn up for a Crusader Hall but it was not built until after the war during the 1950s. Leeds Reformed Baptist Church began to use the Hall for Sunday Services in 1974 and purchased the building from The Crusaders in 1980. It was extended in 1981 and more recently 20 Cottage Road was acquired to accommodate the Sunday School. Leeds Reformed Baptist Church is an independent evangelical church founded in 1972 when about 25 people left Harehills Lane Baptist Church including the Minister, Reverend A. P. Parkinson.

The Twentieth Century: Towards the Modern Age
Business and Pleasure, some well known Far Headingley Establishments

Bryan's of (Far) Headingley

In 1934, John Bryan opened a fish friers businesss, Bryan's Modern Fisheries, at 9 Weetwood Lane, a one up, one down stone cottage with a single storey shop which was formerly Mrs Pickering's grocery shop. The cottage was converted to form a cafe with four tables on the ground floor, five tables upstairs and one outside toilet.

Very little changed for thirty years. John Bryan retired in 1959 and his son Albert took over the business. In 1963, both neighbouring cottages, Nos 5 and 7 Weetwood Lane were acquired and the whole site cleared. A new take away shop was built and an adjoining modern restaurant opened with ninety covers. At the same time part of the site was combined with the old forge at 3 Weetwood Lane which the brewery had demolished to form a shared car park.

In 1969 Albert Bryan bought the old Weetwood Laundry premises at 2, 4 and 6 St Chad's Road, but it was not until ten years later that the empty buildings were eventually brought back into use as part of another major improvement scheme. New kitchens and preparation rooms were formed allowing the restaurant seating capacity to increase.

The Bryan family sold the business in 1984 and retired to the east coast. Jan Fletcher became the new owner and began a programme of further improvements. The take away shop was refitted, a new shop front installed, the restaurant remodelled to accommodate one hundred and thirty six covers and the name changed to Bryans of Headingley. In 1994 Jan Fletcher was voted Businesswoman of the year. She received the OBE for services to industry in 1997.

Today Bryans serves ten thousand customers every week. Half a million fish are sold each year and one hundred and fifty tons of potatoes. It is one of the best known fish restaurants in the region and especially popular with a number of local celebrity names including Michael Parkinson, Sir Jimmy Savile and Dickie Bird. In March 1999, Andrew Morton brought Monica Lewinski to Bryan's for a fish and chip supper during her book promotion tour of the UK.

Headingley Picture House with its original glass canopy. *Courtesy: Robert Preedy.*

The Picture House

In 1912, on Monday July 29th, Headingley Picture House opened in converted garage premises formerly owned by Mr Kirk of Castle Grange. Today it is better known as Cottage Road Cinema and is arguably one of the oldest cinemas in the country. It has been a popular film venue for generations of local people surviving the advent of television, video libraries and now multi-screen, out-of-town, car-park centred cineplexes.

John Kirk, himself a reputedly keen motorist had died in 1908 and the Cottage Road property was taken over by Owen Brooks for use as a motor garage and motor-cycle assembly shop[1]. Besides his interest in motor vehicles, Brooks was a pioneer in the film industry, having built the movie camera and projector first used in 1901 in the Tivoli Theatre in Leeds, on which his own news reel films were shown.

In 1912, Owen Brooks was joined in partnership by Reginald Smith and the pair converted the building into the Headingley Picture House, which they successfully ran until Smith's death in 1922. A silent screen cinema, the Cottage Road had no organ, unlike the Headingley Lounge cinema which opened in 1916. Instead a palm court trio played between film performances.

Between 1922 and 1937 the building was reputedly owned by Henry Atkinson & Sons – building contractors[2]. The gallery was installed and a new stone frontage with a glass canopy was built during this period. A Mr Frank Thompson took the cinema over from the Atkinson's briefly and in 1938 the premises were bought by Associated Tower Cinemas. The name was changed to Cottage Road Cinema.

Inside Headingley Picture House.　　　　　　　　　　　　*Courtesy: Robert Preedy.*

In 1972 the company spent £20,000 modernising the premises and in 1999 the frontage was restored, revealing for the first time in many years the original stone-arched entrance. The building seats 468 patrons and is a gem of a cinema.

The original structure on the site is thought to have been stabling dating back to the 1830s.

Source: Cottage Road Cinema 75th anniversary brochure and additional notes from Associated Tower Cinemas.

Glendor (Do-It-Yourself) Ltd

Keith Wilson writes:
'Horace Wilson finished his joinery apprenticeship in the mid 1930's and started up in business from his aunt's stable in Myrtle Square in Meanwood in the days when a hand cart was the only way of transporting tools and materials to a job. During the war he worked at Avro helping to make Wellington bombers and never flew in an aeroplane after that experience.

The firm of H G Wilson was started shortly after the War in the premises now occupied by Russell Interiors in Park Terrace, originally specialising in joinery and property alterations. Plumbing was added and later decorating. At the height of the season up to forty five staff were employed.

An old invoice shows 2" x 1" planed timber at 12/6d (62p) per 100ft which is about the price for 1 metre now.

Mr Wilson's two brothers ran a building business, G L & E Wilson, in Cottage Road which provided bricklaying and plastering, so between them they could tackle most jobs. One of the specialist services was loft conversions with dormer windows, for which Mr Wilson copyrighted a spring-assisted loft ladder under the 'Glendor' name derived from his middle name, Glencoe, and his wife's name, Dora.

The shop at 2 and 4 Weetwood Lane, previously Hopper and Child's Grocery store, was used as a showroom for bathroom suites and kitchen units and was decorated with several samples of wallpaper. Stock in trade for the business was kept there and as, almost by accident, items of stock were sold to customers it gradually turned into a Do-It-Yourself shop. When the business in Park Terrace was sold in 1967 the shop was retained and continues under the Glendor name run by Horace's grey-haired son, Keith'.

Mansfield Garage

Keightley's garage on Moor Road occupies a prominent landmark building within the Conservation Area. Although it has been altered and adapted over the years to suit the present day motor repair business, the building still stands as a monument to the age of the Victorian blacksmith. It was constructed in the

Weetwood Lane Forge in the late 1950s, redrawn by Michael Smith from a photograph. For a plan of the Forge (and Three Horse Shoes Inn see page 169).   *Courtesy: the artist.*

Mansfield Garage 1971.   *Photo: FHVS collection.*

1880s when the blacksmith's trade was at its zenith embracing, as it did, the services of wheelwright, farrier, mechanic, tool-maker, repairer and sharpener. It must have been very imposing even to the late Victorians. The building combines a family house facing Moor Road (no 12), a retail shop (No 10) and the forge itself which has an elevation onto Oddy Place distinguished by large, round-headed ground floor windows, coach doors and a substantial square sectioned stone chimney.

Mr Richard Dalton, for many years proprietor of Mr Askey's old smithy in Weetwood Lane, moved his business to the new premises in Moor Road during the 1880s and sold ironmongery from the shop. At the end of the old century, trade directories tell us he is well established as 'blacksmith' at 10 and 12 Moor Road, whilst Mr William Whitwell has taken over at the Weetwood Lane Forge. The Three Horse Shoes is still run by the Askey family, Miss Ann Askey now being listed as the proprietor at the Inn[3].

By the late 1920s the Whitwell family remain in business at Weetwood Lane, and now also own Mr Dalton's former premises at Moor Road. However, the hey-day of shoeing horses and repairing horsedrawn wagoncarts, gigs, traps and carriages having passed, the building becomes vacant. In 1928 the parents of Kathleen Johnston arrive at Far Headingley from Lincolnshire and move into No 12:

> 'I was eight years old. Attached to the house was a shop and blacksmiths which was not in use when we arrived. We children had the run of this building. The shop at some earlier date had been part of my home. It had no water facilites and part of one bedroom had been partitioned off to extend the room above the shop.
>
> Two ladies rented this shop as dress and coat makers. There was a large door in our hall which led into the shop. Each morning these ladies would come for water and also to use our bathroom. The back door of the house led out into a large cobbled yard, fully closed in by a stone wall and glass roof. There was a large horse stable, a door into the blacksmiths and a door onto a back garden.
>
> Our landlord owned the blacksmith's next to The Three Horse Shoes which still shoed horses. I spent many hours watching these wonderful animals being shoed and loved the Shire horses which belonged to the brewery.
>
> In 1930 my father turned the old blacksmiths into a garage. I remember workmen arriving to dig a pit and install a petrol tank. We had one petrol pump with a large handle. I would rush home from school to serve customers and earned many a threepeeny bit!
>
> My father died in 1943 and the garage was sold'.
>
> Kathleen Johnston, daughter of Harry Wilson, writing in October 1999

From 1945, the new tenants were Mr Keightley and his son Donald. Under the Keightley's ownership, the business became well established but it was not until 1960 that the freehold was finally acquired. Mr James Whitwell meanwhile had gone into partnership at the Weetwood Lane forge with his former apprentice Arthur Hartley. A drawing of the old forge appears on page 153 and is taken from a photograph dating from the late 1950s when the business was being conducted in the style of 'W A Hartley, blacksmith'[4]. Weetwood Lane forge had been a feature of Far Headingley for over 125 years serving a transport industry that relied on well shod horses. It was swept away in the early 1960s ironically to form a car park.

Across the road from the Mansfield garage forecourt was a block of fourteen back to back cottages with communal toilets at the bottom of the steps which now lead to the cinema car-park. This was Oddy Row, an amazing example of cramped, overcrowded and poor housing in a neighbourhood noted for its grand villas and comfortable living – typifying the mix of people who made up the community of Far Headingley.

Oddy Row was demolished in 1962. The site stood bereft of buildings for many years and was used as an extended car park for Mansfield garage. In 1987, Mr and Mrs Donald Keightley built their present home on the site. It fronts directly onto Moor Road, but passers-by will note its name (and address) – No 2 Oddy Place – a reminder of the houses it replaced.

Cottage Road Wash House (demolished)

On the site of the cinema car park in Cottage Road stood two cottages, a large hen yard and a single storey, stone building, known locally as Cottage Road Wash House, but listed in the directory as 21 Cottage Road, Mrs Ellen Moxon, laundress.

> 'Cottage Road wash house was a large building and employed many women. I went inside on many occasions. A lady owned it and worked there among these huge Amazonian women (as they appeared to me) in clogs, aprons and boots.
>
> In the grounds they had hundreds of chickens with hen hutches surrounded by wire mesh. My mother and neighbours saved all their stale bread and greens for these hens which I would deliver to the owner of the wash house. It was like entering a different world. The noise and steam and women shouting to make themselves heard, all slopping about in soapy water. The owner would be on a high stool and would beckon me over to her. She was very fat and wore the same attire as the other women. I remember she had a nice smile and always pulled out a sixpence for me from underneath her rubber apron'.
>
> Mrs Kathleen Johnston reminiscing in October 1999

Mr Alfred Johnson, who grew up at 7 Weetwood Lane remembers 'Moxon's laundry' and the great wicker baskets that contained the laundry brought in from the larger Headingley houses.

Mrs Moxon's Laundry was demolished sometime prior to the 1939 outbreak of war. Among the other well known laundries at this time was Weetwood Laundry on St Chad's Road, owned by Mr and Mrs Herbert Farrar from about 1922. In 1944 the business was taken over by a Mr Lockwood. The buildings now form part of Bryans Fish Restaurant.

The Moor Road Dairy

Another well known landmark in the pre-war years was Tomlinson's Dairy at 4 Moor Road. Dairy products were sold from the shop and a creamery was run from a small detached building demolished in the mid 1980s. Milk was delivered in churns, bottled and distributed round the neighbourhood.

The principal manufacture, however, was home made ice cream. 'They sold *delicious* ice creams when I was a child' says Christine Baker of Linden Court, 'and opposite, slightly to the right, was Davenports (No 21) who sold biscuits'. This sounds like the perfect combination of shops for hungry children!

In 1935 a modern shop extension was added making a striking 19th/20th century change to the streetscape. The premises remained as a shop – latterly a general store and off licence – until the mid 1980s when the whole block was acquired and converted to self contained flats. A separate block of flats was constructed on land to the rear and the creamery demolished for access to the new development.

Walker's Dairy, Cottage Road – and convenience shopping in the 1940s

In 1937 Richard and Edith Walker established their dairy business in Cottage Road, No 12, a small terraced house opposite the Cinema. A tiny passageway between Nos 12 and 14 leads to the back yard where the Walkers had their dairy, a large brick building in which milk bottles were washed, sterilised, re-filled and capped ready for the next delivery round:

> 'It was quite a big business. My father delivered milk throughout the whole area. We had four vehicles – a wagon, which was used to bring milk in large churns from the family farm at Wike near Harewood, an electric delivery truck, a small van and a Hillman car which took six crates of milk.
>
> At the front of the house, there was an extended wooden porch over the Cottage Road door, where we kept a big refrigerator for people who called at the house for their milk and cream and eggs'.
>
> Mary Coggill (nee Walker) reminiscing in January 2000.

Mary Coggill was a teenager in wartime Far Headingley and, in conversation, offered this 'snapshot' of the village at that time. It was an age when convenience shopping *was* convenient and when the world seemed to be full of sweet shops:

> 'Opposite us in Cottage Road, next to the cinema was Jacksons fruit shop. People would queue from early in the morning to get fresh fruit and vegetables from Jacksons. Mrs Jackson used to grow mushrooms in one of the garages in the yard at the back of the shop. She also kept rabbits in a shed next to the garage. Mushrooms and rabbits, they were all for sale in the shop. It wouldn't get past hygiene and safety today, but nobody had a problem with it in those days.
>
> At No 16 Cottage Road was Mr Tommy Bateson, the verger at St Chad's, a lovely rosy-cheeked man. He lived there with his two sisters. After my father died, he would

Tomlinson's Dairy, Moor Road in 1935 just before it was altered. *Courtesy: Leeds City Library*

Tomlinson's Dairy, Moor Road in 1935, just after the new shop frontage had been installed. A local lad just getting himself into the picture. Note also the earlier building on the present day sub-station site. Leeds Corporation Electricity Board acquired the site in 1929. Yorkshire Electricity Board (now Yorkshire Electricity) was not created until 1948. *Courtesy: Leeds City Library*

Weetwood Lane and Moor Road in 1930. The corner block (another sweet shop!) is Victoria Buildings dated 1841 and beyond that, cottages and workshops since demolished and now a car park. They include upholsterers and a cycle repair shop. *Courtesy Leeds City Library.*

call in carrying a glass of something decidedly alcoholic, covered with a cloth, and he would say to my mother, 'Now, Mrs Walker, this is just for you', and he would make her sit down by the fire and relax for a moment. He often did this. My mother loved it.

At No 18 was Mr and Mrs Frank Shepherd. He was a bespoke tailor and Mrs Shepherd was a dress-maker. There was another dress-maker, Mrs Wade, at 3 and 5 Cottage Road.

At No 20 was a fish shop which became a betting shop after Mr Steels, the cobbler, moved his business there from round the corner in Otley Road. Then you came to Wilson's the builders, then a terrace of four houses and then a general store on the corner of Heathfield Terrace.

Moorhouses, on the corner of Cottage Road and Otley Road was a lovely shop, it was a high class provision merchants. People came from miles around to get their groceries from Mr Moorhouse. Next to Moorhouses was a sweetshop, Mr Cook's butcher's shop, a greengrocer, Field's the bakers, a Chemist's shop and Mr Geldard's Post Office. There was another sweet shop in Cottage Road, attached to the back of the New Inn. It's been pulled down now with two small cottages which stood behind the shop facing onto an alleyway. And next to the sweet shop in Cottage Road was Mrs Brogden's haberdashery (No 8). You could get anything from Mrs Brogden's shop.

Fronting the Otley Road was the New Inn, then Hirst the baker, (the Hirsts lived in the big house next door), then there was Mr Dawson's sweet shop – another sweet shop – at the end of Victoria Terrace. All down Burton Crescent, the posh people lived, every house with maids and chauffeurs and gardeners. Mr (Mark) Altman lived in the big house on the corner (Parkhurst). He owned a dancing school in Great George Street, opposite the Infirmary and next to the Altmans was Mr (Edgar) Firth the estate agent, now the dentists (Holly Dene, the old Parsonage House)'.

Bottom left: Weetwood Lane from Otley Road in 1930. A photograph full of interest. It shows a second block of shops north of Back Baileys Place and a garage building, all on the site now occupied by the electricity substation. The garage was originally Mr Dyke's cab hire business. The fruiterer at 6 Weetwood Lane displays, and serves, his produce through the sliding sash shop windows (which remain today) and whilst one delivery bike is parked outside the grocer's shop, another is being loaded up outside the fruit shop. Far Headingley village was well provided with shops - parades of shops and corner shops. In the 1930s another parade of shops would have been built on the land in front of St Chad's Church had the Church not stepped in and secured the land as a peace garden. Local retail businesses were clearly thriving. Headingley too had a good range of shops, but no more extensive than Far Headingley. It was not the district centre it has since become. As shopping became concentrated on Headingley (the Arndale Centre, St Anne's parade - both 1960s), and then 'out of town', local convenience shops in Far Headingley began to close.

4 and 6 Weetwood Lane are worth a closer look. Note the alignment of the chimneys. They are at an angle to the frontage because they rise above the end gable wall of a house which once stood independently on this site facing due south over a small garden. The house and garden remain to this day, but totally concealed by the Weetwood Lane shops which were added much later and replaced an earlier single shop extension. In the case of No 6, the building is literally wrapped around the gable end of the old house. Openings were made from the house into the shop. It was a very artful way of infilling to create another run of shops The back elevation of the house, which probably dates from before the 1829 Inclosure Act can be clearly seen from Back Baileys Place. *Courtesy: Mr Keith Wilson.*

The Catholic Care Home

31 Moor Road (West Grove) was purchased by the Roman Catholic Church Rescue Society and opened as a care home in 1940. No 29 was purchased the following year to provide additional space and to act as an annexe to the main house.

Today, West Grove houses the diocesan's administrative offices of Catholic Care, while No 29 Moor Road remains a self contained care home for disadvantaged young people. Whilst living there the children become very much a welcome part of the local community.

Personal Banking in the 1950s

By the end of the century, we had entered the age of mobile phones and internet banking, rendering a visit to the bank almost obsolete. A 'hole-in-the-wall' cash dispensing machine is the nearest many of us get to a bank these days, and that's probably a former building society converted to a bank in order to enter the lucrative financial services market. It wasn't always thus. Mrs Bush of West Park remembers the Misses Gaunt:

> 'The Misses Gaunt were two sisters who lived in one of the large detached houses on the Otley Road at West Park. In the 1950s they were elderly, old fashioned ladies, even by the standards of the time. They were always seen together, never apart. You couldn't miss them. They wore long black dresses and high black satin hats anchored with big hat pins.
>
> On their way to town they regularly called at their bank, a branch of the NatWest on Woodhouse Lane, near the BBC. There they would ask for young Mr Lockhart, the cashier and enquire as to the amount of their savings. 'Mr Lockhart, how much money do we have in the Bank?' Mr Lockhart would check the balances and inform the sisters accordingly. 'Thank you, Mr Lockhart. May we see it?' Obligingly, the cashier dutifully went to the safe, took out notes and coinage to the value of their balances and placed it on the counter. Having verified that their money really was safely in the bank, they bade Mr Lockhart good day and went on their way.
>
> Bryan Lockhart has never forgotten the Misses Gaunts. He used to dread their visits!

Left Two views of the Otley Road shops above Cottage Road c 1900 and 1911. In the earlier one it is still predominantly residential with a nice line of bay fronted houses behind railed front gardens. Naylors, the corner shop has its corner entrance and next door is the shop keeper's house. The exquisitely ornate tram wire post is also a pleasure to see and note the simple frontage to the Three Horse Shoes - no bays and an arched front entrance.

Within ten years, however, there had been substantial changes. On the 1911 photograph we see that three of the houses have been converted into shops with classic Edwardian facades. Converting first floor bedrooms has been achieved by moving the original ground floor bays to the first floor. Although too tall to avoid breaking the eaves line, the result works quite well. The adjoining shops have also been extended to the pavement frontage but without any first floor residential embellishments. *Both photos courtesy: Ian Ballantine*

St Chad's Parade Otley Road in 1934 standing on the site of Cardigan Cottage. Originally built as a single storey block, the two first floor flats we see today were added later. Note also the tram depot and foreman's house in the background.   *Courtesy: Leeds City Library.*

Leeds Industrial Co-operative Society, the Co-op, at West Park in 1937. For many years a large illuminated sign fixed to the first floor of the building carried the famous early advertising slogan "Shop at the Co-op". It could not the survive the attraction of supermarket shopping and closed in the 1960s.   *Courtesy: Leeds City Library.*

More Memories of Life in Far Headingley

Alfred Johnson was born in 1922 and apart from his call up during the Second World War has spent all his life in Far Headingley Village. He grew up first at number 7 Weetwood Lane, and then numbers 5 and 7 combined, small cottage houses squeezed, at that time, between Mr Farrar's bespoke laundry on St Chad's Road and Mr Whitwell's forge behind the Three Horse Shoes. He went to St Chad's School and joined the Church choir. On leaving school he was apprenticed in the building trade and went into business as a carpenter and undertaker, a then common combination of business services. It is a little disconcerting to hear him talk of the many local personalities he has 'put away' over the years, but his recall of the people who inhabited Far Headingley between the wars is impressive and puts the listener very much within human touch of by-gone days.

There was Mr and Mrs Farrar who ran the laundry, collecting and delivering by van. James Whitwell, the blacksmith lived at No 3 Weetwood Lane next to the old forge and 'made wheel hoops with Arthur Hartley who continued the business after Mr Whitwell's death'.

5 and 7 Weetwood Lane. The home of Alfred Johnson from the 1920s until it was acquired and demolished in the 1960s. Bryan's Fish Restaurant now stands on the site. This photograph is dated c 1910. No 5 is the local police constable's house, P.C. Barlow. The lamp in the walled garden is thought to be the constabulary "blue" lamp. G Dykes, a relative of Alfred Johnson's mother, Fanny Dykes, seems to have had a number of business interests. Not only is he taking orders for coal from King & Kenworthy, but he is the proprietor of a cab hire business on the opposite side of Weetwood Lane. Next to the upright cart is the coal house to Weetwood Forge with a street opening so that coal could be delivered straight to the blacksmith's bellows. The forge chimney rises above another of Mr Dykes' signs. *Courtesy: Ian Ballantine*

Across Weetwood Lane was an old garage. It had been Dykes' cab hire premises. Related to the proprietor were Robert and Henrietta Dykes, Alfred's grandparents. They lived at Cardigan Cottage on the corner of St Chad's Road and Otley Road. From the garden of the cottage Fanny Dykes, Alfred's mother, had watched a constant stream of ambulances take wounded soldiers up to Beckett's Park military hospital during the First World War. She married George Johnson who came to Far Headingley with her family when they 'retired' from farm work at what is now Bodington fields, Lawnswood.

Alfred's grandparents died in the early 1920s when he was very small and he has no recollection of Dyke's Cab Hire nor the parade of shops adjacent, all of which were subsequently demolished. George Johnson and Fanny established themselves at 5 Weetwood Lane and George took a job as boilerman at Chorley and Pickersgill's Cookridge Street printing works. 'When he came home' remembers Alfred, 'the poor man was so drained, he'd call in first at The Three Horse Shoes to quench his thirst. We knew where to look for him if he was late for his tea'.

Another well remembered character was Thomas Bateson 'who claimed to have been carried into St Chad's church as a babe in arms on the day it was consecrated, served as verger for forty five years, and now lies in the churchyard next to Sir Nathan Bodington'[5]. As a youngster Alfred would help Tommy Bateson light the gas mantles in the church drive lamps and when he began his apprenticeship as a joiner, Tommy gave Alfred a small gift of money to buy some tools and a copy of the trade bible, Mitchell's Technical Building and Carpentry. Sixty four years later, he still has the book and some of the tools.

As the local apprenticed joiner, Alfred was soon visiting many of the large houses in Far Headingley to do small repairs. Mrs Jessie Middleton (of Leeds solicitors, Middletons), at Moor Grange on Moor Road 'lived alone but she and the house were well looked after by maids and gardeners'. Mr Braithwaite, the surgeon at Burton Grange, took a keen interest in his garden and liked to wander round with his two gardeners before going off to the hospital or to his consulting rooms in Park Square in his chauffeur driven car[6]. Mr Smith, a textile mill owner at Burton Lea, would open his house on Christmas Eve to carol singers from St Oswald's, before Midnight Communion in the church. Mr Altman, the Leeds dancing school proprietor, at Parkhurst, liked to sit out and admire the view from the railed deck of the house roof.

Warden of St Oswald's Mission Church, lay reader, and regular bell ringer at St Chad's Church, Alfred Johnson represents in so many ways the heart and soul of the Parish. 'I don't know how many times I've climbed the fifty nine church tower steps to help ring those bells – thousands'. Thankfully, he's still doing so.

George Thomas Johnson 1878-1954. photographed from the roof of Chorley and Pickersgill's printing works, The Electric Press in Cookridge Street, where he was boilerman. In the background are the slate roofs of the surrounding buildings and the soot blackened tower over Brodrick's Town Hall. Cuthbert Brodrick lodged in Far Headingley, Joseph Pickersgill lived on Weetwood Lane (Bardon Hill), and so did George Johnson, at a more modest abode – No 7.

Courtesy: Mr A Johnson.

WEETWOOD LANE CORNER, HEADINGLEY

Public Houses in Far Headingley
The Three Horse Shoes

On July 5th 1832 John Askey, a blacksmith, bought 'a parcel of land on Headingley Moor' containing 860 sq.yds. with frontages to the 'Leeds and Otley Turnpike and Addle Road'. According to the Purchase Indenture, he paid £136.10s and George Askey stood as Trustee. The sellers, for the record, were Henry and Elizabeth Charlesworth Windsor Mitchell, who had secured the title after the Act of Inclosure (1829).

Very soon John Askey was established as a blacksmith and inn-keeper[7]. His inn, The Three Horse Shoes, occupied a strategic position, at an important fork in the road, directly facing traffic travelling along the road from Headingley. At the rear of the inn, was the forge off Weetwood Lane (then Addle Road). It was a combination of businesses that could hardly fail with many customers no doubt taking a draught of ale while Mr Askey repaired a broken wheel or re-shoed a horse. And such was the rapid growth of Headingley Moor village that his local customers must have been multiplying by the years. To cap it all, by the end of the 1830s the inn had become the terminus for the omnibus to Leeds and the road had been turnpiked. Sight of the title documents, however, indicates that it was still a precarious trade. Numerous mortgage agreements accompany the deeds.

John Askey gives his occupation as Inn-keeper in the 1841 census. He is 35 and married to Elizabeth (also 35). They have four children Hannah (14), Sarah (11), John (5), and Elizabeth (2).

Top left: Weetwood Lane and Otley Road junction c1905. Tetley's have acquired Mrs Askey's business and have decided to make the most of the advertising potential offered by the building's strategic site. A horse drawn milk cart is parked outside the front entrance in the disputed forecourt and a barber's pole indicates that the hairdresser is still in business in his tiny wedge (see the 1903 Three Horse Shoes floor plan). Opposite, on Weetwood Lane, is a house and shop, now the site of 4 and 6 Weetwood Lane (Glendor's DIY and the Art Shop). Studying the photograph, my own view is that this was originally a simple double fronted house built by a smallholder to face south over Headingley Moor and the old Headingley Lane – probably predating the Inclosure Act of 1829 and therefore an early encroachment building. At some point it was extended onto Weetwood Lane to form a house and shop (note the doubled chimney stack). This extension was demolished soon after the Great War and replaced by new shops (Glendor's DIY and the Art Shop). The house itself remains but is now entirely concealed from public view.

Early motor cars are beginning to make an appearance, several are parked outside Mr Dyke's cab hire premises in Weetwod Lane, but there is no concern about the vulnerability of the gas lamp which forms something of a traffic island. This is long before the days when pavement railings were required. *Courtesy: Ian Ballantine*

Bottom right: The same view in the 1920s. A brewery dray and two smart motors are parked in the forecourt and a public telephone has arrived, housed in the early telephone booth standing by the gas lamp. *Courtesy: Ian Ballantine*

Twenty years later the 1861 directories indicate that Elizabeth Askey is the proprietor, presumably running the business after John's early death, but after only a few years the directories once again note John Askey as the inn-keeper. This is the son who was five at the time of the 1841 census and whose home was to be The Three Horse Shoes Inn for his whole life. Not an unusual circumstance in those days. He died in 1892, aged fifty seven, 'bequeathing all his personal estates in Trust for his wife, Ann, and after her death in Trust for all his children in equal shares'[8]. Ann Askey kept the inn for a further eleven years, but on her death in April 1903, at the age of sixty four, arrangements were immediately made to sell the property and pay off creditors:

> 'We understand that The Three Horse Shoes Inn estate, Far Headingley, which was offered for auction by Messrs Oliver and Appleton on the 26th ult., has been sold privately. Although the price has not been divulged, it is stated to be very satisfactory to the trade'.
>
> Yorkshire Post 12.6.1903

The purchaser was Joshua Tetley & Son and the price paid £11,100, though from this distance in time it is not easy to deduce whether this was 'very satisfactory to the trade' from the licencee's or licencor's point of view. A report and valuation of the property was prepared for the brewery on May 26th 1903 and included a ground floor plan which shows the arrangement of the bar rooms, brewhouse stabling and yard. The blacksmith's house and workshop are independent of the inn (although included in the sale) as is a small cottage on Otley Road. The cottage became a shop, then a surgery and was finally absorbed into the main building during major alterations in 1992 retaining the old shop front.

Note also on the plan, the extraordinarily shaped 'hairdresser's shop' next to the Tap Room, and the thin garden wedge with coachhouse on the Otley Road side, all now part of the enlarged public house.

The first tenant manager was Mr Scott, and in 1905 parking on the forecourt was becoming an issue. A brewery memo notes:

> 'On Thursday last Supt. Dyson called and told me that the Chief Constable had instructed him not to allow traps to stand any length of time on the space in front of the house - Mr Scott gathered that someone had been complaining. On Saturday afternoon last two Constables came in and enquired for the driver of a horse cart standing there - the horse was securely fastened but the Constables interviewed the man and took his name and address. The Constables told Scott that they had received instructions not to allow vehicles to stand there for any length of time and that it was their duty to report the matter if vehicles did stand there'.

The brewery consulted its solicitor, Mr Simpson:

> 'Mr Simpson says that if (we have) any trouble over this with the police ... we should have no fear of coalescing – especially before our present Stipendiary. We don't admit that in allowing this we are in any way exceeding our rights'[9].

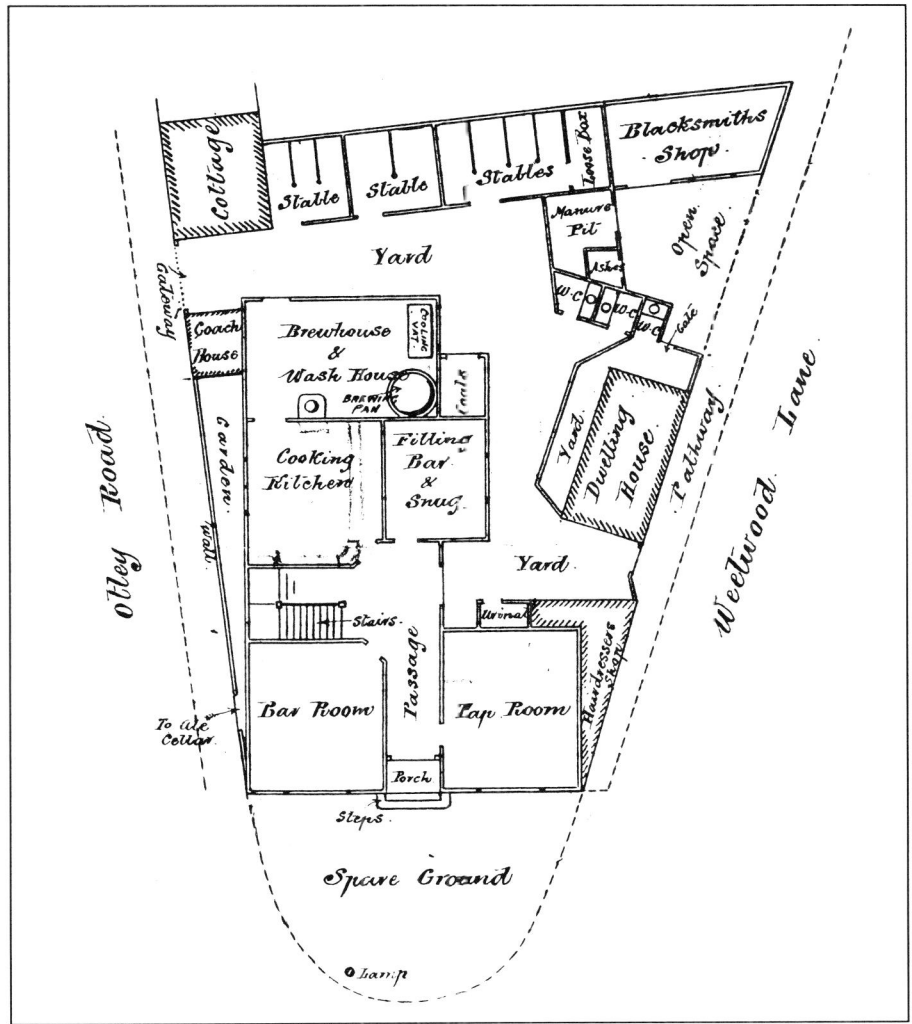

The Three Horse Shoes. The ground floor plan taken from a surveyors report dated May 25th 1903. Lots of fascinating things to note here. Not only the "Hairdressers shop", coach house, stables, garden(!) and public rooms but smaller details like the lack of the heavy square bay windows on the frontage, added after 1903. Most of the early 1830s (late Georgian) houses in Far Headingley were built with simple, regular fenestration and central doorways, The Victorians typically added large angled bays to the ground floor (like the New Inn) but in the case of The Three Horse Shoes the bays were clearly added much later.

The Three Horse Shoes appears in local directories as an "Inn" from the 1830s, whereas the New Inn and The Woodman (Hotel) are not named, merely referred to by address and occupier - "beer" or "beer and spirit" retailer. A true inn provided lodgings for travellers and stabling. It would be a respectable establishment with set-aside accommodation for gentlemen and their ladies. The plan shows a detached dwelling on Weetwood Lane (number 5) - the innkeepers private house (later tied to the separate forge business). In the main building itself we see the original location of the broad staircase which led to the first floor bedrooms directly off the public area. To the rear of the property was stabling for 10 horses. It was the latter day motel, and quite different from its near public house neighbours, The Woodman and New Inn.

Print courtesy Punch Inns.

The Three Horse Shoes is a popular name for an inn attached to a blacksmiths. The superstition that the devil rides on horseback (or is himself cloven hooved) and might come for shoes gave ground to the custom of keeping shoes in sets of three. In this instance, of course the name is doubly appropriate in that the inn was the terminus for Mr Wood's three horse omnibus.

From 1903 to 1999, the Three Horse Shoes was a Tetley house. Towards the end of the twentieth century however, company mergers, which included Tetleys, had produced a giant international brewing conglomerate. The decision was taken to shed the public houses and in 1999 many Tetley houses, including The Three Horse Shoes were acquired by Punch Inns Ltd. of Burton upon Trent. By the end of 1999 the building had undergone another major refit aimed at attracting the area's student population.

The forge as we have seen (page 154) became a separate business, the last blacksmith being Mr W A Hartley who lived at No 5 Weetwood Lane adjoining the inn and retired about 1960.

The New Inn

A privately owned wines, spirits and beerhouse, the New Inn was acquired from Messrs Wardle, Kerr and Glover by Bentley Yorkshire Breweries[10] on 30th December 1893. The deed of conveyance at the time refers to 'all that messuage or dwelling on the said land and called the New Inn with the brewhouse, stabling, outbuildings and yard, and also that messuage or dwelling house and shop erected thereon'. In more recent years the shop and cottage at the back of the inn have been demolished and the site laid out for parking.

The directories indicate that beer was being brewed on the premises from the 1870s. William Scaife is listed as beerseller during the 1870s and 80s, and the property is simply referred to as a 'beerhouse' in Whites directory of 1875. The establishment, however, goes back much earlier than that. According to the 1841 census, the New Inn, Moor End (Headingley Moor) is run by Joseph Coates, aged forty, farmer and publican. John Askey built his Three Horse Shoes Inn and forge very soon after the land enclosure. But not much later it seems, a 'New' Inn was open for business at the corner of the Cottage Road.

The New Inn became a Whitbread house when that company acquired Bentley Yorkshire Breweries in 1968. It had a brief spell as O'Hagan's New Inn in the 1990s and was themed as an Irish bar, but returned to its original name, The New Inn, in 1999.

Above the entrance to the New Inn a clockface bears the legend 'no tick', a neat way of reminding even the best customers that there's no drinking on the landlord's credit.

Woodies / The Woodman

Duttons Brewery Ltd[11] acquired The Woodman Inn from Helenor Daniels (deceased) in July 1925. The deeds describe a site extending to 363 sq.yds. and including 'all that beerhouse known as the Woodman Inn with brewhouse, garage and outbuildings. And also those shops, dwellinghouses, cottages and other buildings known as 102 and 102A Otley Road and 1, 2, 3, 4, and 5 Woodman Yard.'

The Otley Road shops remain, but Woodman Yard was cleared, the pub extended and the rest of the land given over to parking.

The Woodman became a Whitbread house when Dutton's was acquired by Whitbread in 1964. The pub name was changed to Woodies after a 1970s re-fit, and again to Woodies Ale-House after a 1980s refit.

According to the directories beer was being retailed from premises on this site from the 1880s. In 1882, George Winterburn is given as 'beer retailer'.

No tick at the New Inn. A sketch by Mike Smith.
Courtesy: the artist

A three horse-drawn tram (no date) outside the Woodman Hotel which appears to be a Tetley's tied house at this time. The building has undergone many alterations in subsequent years. The column and pediment framed entance has disappeared, the sash windows removed, the window openings enlarged and small paned frames installed. And the most dramatic change of all - the upper storey has been timber framed and rendered. *Courtesy: The Leeds Transport Historical Society.*

A photograph was taken of a horse tram standing outside the building at about this time. The pub appears to be a tied house, there being a large Tetley sign above the door and 'Teltey's Pale Ale' in white lettering on the sash windows. The unspoiled building is in its original form with sliding sash windows to either side of a pedimented central doorway. In subsequent years the window openings and doorway have been enlarged and multipaned window frames installed. At first floor level, the windows have again been altered. In addition, a small bay window has been fitted to the central window and the walls coated with rendering and timber framework.

With Weet*wood*, Lawns*wood* and Mean*wood* closeby, The Woodman was probably an obvious choice when selecting name options from a handbook of British pubs.

Notes

[1] Owen Brooks is also remembered for his home-made red motor cycle with wicker work 'chaise longue' side car, carrying the number plate 'U1'. The plate was later acquired by Leeds Corporation and remains the registration number of the Lord Mayor's civic car.

[2] According to Colin Gordon, 'the Atkinson firm had shares in Cottage Road cinema, having refurbished the interior'. *A Richer Dust* by Colin Gordon (Elm Tree Books 1978) is the story of Alfred Atkinson (1864-1945) an enthusiastic amateur photographer who captured the essence of late Victorian and Edwardian life with his camera. His father had founded the building firm of Henry Atkinson and Sons in Leeds in 1856. When Henry Atkinson died in 1892 the business was continued by his two sons Isaac and Alfred. The

company grew substantially and won some major contracts including the Beckett's Park Training College. Isaac died in 1912 and Alfred became head of the firm. Still devoting much of his time to photography and travel, he increasingly left the business to paid managers. By the 1930s the firm was beginning to fail and a disastrous speculative hotel development in Brighton proved too much for the creditors. The firm went into liquidation in 1937. Mr Thompson acquired the cinema that year and quickly sold it on to Associated Tower Cinemas.

[3] Weetwood Lane Forge was held on lease from the Askey's. In 1903 the property, including the forge, was sold to Joshua Tetley & Sons.

[4] Margaret Barnshaw of Castle Grove Avenue, writing in April 1999 remembered as a small girl bringing her tricycle to be repaired at Mr Hartley's blacksmith's shop in the early 1950s.

[5] W A Wightman writing in St Chad's Parish Church Centenary booklet.

[6] Interestingly, Alfred remembers that Mr Braithwaite's garden included a large plot on the opposite side of Burton Crescent behind Parkhurst, where he had fruit trees and vegetable garden. Burton Dene and Shaw Dene flats were subsequently built on the site.

[7] The first directory entry appears in 1834: John Askey, blacksmith and victualler, The Three Horse Shoes.

[8] One of the children, Maud Askey, predeceased her parents. She died in April 1885 aged seventeen. She is buried at St Chad's Church with John and Ann Askey. In the 1903 settlement papers reference is made to Florence Adelaide Askey, spinster of The Three Horse Shoes, and Henry Askey of 10 Ellis Terrace.

[9] From an internal memo held with other archives papers at Punch Inns.

[10] In 1892 Henry Bentley & Co., of Woodlesford merged with Yorkshire Breweries Ltd., to form Bentleys Yorkshire Breweries.

[11] Dutton & Co founded in Blackburn in 1897. The company acquired the Willow Brewery (Kirkstall) in 1928 and Kirkstall Brewery Co Ltd in 1936.

This view is of the Otley Road/Otley Old Road Junction c1910 above the present day Lawnswood roundabout. The post card is entitled "Otley Road, Headingley" which would seem perfectly appropriate before the road, and district, was severed by the outer Ring Road.
Courtesy: Miss N L Cook.

New suburban "homesteads" fronting the Otley Road (Nos 235-241) c1915.
Courtesy: Ian Ballantine.

The Twentieth Century: New Roads and New Development – From Rich Gardens and Large Estates to Public Parks and Housing

The Ring Road and Residential Expansion North

With the development of the motor car, came the opportunity for much greater individual mobility. People wanted to be away from the densely populated and smoky city centre. The demand was for new out of town garden suburbs.

The problem of overcrowded housing and poor living standards due to slum conditions had long been recognised. In 1909 Asquith's Liberal Government introduced a Town Planning Act with new requirements for house building densities – twelve houses per acre. Victorian Leeds had whole suburbs of forty or fifty houses per acre. After the First World War, Leeds Corporation set about planning new areas for housebuilding to enable the gradual demolition of 'slum' areas. It would involve a massive dispersal of the population. New roads were required and good transport links[1].

There soon developed the idea for an outer Ring Road encircling the whole city. The route of the new road would carve through Far Headingley parish on an east west axis and open up new land for house building, particularly on the north side along Spen Lane and the old Otley Road:

> 'If Leeds is to retain its population people can hardly be expected to spend a great portion of their time in travelling to and from the centre of the city at the comparatively slow speed of tramcars running on tracks laid in the old way in the centre of the carriageway; therefore some means must be adopted by which the desired result may be secured before the areas are built up.
>
> The Ring Road is designed to enable large areas to be utilised for housing the population and to furnish the means, through them of quick transport; it is also intended to supply the good cross-communications between different suburban areas which are so conspicuously absent at the present time, and to allow traffic to pass without entering the city, and so relieve congestion in the central area.
>
> On the north side of Leeds, two short lengths of the Ring Road have been started: one leading from Otley Road to Weetwood Lane (*cutting through the rear of Weetwood Hall grounds*), and the other from Harrogate Road towards the Adel Beck'.
>
> The Yorkshire Post 11.4.1921

After completion of the Ring Road, new housing at Lawnswood, Cookridge and parts of Adel rapidly developed.

Far Headingley Depot in 1935. *Courtesy: Leeds City Library.*

Demolishing Far Headingley Bus Depot in 1992. This part of the site lay fallow for 8 years during which time Far Headingley Village Society campaigned with others against plans for offices and a public house. McCarthy and Stone eventually acquired the site in 1999 for phase 2 of their Orchard Court development of retirement homes. *Photo: David Hall.*

Local Transport and Far Headingley Depot

Notwithstanding the advent of the motor car, trams and buses would remain the main means of cross city transport during the first half of the twentieth century. In 1935 the Far Headingley tram sheds were substantially rebuilt and enlarged with space for forty trams. When the trams were finally withdrawn from service in 1959 the building became a Leeds Corporation bus depot. Enlarged again during the late 1970s, it filled the whole site bounded by Otley Road, Weetwood Lane, St Chad's Road and Hollin Road with the exception of St Chad's Parade. Buses were garaged, maintained and washed here.

In 1992, having been acquired by the newly privatised Yorkshire Rider bus company, the depot was assessed as a surplus asset and demolished for its redevelopment value. Orchard Court, a private sheltered housing complex was built on approximately half of the site in 1993, and plans were lodged for a new Tom Cobleigh public house on the remainder. Strong local objection to the latter, however, resulted in Leeds magistrates withholding a beverage licence even though planning consent had been granted by the Council. Edmund Brudenell visited Far Headingley in November 1997 and gave the campaign valuable publicity. His ancestor, Lady Cardigan, had conveyed the site in 1873 to Leeds Tramway Company subject to a condition that no public house was to be built on the site. It was a restrictive covenant, he told BBC Look North and the press, that should still be respected.

Eventually the brewery interest was withdrawn and the land was sold on to McCarthy and Stone. In 1999 a planning application was submitted for a development of retirement homes to complement Orchard Court and in 2000 the site has come back into use as attractive and valuable community housing.

The last tram ran in Leeds in 1959. As a public transport system, trams had become outmoded and inflexible. The bus could more easily respond to changing travel patterns and new routes could be developed without the need for rail and cable. What's more, personal transport by private car was the quest and road space had to be maximised. That we succeeded in creating a car borne population is evident to any observer of late 20th century Headingley. Traffic congestion causes long delays and poor air quality. Proposals for a Headingley By-pass were argued over for forty years, and more recently Leeds City Council sought planning consent and funding for a new tram system through Headingley, the so-called Supertram. Government support for the project however has not yet been forthcoming and as we turn into the 21st century, traffic congestion remains a serious, quality of life, problem for residents.

The bicycle offers the quickest transport option into town from Far Headingley at most times of the working day, and walking can be faster than driving through the mile long Headingley bottle neck during peak times.

The Otley Road entrance to Beckett's Park . . .

Beckett's Park

In 1907 Gervase Beckett and his family left Kirkstall Grange for Helmsley. The vacated estate consisted of 464 broad acres on the edge of Leeds. It had been undiminished by piecemeal disposal, and remained largely the same domain acquired by William Beckett in 1829. It was now to be offered for sale by the 2nd Lord Grimthorpe, Ernest Beckett.

The Corporation of Leeds, a City by royal charter since 1897, saw the opportunity it presented and commissioned a committee report which recommended purchase. The committee considered 92 acres of land would provide a public park. The mansion house and land immediately adjoining were suitable for Training Colleges, and the remainder, about 290 acres, could be sold for building land. On the question of the public park:

> 'The land referred to is part of the Park Land of the Estate to the south of Kirkstall Grange and would not require any laying out, but should be utilised in exactly its present condition and could be maintained in that way without any annual cost'.
>
> Extract from the report of the Special Committee, appointed by the Council to consider the purchase of Kirkstall Grange Estates, 1907.

A bold and optimistic statement on maintenance costs which today's Parks Department must wonder at. Notwithstanding, the land was bought by the Corporation and opened to the public with the given name Beckett's Park.

... and the laying out of St Chad's Drive in 1932.   *Courtesy: Leeds City Library.*

In 1932 came another great change to the built environment around Far Headingley Village with further sales of the former Beckett estate. Land on the west side of Otley Road including the gate house and drive to Kirkstall Grange was sold for house building. Ideal Homes Ltd. began to develop the Beckett's Park housing estate – handsome, modern, well appointed, brickbuilt, 20th century houses – dream houses to most residents living in Far Headingley's old stone dwellings.

William Beckett's attractive 1830's gatehouse became dwarfed by its new brash suburban neighbours, the park drive was widened and made into a residential street, St Chad's Drive, and the cast iron gates, railings and stone piers – so long a feature of the Otley Road frontage – were taken down and removed to the end of the new road, marking the formal entrance to the Training College and public park.

West Park and Reservoir Hill

As we have seen, Headingley Golf Club was established in 1892 as a nine hole course at Moor Grange, Spen Lane. Formerly a grange of Kirkstall Abbey, Moor Grange had been a tenanted farm belonging to the Manor of Headingley and thus belonging to the Cardigan estate. The golf club opened at a time when golf was becoming a booming and fashionable sport. By 1900 the club had

Thoroughly in the country – the Otley Road in 1904 just above the Spen Road junction. Note the telegraph poles which are probably the same poles seen on the later 1910 view. In the later photograph, however suburban housing and the tram extension have arrived.

Courtesy: Miss N L Cook.

The tram terminus at West Park c1910. The tramway was extended up to West Park from The Three Horse Shoes in 1908, and further extended to Lawnswood in 1913.

Courtesy: Miss N L Cook.

over two hundred members and club officials were looking at ways to enlarge the course by a further nine holes. They turned their attention to farmland on the opposite side of Spen Lane, shown as the Ox Moor on the 1715 Cardigan estate map, immediately north of the Beckett estate. Negotiations, however, failed. The land, now considered prime building land was too expensive for the golf club which had to look elsewhere. It eventually acquired a new site at Adel where it relocated in 1906. By this time, house builders had already moved onto Ox Moor.

Present day Spen Road follows the course of an old road which cut across the Ox Moor and joined Spen Lane at the entrance to Moor Grange. Even before the departure of the Golf Club, land to the south side had been sold off and was under development. The 1909 edition of the Ordnance Survey (surveyed in 1906) shows Arncliffe Road, West Park Drive, West Parade and the cross streets from Darnley Road to North Parade plotted and part laid out. A new quarter of fashionable Edwardian 'homesteads' was taking shape west of the Weetwood Park estate, to be known as West Park.

By 1913, an elegant parade of shops had been completed on the Otley Road frontage (also former Cardigan land) and post card views were on sale from the recently opened West Park Post Office.

To the south of West Park Parade was the Beckett estate, open farmland at the beginning of the century, offering wholly rural views to the residents of the tall Victorian villas fronting the east side of the Otley Road. In 1905 Ernest Beckett sold land to Leeds Corporation for the construction of additional filter beds associated with the water treatment works on the other side of the road and in 1907 the estate itself was on the market. As we have seen, Leeds Corporation stepped in again and acquired the house and part of the estate for the college and park. Meanwhile, land north of the new filter beds was sold for housebuilding.

The filter beds at West Park remained fully operational, and a notable local landmark, until a new water treatment process was commissioned on the original waterworks site in the 1980s and 90s. A new fully automated plant costing forty three million pounds was installed, capable of supplying twenty six million gallons per day, six times the mid Victorian consumption. The original reservoir was reconstructed underground, holding 9.9 million gallons. It still supplies, by gravity, the Woodhouse Service Reservoir, and now, by pump, the Tinshill Service Reservoir taking water to Cookridge and Horsforth.

The sand filter beds on the west side of the main road were closed and the site was acquired from Yorkshire Water in 1999 by Crest Homes. An application for planning consent to build 246 dwellings was submitted to Leeds City Council in the midsummer of 1999 raising objections on the grounds of over intensive development and loss of character to the surrounding area. Nonetheless, permission was granted for a slightly modified scheme and building work began in 2000.

Aerial view of Reservoir Hill in the 1920s/30s. The ordered geometric pattern of the "new" filter beds contrasts with the more organic shape of the original reservoir on the far side of the main road. In the bottom right, the old vicarage can be seen. The Drummonds are substantially developed on the south side of the filter beds, as is the housing on the north side at West Park.
Courtesy: Ian Ballantine.

Spen Road West Park c. 1910. *Courtesy: Ian Ballantine.*

West Park housing opposite James Oxley's Spenfield Mansion. In the background is the incomplete shopping parade. Beyond is open countryside. Date: 1914. *Courtesy: Ian Ballantine*

A closer look at the impressively gabled facade and the matching frontages of the new shops at West Park in 1913. *Courtesy: Ian Ballantine.*

New suburban housing, Otley Road West Park c1915. Two locals are seen chatting at the corner of Ancaster Road.
Courtesy: Ian Ballantine.

New suburban housing at Welburn Avenue West Park c1915.
Courtesy: Ian Ballantine.

Castle Grove and The Masonic Hall Company

In an earlier chapter we left Castle Grove in the comfortable ownership of Mr and Mrs John Kirk, after its lavish reconstruction in 1896.

John Kirk died 'after a long illness' in 1908, aged seventy three, leaving Castle Grove to his sons. They chose not to, or were unable to, sell the house and installed a caretaker, Mr Frank Heaton. The gate house was let to John Gouldthorp whose occupation is given as tram conductor.

The situation remained unchanged until 1920 when the Kirk family sold Castle Grove to Edward Bain, a Leeds surgeon, for £7,750. His chauffeur, George Heslup occupied the gate house. Edward Bain had worked at the temporary Military Hospital at Beckett's Park during the Great War before taking up an appointment at Leeds Infirmary. He is now remembered by a memorial plaque in the main entrance of Leeds General Infirmary.

Arthur Hopwood has this memory of Castle Grove in the 1920s:

> 'During the late 1920s my elder sister and I visited Castle Grove on a number of occasions. Our Uncle Will (Mr G W Hopwood) who lived with us in Highbury Terrace, was one of Dr and Mrs Bain's two gardeners.
>
> Mrs Bain was very fond of entertaining and on occasions instructed her gardeners to flood one of the well kept lawns in times of frost, to make it suitable for skating. In the summer, we would be treated to Castle Grove tomotoes, apples and pears. But much more memorable were the picnic baskets. My uncle was very friendly with one of the Castle Grove maids - whom he later married - and in the 1920s and 30s, when he took me to see Yorkshire play at Headingley, what a joy it was and how late in the day the lunch interval seemed to a hungry young lad!'.

Arthur Hopwood reminiscing in December 1999.

In 1930, 'The Doctor', as he was known by patients and staff, sold Castle Grove for £5,300 and moved to Scarcroft. The house was bought by Mr Marshall Clegg a wall paper merchant, the low price partly indicative of the economic depression of the late 1920s but more due to spreading suburbia. The adjoining villa, Moor House had already been demolished to make way for the Moor Park housing estate.

> 'When Mr Marshall Clegg bought Castle Grove it was a house of significance but no doubt somewhat old fashioned. Nearly forty years old, built for a lifestyle which disappeared during the First World War, and becoming surrounded by more up-to-date although smaller residences such as the adjoining Moor Parks. We will never know if he bought Castle Grove for speculation and as a site for semi-detached houses, but he has the historical fame of being head of the last family to live there'.

E Richard Vaughan. *A History of Castle Grove*

Mr Clegg's chauffeur, John Danby, now occupied the gatehouse.

Marshall Clegg was a self made businessman, rising from a shop assistant in a general store to the proprietor of the West Riding Wallpaper Company with a chain of over sixty shops. However, he did not settle at Far Headingley for very long. Within four years he had sold Castle Grove for one hundred pounds more than he paid. A building firm, Pickard and Co., purchased the property, retaining part of the grounds for house building, and disposing of John Kirk's late Victorian splendour to a consortium of four Leeds Masonic Lodges, which came together especially for the purpose, forming themselves into the Castle Grove Masonic Hall Co. Ltd.

The architectural practice of Braithwaite and Jackman was commissioned to produce designs for a large dining room with kitchen and servery on the ground floor and a Lodge Temple room on the first floor. The rest of the house was re-arranged to provide instruction rooms, cloakrooms and a bar. The foundation stone for the new work was laid by the Earl of Harewood on December 11th 1934 and for the first time electricity was connected to the building.

The four Lodges transferred their meetings in October 1935 and by the end of 1935 not only had Castle Grove house become a Masonic Hall, but a slice of its generous garden had been taken for regimental, semi detached housing. The gatehouse was also demolished at this time.

Moor Park Housing Estate

As late Victorian demand for the Far Headingley villas waned, the large garden plots became attractive propositions for speculative builders. The Tetley family sold Moor House in Moor Road in 1899.[2] Soon after, it was demolished together with the coach-house, stables and two lodges. Moor Park Avenue and Moor Park Drive were laid out on the site. An adjacent vacant plot belonging to another brewing family (Samuel Smith's of Tadcaster)[3] was also sold and laid out as Moor Drive and Moor Park Villas, leaving the unmade lane which originally separated the two parcels of land, High Close Road, as a footpath access through to Hollin Drive and Meanwoodside.

Many of the houses were built between the wars by Pickard & Co. developers also of Castle Grove Avenue.

Reservoir Hill, Otley Road facing south c1900. In the carriage is Mr and Mrs George Cook. Mr Cook was the proprietor of G Cook and Son, Headingley butchers. The house on the left foreground is now a dentist and Richmond House School is next door.   *Courtesy: Miss N L Cook.*

Reservoir Hill, Otley Road facing north c1900. The Water Board has not yet encroached onto the west side of the road. The smart Victorian villas on the east side enjoy views straight across the Beckett estate farmland.   *Courtesy: Ian Ballantine.*

The Hollies and Meanwood Park

After the First World War, as we have seen, William Brown donated (in 1921) The Hollies and thirty acres of grounds to the City of Leeds to be maintained as a public park in memory of his late son, Harold, killed at the end of The Great War in 1918. To acknowledge the gift the Lord Mayor of Leeds attended a reception at the house in June 1921:

> The Hollies, Weetwood Lane, was handed over to the City of Leeds today by Mr G W Brown as a memorial to his son killed in the war. The grounds will be developed as a park. Eight acres of terraced woodland, the house, two acres of gardens, three acres of meadow estate covering thirty acres in all including nine and a half acres on the eastern side of Meanwood Beck specially purchased by Mr Brown to give access to the estate from Meanwoodside.
>
> Yorkshire Post 24.6.1921

A further acreage was added when Leeds Corporation bought Meanwoodside from the Kitson Clark estate in 1954. Jointly, this parkland creates a substantial swathe of public open space – woodland, meadow, valley walks and playspace. It brings the countryside deep into the city. It is a very valuable amenity to local residents. Though Meanwoodside house was demolished in the 1950s, leaving only forlorn looking outbuildings, many of the Weetwoodside villas remain and one is easily reminded of the luxuriant grandeur that once belonged to the fortunate few. For the wealthy, Far Headingley was indeed a verdant paradise.

Notes

[1] In 1898 Ebenezer Howard published his *Garden Cities of Tomorrow* which envisaged new satelite townships close to major English cities where he recommended a net residential density of eighty people per acre. Modern thinking would consider this too low to sustain local shops and services but it is indicative of the reaction against overcrowded housing.

[2] for a description of Moor House see page 83.

[3] but originally of Meanwood.

FROM RICH GARDENS TO PARKS AND HOUSING 189

Woodland walks along the millstream at Hollies Park, c. 1920s.   *Courtesy: Ian Ballantine.*

Meanwood Valley. A photograph by Godfrey Bingley dated 27th June 1887.
Courtesy: Leeds University.

The Twentieth Century:
More surprising literary connections

Arriving from Oxford in 1921, to take up a post in the English Department at Leeds University, J Ronald Tolkien and his wife, Edith, settled briefly at Hollybank just north of Shaw Lane. After a short stay they moved to St Mark's Terrace, Woodhouse, to be nearer to the University, but in 1924 they moved back into the Far Headingley parish when Ronald Tolkien was made Professor of English Language. They bought a house at 2 Darnley Road in West Park, a handsome Edwardian semi-detached property, distinguished by a turretted bay on the corner of the party house (3 Spen Road).

Always a great story teller, Tolkien would regale his children John (then 7) and Michael (4) with fantastic bedtime tales which would eventually lead him to pen *The Hobbit* in 1937 and *The Lord of the Rings* in 1954. His third son, Christopher was born in 1924.

Within two years Tolkien was offered the professorship of Anglo Saxon studies at Oxford and in 1926 the family left Leeds:

> 'My earliest memories of my father as a story-teller go back to Darnley Road during 1924 and 1925. When I was unable to sleep he would sit upon the bed and tell me wonderful stories which he never wrote down'.
>
> John Tolkien, *The Tolkien Family Album*, Houghton, Mifflin Co., Boston 1992

The semi-detached houses on the left (by the tree) are 3 Spen Road (turretted) and 2 Darnley Road. J. R. R. Tolkien lived at 2 Darnley Road between 1924 and 1926.

Courtesy: Miss N L Cook.

Another literary resident of Hollybank on the Otley Road was the travel writer John Hillaby. He grew up in Far Headingley and 'at Apperley Bridge' he writes, 'I worked out my years of indiscretion in a school for Methodists', Woodhouse Grove. He touches on his life in Leeds in one of his books:

> 'They, rich conservative merchants of wool, built themselves huge Italianate mansions of gritstone surrounded by screens of rhododendrons on that roller-coaster of a road between Woodhouse (Wood'us) Moor and the old tramsheds opposite St Chad's in Headingley. And there we, the Hillaby's, lived in a third of a large house with me trying to keep up with the spoilt brats of the surgeon next door'.
>
> *John Hillaby's Yorkshire,* Constable & Co 1986

When John Hillaby was growing up in Yorkshire, several of the gritstone mansions had already been taken over by the University as halls of residence. The University was becoming a major property owner in the parish. The comparatively modest detached stone house standing at the corner of Moor Road and the south side of Cottage Road was among the Universities acquisitions and is now part of the Tetley Hall complex. For many years it was used to house the Gregory Fellows.

Eric Gregory was born in Scotland, but lived most of his life in Yorkshire. He was a printer, and his firm Percy Lund Humphries and Co Ltd had its presses in Bradford. He was a life-long friend of Henry Moore and a patron of the arts.

After the Second World War, Eric Gregory began to sponsor fellowships in the creative arts at the University of Leeds. He died in 1959 but the Gregory fellowships continued right through to the 1980s, funded directly by the University, until they were subsumed by The Henry Moore Foundation.

For a time there were Gregory fellowships in Sculpture, Painting, Poetry and Music. Many artists came to spend time at the University and were housed in one of the converted flats in Moor Road House. Terry Frost, the painter was here between 1954 and 1956, Hubert Dalwood, the sculptor (1955-1959) and Oleg Prokofiev, son of the famous composer Serge Prokofiev, held the Gregory Fellowship in Painting between 1972 and 1974.

On the selection committee with Eric Gregory was another famous name – T S Eliot, dramatist, poet and author of *Mr Possum's Practical Cats*. The great American poet's association with Far Headingley, however, extends beyond the Gregory Fellowship. His wife Valerie grew up here.

Thomas Stearns Eliot was born in St Louis, Missouri, in 1888, but he migrated to Edwardian England and became 'English in everything but accent and citizenship' according to one biographer. He married Vivienne Haigh-Wood, but the marriage ended unhappily in 1915. The story of this troubled relationship became the subject of the 1990s film *Tom and Viv*. Thomas met his second wife, a Far Headingley girl, after the Second World War. Valerie Fletcher was born in 1926 and raised at the family home, 49 Weetwood Lane. Her father James Fletcher was manager of an insurance office. After training as a secretary in Leeds, she moved to London and a job with the publishing house of Faber and Faber – Thomas Eliot's publishers.

Through these connections, Thomas Eliot met Valerie Fletcher and became a regular visitor to Far Headingley. They were married on January 10th 1957.

At the time of T S Eliot's second courtship, an impressionable young boy was growing up in Far Headingley destined to become an equally famous playwright.

Alan Bennett was born in Armley in 1934 and moved to Far Headingley in 1946 when his father, Walter Bennett, became the local butcher. In his book 'Writing Home', Alan Bennett recalls his links with the great American writer, which were not, it has to be said, through a Gregory Fellowship:

> 'I was born and brought up in Leeds, where my father was a butcher. As a boy, I sometimes went out on the bike delivering orders to customers, one of whom was Mrs Fletcher. Mrs Fletcher had a daughter, Valerie, who went to school then to London, where she got a job with a publishing firm. She did well in the firm, becoming assistant to one of the directors, whom, though much older than she was, she eventually married. The firm was Faber and Faber, and the director was T S Eliot. So there was a time when I thought my only connection with the literary world would be that I had once delivered meat to T S Eliot's mother-in-law.
>
> A few years later, my mother came in one day and said: 'I ran into Mrs Fletcher down the road. She wasn't with Mr Fletcher, she was with another fella – tall, elderly, very refined looking. She introduced me and we passed the time of day'. It wasn't until sometime later I realised that, without it being one of the most momentous encounters in western literature, my mother had met T S Eliot. I tried to explain the significance of the great poet, but without success, *The Waste Land* not figuring very largely in Mum's scheme of things.
>
> 'The thing is', I said finally, 'he won the Nobel prize'.
>
> 'Well', she said, with that unerring grasp of inessentials which is the prerogative of mothers, 'I'm not surprised. It was a beautiful overcoat'.
>
> *Writing Home* by Alan Bennett, Faber and Faber 1994

Alan Bennett went to Leeds Modern School for boys (now Lawnswood School) from 1946 to 1952. He lived with his parents in the house attached to his father's butchers shop at 92A Otley Road between 1946 and 1957. In 1957, Mr Bennett sold his business to Mr Waters and removed, with his family, to Wood Lane. The house in Wood Lane became Alan Bennett's home until 1966. Water's butchers is still trading at 92A Otley Road at the close of the century.

> 'After the war we moved to Far Headingley, where Dad, having worked all his life at the Co-op now has a shop of his own just below the tram-sheds opposite St Chad's. We live over the shop, so I sleep and wake to the sound of trams: trams getting up speed for the hill before Weetwood Lane, trams spinning down from West Park, trams shunted around in the sheds in the middle of the night, the scraping of wheels, the clanging of the bell.
>
> To be on a tram sailing down Headingley Lane on a fine evening lifted the heart. I went to school by tram, the fare a halfpenny from St Chad's to the Ring Road. A group of us at the Modern School scorned school dinners and came home for lunch, catching the tram from another terminus at West Park.

Moorville, Moor Road. The Kettle family house from 1946 to 1970. A detail of the gate arch sketched by Michael Smith.

Courtesy: the artist.

We were all keen on music and went every Saturday to hear the Yorkshire Symphony Orchestra in the Town Hall, and it was on a tram at West Park that another sixth-former, 'Fanny' Fielder sang to me the opening bars of Brahms's Second Piano Concerto'.

Writing Home by Alan Bennett

Another customer to whom Alan Bennett almost certainly made deliveries for his father was Arnold Kettle who lived at Moorville, on the corner of Cottage Road and Moor Road, between 1946 and 1970. Arnold Kettle taught English Literature at Leeds University and was well known as a Marxist and as a member of the Communist Party at time when such views and activities were highly controversial.[1] He was respected by eminent authors of the day and was a noted literary critic with a worldwide reputation in his field.

Arnold Kettle's son, Martin, was born in 1949. He grew up at Moorville and became a distinguished journalist. In 1993, when associate editor of *The Guardian*, Martin Kettle recalled his childhood memories of growing up at Moorville:

'The garden where we played cricket, the copper beech where we built a tree house, the holly tree in the corner where I spent hours secretly watching the comings and goings in Moor Road, the snow and tobogganing down from the big hall at the top of the hill across Moor Road and into Cottage Road, the conker trees, the madcap bicycle rides round the house and out onto the pavement with my brother, pocket money being spent on sweets at Hemingways, Saturday fish and chips from Bryans before it became a restaurant, with extra scraps, the smithy at the bottom of Weetwood Lane, Barbara with the twisted lip from the little dairy in Cottage Road with whom I used to go delivering milk many mornings, the day our cat was run over and buried in the corner of the garden; the walls, the stone, the dirt, the leaves, the feel of the great green drainpipes I used to climb, the balcony and the house itself, a great square house with four big rooms on each floor, stained glass in the hall, tiles on the floor, the banisters we used to slide down, the coal in the garage, the day we got our first TV. Stop me, stop me. Merely to ask me about Far Headingley is to invite me to become unutterably nostagic and affectionate.'

London, October 13th 1993

Claremont Drive, New years Day 2000. St Anne's Villas (near distance) and St George's Terrace (middle distance). A scene little changed since these houses were built between 1854 and 1861 on land purchased by George Veevers, a Leeds solicitor, in 1853. To the right is Claremont Drive, originally a carriageway leading from Shaw Lane. Tennis courts on the other side (far right) are now replaced by red brick villas of the Edwardian period.

Photo and caption: Chris Hammond.

Phyllis Atkinson was born in 1902 and lived at 29 Claremont Drive all her life. Her father built the red brick Edwardian villas including No 29 before her arrival and nearly 100 years later she could recall that Claremont Road was originally known as Tennis Court Lane. Phyllis Atkinson died in January 2000. George Corson lived at 4 St George's Terrace in the 1860s.

St Chad's Gardens, Otley Road, January 2000. A line of four dutch baroque style, brick and terracotta houses, flamboyantly decorated. 1885. Grade II listed. Built on land acquired from the Cardigan estate in 1878 by Thomas Simpson. *Photo: David Hall.*

Next door to Moorville is Mazebrook, one of a pair of early houses with deep garden frontages to Cottage Road and rear service yards on Moor Road. This was the home of art critic William T Oliver from 1937 to 1965. During the war years the house was commandeered by the Headingley Home Guard. Mr Oliver moved back just before the end of the war. His son, Patrick, remembers finding munitions, including tear gas bombs, left in the cellar. Bill Oliver was Chief Assistant Editor at the *Yorkshire Post* and, for a time, Deputy Editor. He retired in 1968 but continued as the newspaper's highly respected Art Critic. During his years at the *Yorkshire Post* he nurtured and encouraged artistic talent. The film and theatre actor, Peter O'Toole, then photographic assistant at the *Yorkshire Evening Post*, and a personal friend of Patrick Oliver, was a frequent house guest, and when a young reporter from the *Bristol Evening Post* spent a week at Mazebrook, Bill Oliver was so impressed that he offered him a job at the *Yorkshire Post*. The young man declined. He was aiming to write for the theatre not the regional press. He was Tom Stoppard.

Next door to Mazebrook is Wheatlands, where Frank Lisle a well known local artist and principal of Leeds College of Art, lived between 1955 and 1983.

Opposite Wheatlands is a handsome, late Georgian villa, No 46 Cottage Road (sometime known as Moor Cottage). It was the home of Mr and Mrs Philip Wade for many years. Philip Wade was a keen collector of gramophone records and became something of an early disc jockey. During the war, he regularly drove to Harewood House, then serving as a military hospital, to play records to the war wounded. As a result a war time friendship developed between the Wades of Far Headingley and the Lascelles of Harewood. The Princess Royal became Godmother to Phililp Wade's son, and would visit Cottage Road with her young boys, the present Lord Harewood and his brother Gerald Lascelles.

Other writers, broadcasters and performers associated with Far Headingley include playwright Kay Mellor, born and brought up locally and now resident in Weetwood; film star James Fox who lived at 27 Arncliffe Road in West Park between 1974 and 1980 whilst taking time out to work with the University's Christian Mission; Archdeacon Francis House, Head of Religious Broadcasting at the BBC 1947-1955 and writer on the Russian Orthodox Church, who has lived in retirement at Drummond Court since 1978 whilst acting as honorary priest at St Chad's; Barry Overend, Vicar of St Chad's since 1986, well known for his religious 'Life on an Angle' broadcasts for Radio Leeds; and David Jenkins, the politically outspoken Bishop of Durham, who lived in Drummond Avenue whilst Professor of Theology at the University of Leeds and acted as honorary priest at St Chad's – his searching sermons, softly spoken, freely extemporised and delivered with such energy and wit.

Inevitably, however, we are led back to the University. Far Headingley is a University parish known for its resident population of students, professors and academics. It is perhaps appropriate to end this section, therefore, with another reference to Professor Arnold Kettle and his wife, Margot. Writing in the University Review in 1997, Martin Kettle records that his parents ...

> came to Leeds in 1946, the year of their marriage, and lived for the next twenty four years in Far Headingley, in a big and characterful gritstone house on the corner of Moor Road and Cottage Road in which I and my brother grew up.
>
> All sorts of fascinating left-wing and literary figures of the age seemed to visit them there. Among the people I remember coming through the house were C P Snow, Pamela Hansford Johnson, John Braine, Doris Lessing, Alan Sillitoe and Hugh Macdiarmid. But my abiding memory of literary Leeds at that time is all about the students, for whom my parents and their colleagues seemed to be infinitely solicitous and indefatigably supportive. When Arnold died in 1986 and Margot nine years later, my brother and I received letters and condolences from all around the globe from people who had passed through Leeds in those years'.

Leeds University Review 1997.

Note

'*Arnold & Margot Kettle Remembered*', Martin Kettle, Leeds University Review 1997.

MORE SURPRISING LITERARY CONNECTIONS

Mazebrook, W. T. Oliver's home between 1937 and 1965. *A 1975 sketch by Mike Peace.*

Moorville, Moor Road in 1976. The home of Professor Kettle and his family. *FHVS collection*

Into the Twenty First Century: Care for the Present, Regard for the Future

The Far Headingley Village Society

By the end of the 1960s many of the old cottages and houses, which make up the core of Far Headingley 'village', had fallen into a poor state of repair. Building Societies were reluctant to offer mortgages on property considered to have reached the end of its useful life and the area took on an air of neglect. Wholesale demolition was on the cards as the City Council considered major redevelopment of the Cottage Road area. In 1971, sixty-six houses were condemned as unfit and scheduled for clearance.

But, this was also a time when the charm and character of old property was beginning to be appreciated and its importance in heritage terms recognised. In the New Year of 1971 local residents came forward with proposals for a Conservation Area. This would offer protection against redevelopment and qualify property owners for renovation grants. The Council agreed to designate the Cottage Road area as a Conservation Area but did not agree to withdraw plans to demolish the sixty six houses.

A public meeting was held in November 1971 to establish The Far Headingley Village Society, elect officers and agree its objectives:

> 'to promote the conservation and improvement of Far Headingley Village and districts adjoining for the benefit of the inhabitants and of all those who make use of its amenities'.

Immediately the new committee got down to the job of challenging the demolition plans. They produced their own report on 'The Cottage Road Conservation Area – the housing situation and the proposed clearances'[1] which analysed the potential for improving houses classed as 'unfit' and outlined a policy for rehabilitation and conservation. It was a direct response to the Council's own report 'Conservation and Clearance' prepared by the City Architect in September 1972.

The Council conceded that twenty-one of the sixty-six houses were capable of improvement with the aid of grants. A partial reprieve, but the remaining forty-five could not be improved sufficiently to meet modern building regulations. No grants would be available.

On the basis of the City Architect's report, The Cottage Road Area was approved as Conservation Area No 5 by Leeds City Council in September 1972 and a pamphlet was issued to householders who qualified for improvement grants. The work of the Society, however, continued - more surveys, more lobbying, more consultation within the community, more published reports

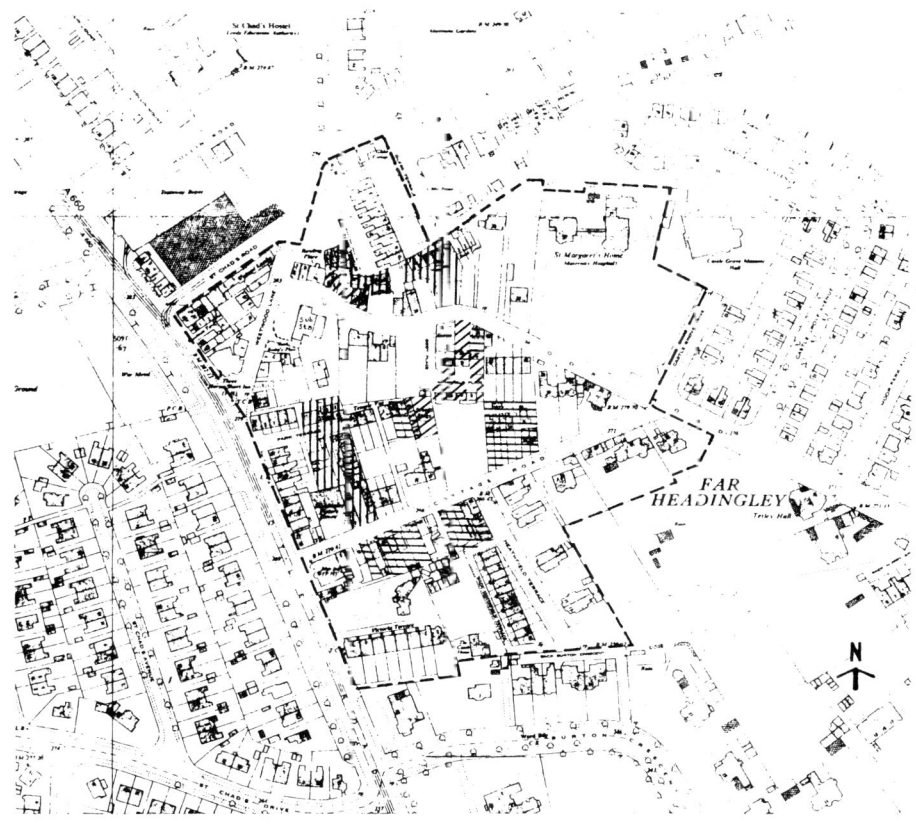

COTTAGE ROAD CONSERVATION AREA

Planning Brief

Clearance Proposals

Notation

Properties for Clearance	
Properties for Retention and Upgrading	
MINOR IMPROVEMENT	
MAJOR IMPROVEMENT	
CONSERVATION AREA BOUNDARY	

Plan No. PP/9A4/107

The 1972 planning brief prepared by Leeds City Council showing the original Conservation Area boundaries and the extent of the demolition proposed. – Ellis Terrace, Park Terrace, Sowdens Yard and Smith's Cottage were all to be swept away. In 1975 the boundaries were altered to include Castle Grove and the whole of the bus depot block. Cottage Road Conservation Area was subsumed into Headingley Conservation Area in 1984.

and during the following two years nearly all the forty five 'unfit' houses came off the condemned list and received grants – notably Ellis Terrace, Park Terrace and Smith's Cottages. A tremendous tribute to the hard work of the Society in its early years.

Today, Far Headingley Village Society continues to meet bi-monthly to discuss planning applications and other issues affecting the area. It organises an annual Yard Sale, sponsors summer flower baskets, runs a sun flower competition each summer, and holds its Annual General Meetings every November. It is an affiliated member of Leeds Civic Trust.

The Society takes a continuing interest in researching local history and in this respect it is probably apt to apologise here for any mistakes that may have crept into this book. If anyone has more information, Society members would be pleased to hear from them.

In addition to Far Headingley Village Society, there are two other active residents associations in the area at the time of publication – Fox Hill Residents Association, also affiliated to Leeds Civic Trust and Weetwood Residents Association.

In 1971 Far Headingley Village Society appointed the following officers and committee:

Mrs Alison Ravetz	Chairman
Mrs June Lisle	Joint Secretary
Mrs U Laredo	Joint Secretary
Mr W Adamson	Treasurer
Mr W Bedford	Liaison Officer
Mrs Judith Dryhurst	Joint Public Relations Officer
Mr Jim Dryhurst	Joint Public Relations Officer
Mr D Gabb	
Mr Donald Hood	Housing Group
Mr J Inman	Housing Group
Mrs A Latham	
Mr R Mascall	
Mr J Myers	Roads Group
Mr Jerry Ravetz	Roads Group
Mr Peter Snodgrass	Liaison Officer
Mr G Whiteley	Roads Group
Mrs J Whitworth	Townscape Group

The three local Councillors Dr R D Hall, Mrs B Peart and Mr S Rostron were co-opted. The Constituency's Member of Parliament was Sir Donald Kaberry MP, Conservative.

For the Millennium year the officers and committee elected to serve were:

Mr David Hall	Chairman
Mr Donald Hood	Joint Secretary
Mrs Posy McTurk	Joint Secretary
Mrs Yvonne Oughton	Treasurer
Mr John Coles	University Liaison
Mrs Pam Davies	Police Liaison
Mr Andrew Davies	
Mrs Julie Fordy	
Mrs Sue Hall	
Mr Bob Holt	
Mrs Clare Nash	A66c Committee
Mrs Mu Tucker	
Mrs Margaret Wilkinson	

Mrs Sue Thornton was co-opted to join the committee during the year.

The three local councillors were Judith Blake, Brian Jennings and Stewart Golton. The Constituteny's Member of Parliament was Mr Harold Best MP, Labour.

Note
[1] Written by Alison Ravetz, a noted Town Planning Specialist.

Nicholson's Cottage Road/Heathfield Terrace corner shop in the 1970s.

Courtesy: FHVS Collection.

Who's Who, and Who Was Who, in Far Headingley

A brief guide to some of the personalities encountered in the main text.

Prince Alamayou (1861-1879). Eldest son of King Theodore of Abyssinia. He was 'rescued' by Captain Speedy and brought to England after the storming of Magdala by the British in 1868 during which his father had committed suicide. Educated by the state and under the personal protection of Queen Victoria, Prince Alamayou arrived in Far Headingley in 1879 as the house guest of his tutor Cyril Ransome. He caught a severe cold and died at 1 Glebe Villas Hollin Lane within a few weeks. He was buried at St George's Chapel Windsor, much grieved for by Queen Victoria.

Sir Thomas Clifford Allbutt (1836-1925). The doctor attending Alamayou at Hollin Lane in 1868, a wealthy physician celebrated as the inventor of the clinical thermometer. In the mid 1870s he purchased Carr House on Stonegate Road, from the Oates estate and commissioned the building of Carr Manor around the structure of the original 17c farmhouse. Carr Manor was completed in 1881 and Clifford Albutt lived there until 1889. It is now the judges' residence in Leeds but Clifford Albutt's initials can still be clearly seen in the decorative scroll designs within the wrought iron gates.

In 1868 Clifford Allbutt became a close friend of the writer Marian Evans, namely Mrs George Lewis, universally known by her pseudonym, George Eliot. Her biographer, Rosemary Ashton refers to Allbutt as …

> 'a young doctor in Leeds, an idealist whose chance reading of Comte while an undergraduate in Cambridge had made him look to science and the socially useful occupation of medicine. Allbutt made (George) Lewis's acquaintance at a meeting of the British Medical Association in Oxford in the summer of 1868. In September 1868 both Lewises visited him in Leeds'.

Clifford Allbutt was also the 'genial' friend of Thomas Hardy. From 1892 he was Regius Professor of Medicine at Cambridge. He had been a Commissioner in Lunacy and gave credence to Florence Hardy's assertion that Thomas's first wife Emma became clinically mad in her later life.

Thomas Hardy's biographer, Martin Seymour-Smith, also reveals more about the George Eliot connection:

> 'Allbutt himself was a distinguished and humane doctor, who invented the clinical thermometer. When young he had run a notably progressive infirmary in Leeds, around which he had shown George Eliot, whom he also consulted about 'his long engagement'. But he was vain, and thoroughly deserved his inevitable knighthood. His claim that he was the original of Lydgate in George Eliot's *Middlemarch* (the novel's most conspicuous human failure) is taken seriously to this day'.

Thomas Ambler (1838-1920). Leeds architect, best known for St Paul's House in Park Square – an extraordinary Hispano Moorish factory decorated with five terracotta minorets and built for Sir John Barron in 1878. Also the Trevelyan Temperance Hotel in Boar Lane c1866-70 (now the Marryat Hotel), which marked the beginning of the whole rebuilding of Boar Lane. In 1874 he bought land in Far Headingley and laid out Hollin Lane. Glebe Terrace is also attributed to Ambler. For much of his professional life he was associated with Leeds Permanent Building Society as Director and President and made designs for model dwellings for the Society.

Alfred Austin (1835-1913). Born in Headingley Lane. He became a barrister but devoted his life to writing after the death of his father. He succeeded Alfred Lord Tennyson as Poet Laureate in 1896. 'Across the wires the electric message came: / 'He is no better, he is much the same', – *On the illness of the Prince of Wales*.

Arthur James Balfour (1848-1930). Won fast promotion through his uncle, Robert Cecil, giving rise to the popular expression 'Bob's your uncle'. He was Prime Minister from 1902 to 1905 and a house guest of the Hon Gervase Beckett MP at Kirkstall Grange in December 1905. A photograph taken at the time shows Balfour on the steps of Kirkstall Grange wearing a long overcoat and spats. His pince-nez hang from his coat buttons. Standing with him are Gervase and Mabel Beckett whose daughter Beatrice was to marry Anthony Eden in 1923.

Sir Edmund [Beckett] Denison (1786-1874). The sixth son of Sir John Beckett and William Beckett's younger brother. In 1814 he married Maria, the heiress of Lady Denison's estate, and assumed the family name Denison, after Sir Thomas Denison, a former Judge of the Common Pleas. He was chairman of the Great Northern Railway for nearly twenty years and established that company's plant works at Doncaster where he came to reside. He survived his elder brothers and briefly inherited his father's baronetcy. On becoming a Baronet he reverted to the name of Beckett. William having died in 1863, it was Edmund who became the acknowledged patron of St Chad's Church (see main text).

A noted horseman, he was a friend of Sir Robert Peel and has the distinction of having sold the British Prime Minister the horse that threw him whilst on his way to a Great Exhibition meeting. Sir Robert Peel died of his injuries.

Edmund Beckett Denison QC, Lord Grimthorpe (1816-1905). The eldest son of Edmund Denison born at Carlton Hall, Nr. Newark. Educated at Doncaster, Eton and Trinity College Cambridge. A successful (London) barrister specialising in parliamentary and ecclesiastical law, amateur architect noted for his much criticised alterations to St Alban's Abbey, expert horologist renowned for designing the clock at the Palace of Westminster, and student of homoeopathy. He was created a peer in 1886 and took the title Lord Grimthorpe. His professional work as a parliamentary lawyer took up five months of every year. The rest of his time he gave to things that amused him. He died in 1905 leaving a personal fortune of two million pounds. He suffered from an exaggerated sense of his own abilities, according to his biographer, Peter Ferriday, and 'although learned, clever, and splendidly

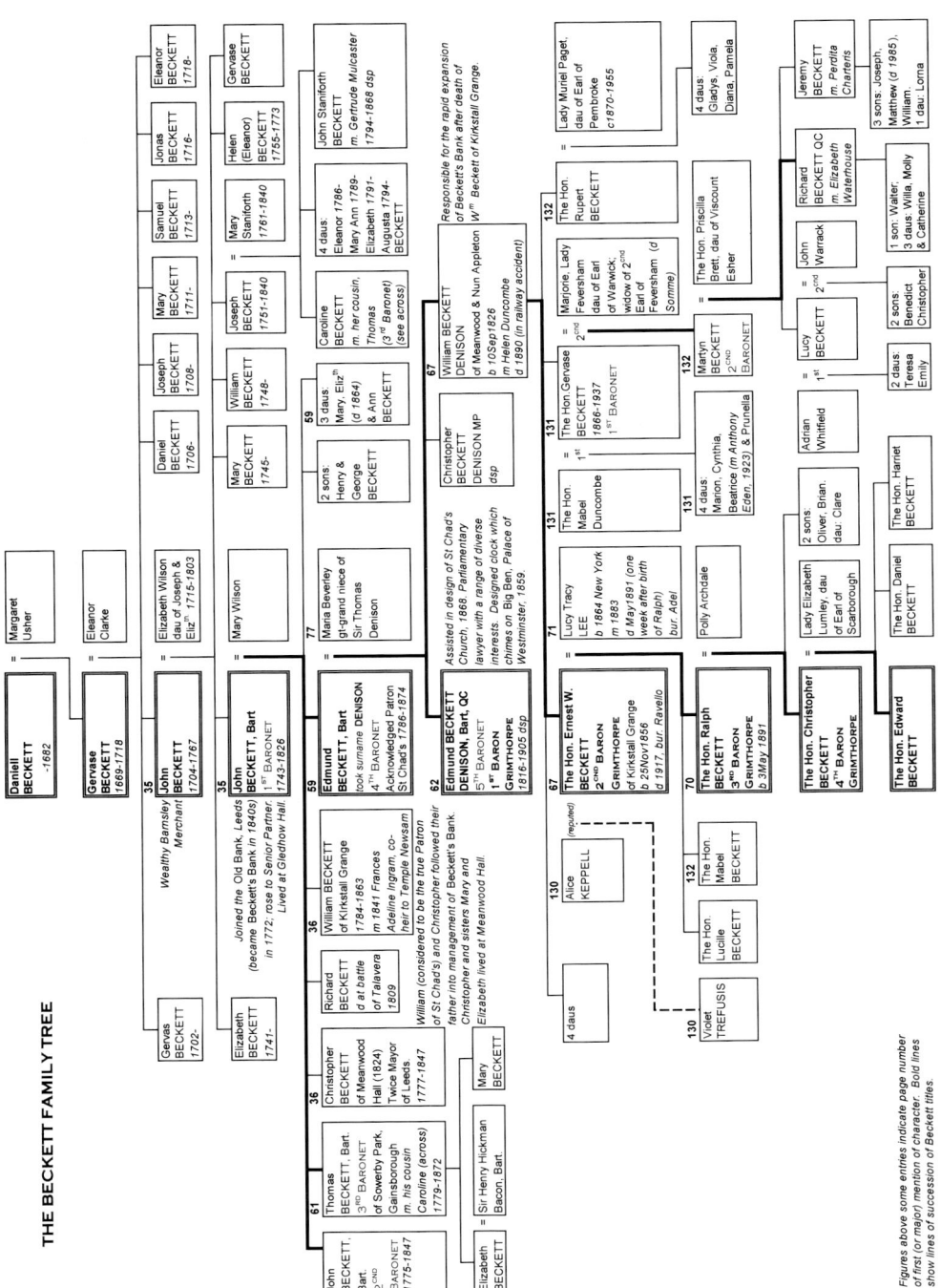

gifted Grimthorpe was brutal, wrongheaded and mischievous'. He assisted in the design of St Chad's Church and led the celebrations at the dedication lunch.

Ernest William Beckett, 2nd Lord Grimthorpe (1856-1917). Eldest son of William Ernest Beckett Denison. He joined the family firm of Beckett & Co in Leeds and was MP for Whitby. In 1883 he married American socialite Lucy Tracy Lee and made Kirkstall Grange his home. Lucy died six days after the birth of their son Ralph in 1891. Ernest enjoyed entertaining the rich and famous, travelled extensively and is reputed to have fathered a love child with Alice Kepple the future King's mistress in 1894. He emigrated to Italy in 1903 and died at his home in Ravello in 1917.

The Hon Gervase Beckett (1866-1937). The last Beckett to live at Kirkstall Grange. He was MP for Scarborough and Whitby from 1905 to 1921 and Leeds North from 1921 to 1930. His third daughter Beatrice (born at Kirkstall Grange) became the wife of Sir Anthony Eden. Gervase moved from Kirkstall Grange in 1908. The visitors book, still in his family's possession, shows some notable week-end guests including Arthur Balfour and Winston Churchill. Gervase became Chairman of Yorkshire Post Newspapers and was also a director of Westminster Bank which absorbed Beckett's Bank in 1920. His younger brother Rupert became Chairman

Sir John Beckett (1743-1826). John Beckett was the elder son of a Barnsley grocer 'gifted with industry, thrift and foresight' who largely through property speculation 'rapidly became the richest man in town'. John moved to Leeds and joined Old Leeds Bank in 1772. He became an Alderman of the City, Lord Mayor and principal partner of the Bank. In 1813 he was created a Baronet in recognition of his services to the commercial community of Leeds. A contemporary is reputed to have said of him 'Sir John Beckett governs the country, inasmuch as he governs Leeds, Leeds governs Yorkshire and Yorkshire governs Pitt.' He had eight sons and three daughters. His son William bought New Grange in 1829, Christopher lived at Meanwood Hall from 1824 with his sisters Mary and Elizabeth. Another brother, Edmund, lived at Doncaster and took the name Beckett Denison after his marriage to Sir Thomas Denison's heiress, Maria Beverley.

William Beckett (1784-1863). The fifth son of Sir John Beckett. He and his brother Christopher followed their father into Beckett's Bank. William bought the New Grange Estate in 1829. The house was modernised and renamed Kirkstall Grange. He lived there for the rest of his life. In 1832 he was called before a Secret Committee of the House of Commons to advise on matters relating to the renewal of the Bank of England's Charter. On his death he left sufficient money to build St Chad's Church and endow its ministry.

Willam Ernest Beckett-Denison (1826-1890). The 2nd son of Edmund Beckett Denison, Willam followed two of his uncles (William and Christopher) into the family bank. He lived at Meanwood Hall after his aunt died leaving the Hall unoccupied, and later moved to Nun Appleton near York. He was responsible for the rapid expansion of Beckett's Bank which merged with and took over other smaller Yorkshire banks. His staff regarded him as a stern but benevolent dictator. He was also MP for East Retford and Bassetlaw. He married Helen Duncombe and had six children Ernest, Gervase and Rupert, and three daughters. In 1890 he was killed by a train, in an appalling accident, whilst walking beside the railway in Dorset.

Alan Bennett (Born 1934). Dramatist, actor, director. He came to prominence as a writer and performer in *'Beyond the Fringe'* a revue performed at the Edinburgh Festival in 1960. His stage plays include *Forty Years On, Getting On, Habeus Corpus, The Old Country, Single Spies* and *Lady in a Van*. His play *The Madness of George III* was adapted for the screen as *The Madness of King George*, to avoid confusing cinema audiences who, the film's American backers thought, having seen 'George Three', would want to know what happened to Parts 1 and 2. Other films include *A Private Function*. He has also written extensively for television including *An Englishman Abroad* and two series of *Talking Heads*. He lived in Far Headingley between 1947 and 1957, and was educated at Leeds Modern School.

Sir Nathan Bodington (1848-1911). Born near Birmingham on May 29th 1848 and educated at Birmingham and Oxford. Principal and Professor of Greek at the Yorkshire College becoming the first Vice-Chancellor from 1904 of its successor the University of Leeds. Before moving to Shire Oak Road he lived at 126 Otley Road (later the home of a young Arthur Ransome). Nathan Bodington was a regular worshipper at St Chad's where he was buried on May 16th 1911. His grave is prominently located near the church tower. His name was given to Bodington Hall, the University's halls of residence at Lawnswood.

Cuthbert Brodrick (1822-1905). Born in Hull and apprenticed as an architect. He came to Leeds in 1853 and during the following sixteen years designed Leeds Town Hall, the Corn Exchange, the Mechanics Institute (The Civic Theatre building) and Headingley Hill Congregational Church. According to his biographer T Butler Wilson 'Cuthbert Brodrick had no residence in Leeds, being content as a bachelor with lodgings at Far Headingley, and the convenience and amenities of his club' (The Leeds Club in Albion Place). He 'retired' to Paris in 1869 but spent the last seven years of his life on the island of Jersey where he is buried.

Lord Cardigan (1797-1868). James Lord Brudenell became the 7th Lord Cardigan on the death of his father (the 6th Earl) in 1837. The family seat was at Deene Park, Northamptonshire, but the family estates were extensive in three counties and included the Manor of Headingley and Kirkstall. He fought in the Crimea war and led the Light Brigade into battle in 1854 at Balaclava. The Charge of the Light Brigade became one of the most celebrated moments in British military history, a disastrous sortie straight into the Russian guns. But Lord Cardigan survived and was regarded as a national hero. His habit of wearing a buttoned up woollen tunic gave rise to the name 'cardigan'. Late in life he married a much younger second wife, Adeline, who survived him for forty seven years. By the time Lady Cardigan died in 1915 the last of the Headingley property had been sold.

Saint Chad (died 672). Born in Northumbria and educated at Lindisfarne under St Aidan. He became the second Archishop of York 664-9. He resigned his See because of difficulties with the fiery St Wilfred. He became the first Bishop of Mercia and Lindsey at Lichfield in 669 and died on March 2nd 672. Bede described his first shrine as 'a wooden coffin in the shape of a little house with an aperture on the side through which the devout can take out some of the dust, which put into water and given to sick cattle or men to drink, upon which they are presently eased of their infirmity and restored to health'. His relics were later removed to the lady chapel at Lichfield Cathedral. We see him carved in oak by the pulpit within St Chad's church holding a church in his hand.

Winston S Churchill (1874-1965). Prime Minister and British statesman was a house guest at Kirkstall Grange in February 1907 the year before the Becketts finally moved from Far Headingley to Kirkdale Manor near York. Churchill's niece Clarissa married Anthony Eden in 1952 two years after his divorce from his first wife Beatrice Helen Beckett, born at Kirkstall Grange in 1904. Winston Curchill was Prime Minister in 1940-1945 (the wartime coalition government) and in post war Britain between 1951 and 1955.

Alf Cooke (1842-1902). Born in Leeds on July 4th 1842 and educated at the Collegiate Institution, Meanwood. He was the pioneer of art colour printing in England and owned Crown Point Printing Works on Hunslet Road, at the time claimed to be the largest in the world. He was elected Mayor of Leeds in 1890 and lived in Moor Road then at Weetwood Hall. Alf Cooke was a regular worshipper at St Chad's church where the two west windows are dedicated to his memory. He was buried at St Chad's on March 27th 1902.

George Corson (1829-1910). Born in Dumfries the son of James Corson, Provost of Dumfries and Chief Magistrate of that town. At the age of twenty he joined his elder brother, William, in Leeds and together they practised as architects. His first house was at Lyddon Terrace (now within the University campus) where he lived with his sister Jean, but in 1861 the Directory gives 'George Corson, architect 5 South Parade and Far Headingley'. He moved to 4 St George's Terrace, Monkbridge Road in Far Headingley and in 1871 built Dunearn in Wood Lane Headingley where he lived until moving to his last home in Woodland Park Road. According to his biographer, T Butler Wilson, 'for many years he attended St Chad's Church Far Headingley, and later St Michael's Church Headingley'. During the 1860s he bought land to the north of Headingley Hall from the Earl of Cardigan but it was not until the 1880s that he laid out Shire Oak Road. In 1885 he was advertising half-acre lots for new houses 'according to his own designs'. By this time he had a reputation for designing Weetwood mansion houses at Foxhill (1862) and Spenfield (1875) plus the Leeds Central Library building, the City's Education Offices, and his great architectural triumph – Leeds Grand Theatre.

In 1874, 10.75 acres of land was purchased at Lawnswood for a new cemetery, part of which lies inside Far Headingley parish. George Corson designed the chapel, the entrance lodge and landscaped the grounds. He died in 1910 and is buried at Lawnswood.

Thomas Cranmer (1489-1556). Took holy orders in 1523 and was consecrated Archbishop of Canterbury in 1534. He declared Henry VIII's marriage to Ann Boleyn legal, broke allegiance to the Pope and pronounced the King of England head of the Church of England. After the death of Henry VIII he was granted the lands which had belonged to Kirkstall Abbey including the Manor of Headingley by Edward VI. In 1556 he was burnt at the stake in the centre of Oxford charged with treason for supporting the succession of Lady Jane Grey, in place of Mary, and for heresy. He was godfather to Elizabeth I.

Hubert Dalwood (1924-1976). Sculptor who produced abstract work formed in concrete, bronze and lead. Born in Bristol, he came to Leeds when awarded a four year Gregory Fellowship in 1955 and continued to live in Cottage Road Far Headingley until 1962, teaching for a while at the Leeds College of Art. Locally, his work can be seen at Bodington Hall, and the Henry Moore Gallery in Leeds.

Sir Thomas Denison (1697-1765). Circuit Judge of the Kings Bench. His estate passed to his widow Lady Anne Denison who lived at Weetwood Hall for a time. The trustees of Lady Denison purchased the Manor of Grimthorpe in the East Riding, which ultimately devolved upon Maria Beverley of Beverley. Edmund Beckett married Maria Beverley in 1814 and assumed the name Beckett Denison in 1816. When his son, also Edmund, was enobled in 1886 he took the title Lord Grimthorpe.

(Robert) Anthony Eden, first Earl of Avon (1897-1977). 2nd son of Sir William Eden, a Durham baronet. In 1923 he married Beatrice Helen Beckett, born at Kirkstall Grange in 1904, the daughter of Sir Gervase Beckett, banker and chairman of the *Yorkshire Post*. In 1925 Anthony Eden toured the Empire partly financed by the *Yorkshire Post* for which he wrote articles converted into his book *'Places in the Sun'*. Described as 'slim, debonair, well dressed wearing a hat named after him and talking with the clipped yet languid accents of the Eton and Christ Church of his day'. Behind an urbane manner he was both tough and sensitive. Their son Simon, a pilot, was killed in Burma in 1945 and in 1946 he separated from Beatrice. The marriage was dissolved in 1950. In 1951 he became Foreign Secretary and in 1955 Prime Minister. He married Winston Churchill's niece Clarissa in 1952. He resigned as Prime Minister on medical advice at the height of the Suez crisis.

King Edward VII (1841-1910). Married Princess Alexandra of Denmark in 1863 and was Prince of Wales before succeeding to the throne on the death of

Queen Victoria in 1901. His mistress, Alice Keppel, also had a liaison with Ernest Beckett, the relationship resulting in the birth of Violet (Trefusis) in 1894. The following year the future king stayed at Kirkstall Grange as Ernest Beckett's guest during the Leeds Music Festival.

Thomas Stearns Eliot (1888-1965). Born in St Louis, he was 'English in everything but accent and citizenship'. He married Miss Vivienne Haigh-Wood of London in 1915, taught at Highgate School and also took a job at Lloyd's Bank. He was part of the Bloomsbury Set, established his own magazine *'The Criterion'*, and was literary editor for Faber and Faber. He became a British citizen in 1925. In 1935 he wrote *Murder in the Cathedral* and in 1948 he won the Nobel prize for literature. In 1957 he married his secretary Miss Valerie Fletcher daughter of James Fletcher from Weetwood Lane, Far Headingley. Alan Bennett remembers delivering meat for his father to the Fletcher's house in Weetwood Lane, or as Alan Bennett puts it his claim to great literary connections as a boy rested on the fact that he 'used to deliver the meat to T S Eliot's mother-in-law'. In 1942 T S Eliot was described thus 'he wears his handkerchief in his cuff, drinks burgundy and sherry, plays chess (not so well) and is afraid of cows and high places. He prefers to mingle with the nobility, with church dignitaries and genteel spirits'.

James Fox (born 1939) Film and television actor. 1960s star of *Those Magnificent Men in Their Flying Machines*, *Thoroughly Modern Millie* and *Performance*. He left acting in 1970 and arrived in Leeds to pursue a Christian vocation. 'My wife and I lived at 27 Arncliffe Road from 1974-1980 and four of our children were born at Leeds Maternity Hospital. We were part of the University's Christian work and attended St George's in town. Our memories of Far Headingley are long and strong and happy'. Since returning to acting he has appeared in a number of films and TV plays including *A Passage to India* and *The Remains of the Day*.

Hon Alderman Douglas Gabb. Prominent local politician. City councillor for Leeds and Lord Mayor of the City (1984/85). From 1963-1976 he ran a small general store at 21 Moor Road. Political agent to Denis Healey (Lord Healey) M.P. for East Leeds 1952-1992 and Chancellor of the Exchequer 1974-1979. Douglas Gabb was an engineer but writing about him in his autobiography, Lord Healey remembers that 'for a time' he was also a milkman. 'He and his wife, Ivy, ran a small newsagents shop. When we first met in 1952, Douglas was somewhat suspicious and prickly – and very left-wing. Today he is one of my closest friends. Always trim and dapper, with sharp features, bright eyes and a wise smile, he symbolises everything that is best in the British Labour movement.' In recent years, an honorary degree was conferred on him by Leeds University.

Cardinal John Heenan (1905-1975). Born in Ilford, Essex. He was ordained in 1930 and became a parish priest in East London. During World War II he worked with the BBC, becoming well known as 'the Radio Priest'. He became Bishop of Leeds in 1951 and lived at Bardon Hill, Weetwood Lane. In 1957 he was appointed Bishop of Liverpool, and Archbishop of Westminster in 1963. On leaving Leeds, he requested that the Bishop's House, Bardon Hill should be converted into a school. St Urban's Catholic Primary School opened at Bardon Hill in 1956 and transferred to a new site in Tongue Lane in 1996 next to Cardinal Heenan High School.

King Henry VIII (1491-1547). Second son of Henry VII. In 1521 he published a book in defence of the seven sacraments in reply to Martin Luther's protestant pamphlets and received from Pope Leo X the title 'Defender of the Faith'. He declared himself 'Protector and Supreme Head of the Church of England' in 1531 and in 1532 abolished the annuities paid to the Pope. He ordered the dissolution of the monasteries in 1536, the same year Catherine of Aragon died and Anne Boleyn was executed. Kirkstall Abbey was granted to Archbishop Thomas Cranmer by Edward VI 'to fulfil the verbally expressed wishes of Henry VIII'.

William Hill (1828-1889). Architect. He set up in practice in Leeds 1851. He had been assistant to Cuthbert Brodrick and some of his own independent work reflects Brodrick's influence, particularly Bolton Town Hall (1865). Other well-known commissions include Yeadon Town Hall (1879) and Portsmouth Town Hall (1884). He designed a number of houses in Far Headingley notably Burton Grange and Oak Lea in Burton Crescent (1874), and also in 1874, Oakfield Terrace Grove Lane. He was one of the shareholders of the Oakfield Terrace Building Club and acquired Plot 2.

John Hillaby (1917-1998). Travel writer who grew up at Hollybank on the Otley Road. A one time correspondent for The Guardian, New York Times and New Scientist, he is best known as a travel writer, *Journey Through Europe, Journey to the Gods* and others. 'If you want a voluable Yorkshireman at your elbow, a compulsive walker, bubbling with wit, reminiscence, anecdote and gossip, with a cultivated eye for beauty in buildings and stone, a scholarly knowledge of birds, beasts and beetles, a feeling for history and a taste for bawdy, here is your man'. The Tablet.

Archdeacon Francis House (born 1908). Originally from Almondbury, near Huddersfield, Francis was ordained in 1935 and joined the staff of the World Student Christian Federation in Geneva. He married Margaret Neave in 1938 and together they worked for the student Christian movement in south eastern Europe. Returning to England at the outbreak of World War II, Francis was appointed Curate of Leeds and later moved to the BBC where he organised religious services in German for broadcasting to Germany, and religious 'interludes' in English for the British Forces Network in France. He left the BBC in 1944 and went back to south east Europe (Greece) via Egypt working in military liaison for the United Nations Relief and Rehabilitation programme. After the war he became Head of Religious Broadcasting at the BBC (1947-1955). In the late 50s he joined the staff of the World Council of Churches, then he became Vicar of Pontefract and Archdeacon of Macclesfield before retiring to Drummond Court, Far Headingley in 1978. His book *'The Russian Phoenix'* an account of 1000 years of the Russian Orthodox Church, was published to acclaim in 1988. Since 1978 he has been an honorary priest at St Chad's where he regularly preaches.

Rt Rev David Jenkins (born 1925). Bishop of Durham 1984-1994. Outspoken and controversial Churchman. Celebrated for his open criticism of Margaret Thatcher's government during the Miner's strike of 1984 and for his broad views on Biblical interpretation. Sections of the press denounced him a heretic and saw God's judgement in the great fire that destroyed part of York Minster only days after he was inducted Bishop of Durham at York. He is also known for his deftly argued theology (he has written a number of books) and deeply spiritual sermons. He was Professor of Theology at the University of Leeds between 1979 and 1984. During that time he lived in Drummond Avenue, Far Headingley and acted as honorary priest and preacher at St Chads.

Alice Keppel (1868-1941). Married George Keppel in 1891 and notoriously became mistress to King Edward VII. She is reputed to have had an affair with Ernest Beckett of Kirkstall Grange who is said to have fathered her child, Violet (Trefusis), in 1894.

Arnold Kettle (1916-1986). Taught English Literature at Leeds University from 1946 to 1970 when he became Professor of Literature at the Open University. Distinguished literary critic, author and committed member of The Communist Party. He lived at Moorville 36 Moor Road where he often entertained interesting literary figures including C P Snow, Pamela Hansford Johnson, John Braine, Alan Sillitoe, Hugh Macdiarmid, E P Thompson, Doris Lessing and G Wilson Knight.

Martin Kettle (Born 1949). Lived at Moorville 36 Moor Road from 1949 to 1970 the son of Professor Arnold Kettle. Educated at Leeds Modern School and Balliol College Oxford. Political correspondent for the *Sunday Times* from 1981, political leader writer for The *Guardian* from 1984, Associate Editor of The *Guardian* and weekly columnist in the 1990s. Since 1977 Washington correspondent for The *Guardian*. See his reminiscence on page 193.

Frank Lisle (1916-1986). Principal of the Jacob Kramer College of Art (Leeds Art College) from 1969 to 1976. A noted portrait, landscape and abstract painter, examples of Frank Lisle's work can be seen in Leeds City Art Gallery and Wakefield Art Gallery. His pictures also form part of many private collections. He lived at Wheatlands, Cottage Road with his wife, June, and family from 1955 until 1983.

Henry Cowper Marshall (1808-1884). Born at New Grange, the 4th son of John Marshall. An Alderman of Leeds and Mayor of Leeds in 1843. He married Catherine Lucy Spring-Rice, youngest daughter of a former Chancellor of the Exchequer. The ill-fated Leeds Zoological and Botanical Gardens belonged to him according to White's Directory of 1853. He lived at Weetwood Hall from the 1830s until he died in 1884.

John Marshall (1765-1845). 'The celebrated flax-spinner, is one of the most remarkable instances, even in this commercial country, of men who have risen by their own talents, perseverance and enterprise, from moderate circumstances (his father is said to have occupied the shop, No 1, at the bottom of Briggate) to the possession of a splendid fortune, and to a degree of honour and influence rarely attained by the aristocracy of the land'. W. G. Rimmer.

In 1805 John Marshall moved to New Grange, from Hunslet, away from the smoke and the bustle of the town. He had married Jane Pollard in 1795. By 1805 they had six children and more were to follow – a family of five sons and seven daughters. A succession of nursery maids and well paid governesses were a permanent feature of the establishment.

'In 1804 he had nearly £40,000; at the end of 1815 he had nearly £400,000. He rented New Grange from Wade's trustees at £500 per annum for the first five years, then £200. He became a spare time farmer, laying out the grounds near the house and rearing sheep in the fields. The house was large, its staff numbered more than a dozen servants. By residence as much as wealth the Marshalls ranked amongst the foremost families of Leeds'. W G Rimmer.

He was one of the founders of London University and Liberal MP for Yorkshire from 1826 to the dissolution of Parliament on the death of George IV in 1830. His opponent on the hustings in 1826 printed bill-posters describing Marshall as 'a Unitarian and a Radical ... an extensive Flax Spinner (who) makes more Thread for the Tailors than any of his Competitors in Trade ... He has amassed great wealth and no small proportion of it is invested in Foreign Funds, French, American etc., as if the Country which has given him wealth could not secure it to him ... He has not 20 Acres of Land in this County ... Has Whiggism come to this?' John Parr, Printer, Leeds, June 9th 1826.

The Marshalls had a second house, Hallsteads, at Ullswater in the Lake District. Eventually they left New Grange and made Hallsteads their principal residence, but still needing a Leeds home, John Marshall bought Headingley House (c1815), close to the Grange, from James Bischoff. In 1828 he built Headingley Lodge nearby, for his newly married second son John.

Whilst landscaping at New Grange in 1815, it is said that John Marshall planted trees to correspond with the disposition of troops at the Battle of Waterloo.

Kay Mellor (born 1954). Internationally renowned filmwriter and playwright. Entirely home-grown talent, Kay was born in Leeds 16, educated at West Park High School and trained to be an actress at Bretton Hall College. Whilst at Bretton Hall she became interested in writing and was soon scripting episodes of *Coronation Street* and *Brookside*. She is best known for her award winning, six part television series, *Band of Gold* and films for the cinema *Girls Night* and *Fanny and Elvis*. Her stage plays include *The Passionate Woman* and *Queen*. Before moving to her present house in Weetwood, she lived in West Park. *Fat Friends*, a six part comedy drama series for television was extensively filmed around Far Headingly in Summer 2000.

Theo Moorman MBE (1907-1990). Renowned artist working woven tapestries and bringing this particular art form to a new level of international appreciation. Born in Hollin Lane Far Headingley, her father was the first Professor of English Language at Leeds University. After his death from a drowning accident in 1919 her mother became Warden of Oxley Hall, by this time a University residence for women. Theo and her mother lived at Oxley Hall from 1921 until Theo went to London to train at the Central School of Arts and Crafts. Her home and studio from 1957 until 1983 was at Painswick in Gloucestershire. She received the MBE in 1977. Among her commissions are tapestries and altar cloths for many churches and cathedrals including a reredos fabric for St Michael's church in Headingley. Her work can also be seen at Ripon, Manchester and Wakefield Cathedrals. *'Theo Moorman - Her Life and Work as an Artist Weaver'* was published in 1992.

Dipak Nandy (Born 1936). Lived with the Kettle family at 36 Moor Road from 1957 until 1962 while a student. He helped to found the Runnymede Trust, the race relations research charity, becoming its first director and was later the deputy chief executive of the Equal Opportunities Commission.

Captain Lawrence Oates (1880-1912). Lawrence Edward Grace Oates was born in Putney but his family were important landowners in Far Headingley, Weetwood, and Meanwood, where he was a regular visitor in the time of his Uncle Charles. His grandfather was Edward Oates of Meanwoodside, his fourth child William Edward being Lawrence's father. Lawrence and his brother Bryan jointly inherited the estate in 1902 after the death of their Uncle Charles (William's younger brother), the last of the Oates family to live at Meanwoodside.

In 1910 Lawrence Oates set out with Capt Scott's Antarctic expedition, and was one of the party of five to reach the South Pole on January 17th 1912. On the return journey the explorers suffered dangerous delay and became weatherbound. Lamed by severe frostbite, Lawrence, convinced that his crippled condition would fatally handicap his companion's prospect of winning through, walked out into the blizzard, deliberately sacrificing his life to improve his comrades chance of survival.

Edward Oates (1792-1865). Inherited Manklins Farm from his father Joseph Oates of Weetwood Hall in 1825 and rebuilt the old farmhouse now known as Hollin House. In 1834 he bought Meanwoodside from the Rinder estate, enlarged and renovated Francis Whalley's derelict cottage, and landscaped the grounds over a period of thirty years to create an American garden in an idyllic setting of ponds and streams. He married Susan Grace in 1836 and had five children. Captain Lawrence Oates was his grandson.

William T Oliver OBE (1903-1991). Deputy Editor of the *Yorkshire Post* and, for forty six years its art critic. He lived with his family at Mazebrook,

Moor Road from 1937 to 1965 vacating the property during the War years, when it became the headquarters of Headingley Home Guard. In later years, author John Braine was a regular visitor to the house as were college friends of Patrick Oliver - playwright Tom Stoppard and actor Peter O'Toole.

St Oswald (604-642). King of Northumbria and Martyr. He fled to Scotland when his brother Edwin seized the Northumbrian Kingdom and became a Christian at Iona. Edwin was killed in 633 in a battle against the combined forces of Penda and Cadwallon. Oswald returned to Northumberland, raised an army and defeated Cadwallon near Hexham in 634. Cadwallon was killed and Oswald's victory was attributed to the hand of God. On the eve of battle Oswald erected a wooden cross at which he knelt and prayed with his army. Having regained the throne, Oswald reigned as King of Northumberland for the next eight years during which time he persuaded (St) Aidan, a monk of Iona, to preach Christianity in the North East of England and bestowed on him the Isle of Lindisfarne (the Holy Island), near the royal castle at Bamburgh. He gave the money to build several monasteries. On August 5th 642 Oswald went into battle at Maserfield, Shropshire, against the pagan King Penda of Mercia and was slain. The Mission church at Highbury is dedicated to St Oswald.

Rev Barry Overend (born 1949) Vicar of St Chad's since 1986. A renowned preacher, Barry was the first recipient of *The Times* Preacher of the Year Award in 1995, co-sponsored that year by the College of Preachers. He is a regular broadcaster (Radio Leeds 'Life On An Angle') and thought provoking writer. He has published three *Life On An Angle* books and contributes to the *Credo* column of *The Times*.

Henry Oxley (1805-1890). Senior partner in the bank William Williams Brown & Co of Leeds and twice Lord Mayor of Leeds – 1865 and 1872. He lived at the large neo-Gothic mansion, Oxley Hall. His son James Walker Oxley lived at Spenfield until his death in 1928.

James Walker Oxley (1834-1928). Partner in his father's bank (see Henry Oxley) from 1861 and senior partner from 1890 until his retirement in 1899 when the Bank, William Williams Brown & Co of Commercial Street merged with Lloyds. He made his home at Spenfield next to his fathers' property – Oxley Hall. Spenfield was built between 1875 and 1877 and designed by George Corson. James Walker was an avid collector of works of art. In 1948 his collection, numbering one hundred and thirty 'exotic' pieces, was bequeathed to Leeds by his son, the reclusive Henry Oxley, at his father's wish. The collection went to Temple Newsam.

Lord Palmerston (1784-1865). John Henry Temple, third Viscount Palmerston. First elected to Parliament in 1807. He sat in sixteen parliaments and was a member of every administration except Peel's and Derby's from 1807 to 1865. He held office for all but half a century. At the age of seventy five he formed his second administration in June 1859. The following year, as prime minister, he was the guest of William Beckett at Kirkstall Grange while carrying out several public engagements in the North of England. He died within two days of his 81st birthday and is buried in Westminster Abbey. As a young man he was described as a man of fashion, a sportsman, a bit of a dandy and also something of a wit. 'Palmerston's jolly 'Ha, ha!' was a thing to be remembered.'

Ralph Paynel (or Paganel) (died 1109). The Norman baron who was granted the Manor of Headingley, together with other confiscated Saxon estates, by Ilbert de Laci his Norman overlord and commander in King William's conquering army.

William Peytvin (William le Peitevin de Haddingeleia). 12th century Lord of the Manor of Headingley. He granted four carucates of land in West Headingley, in the Parish of Leeds to Kirkstall Abbey. The land became the Abbey farms of Kirkstall Grange, Moor Grange and Burley Grange.

Joseph Pickersgill (1849-1920). Race horse owner and turf commission agent who 'kept a book' for King Edward VII when Prince of Wales. He lived at Bardon Hill from 1899 until 1920 where he built 'stables, believed to be second to none in the Kingdom'. His business interests included Chorley and Pickersgill the Leeds printers based from 1900 at The Electric Press building in Cookridge Street.

Walker Rawstorne (died 1867). Church architect. Articled to his father, John Rawstorne, before opening his own practice in Bradford. Among his commissions were All Saints Church Bingley, St Mary's Burley in Wharfedale, St John's Yeadon, St Luke's Eccleshill, and several warehouses at Leeds Road Bradford. He was living at St Annes Villas, Monk Bridge Road when he died.

Arthur Michell Ransome (1884-1967). Journalist and writer of children's books. In his very early years he lived at 6 Ash Grove, Hyde Park and 4 De Grey Road (now below the foundations of the University Parkinson building). When aged six his home was at 2 Balmoral Terrace off Shaw Lane, and three years later the family moved to 3 St Chad's Villas (now 126 Otley Rd). He left Leeds when he was seventeen. He was a reporter on the *Manchester Guardian*, and having learned Russian, was sent to cover the Revolution. He divorced his first wife in 1924 and married Trotsky's secretary Eugenia Shelepina with whom he fled from Russia settling in the Lake District. His most famous book, *Swallows and Amazons*, was written in 1930.

Cyril Ransome (1850-1897) Professor of History and Modern Literature at the Yorkshire College, now Leeds University. Friend and tutor of Prince Alamayou and father of Arthur Ransome. Patron and founder of several local literary clubs and author of a number of books including *A Short History of England*, *English Political History* (with Arthur Dyke Acland) and *Our Colonies and India: How We Got Them and Why We Keep Them*. He had three local addresses, at Hollin Lane, Balmoral Terrace and St Chad's Villas where he wrote history books in his own inimitable style …

'If you were to be suddenly told that the inhabitants of two little islands (Great Britain and Ireland) had taken upon themselves to govern a continent whose area was eleven times as great as theirs, and if it was added that they only maintained in that continent, including the army, one man in two thousand of the population, you would be astonished at their audacity. If you were also informed that the climate of the continent was such that the islanders could not possibly live there without the assistance of the natives, so that a simple strike on the part of all native servants would be sufficient to render their living there impossible, you would be still more surprised. And, perhaps, if you were informed that the islanders regarded this feat as a matter of course, and took very little interest in the affairs of the continent, your wonder would be even greater still'.

From *Our Colonies and India*

Cyril Ransome's unfinished and unpublished autobiograhy can be seen, in its hand written form, at the Brotherton Library, Leeds University.

Sir John Savile (1556-1630). The first Alderman of Leeds in 1626, and a largely absent one. He built the family seat, Howley Hall in Batley parish – blown up in 1730 'with gunpowder' by order of the Earl of Cardigan. He was the son of Sir Robert Savile of Howley who acquired Kirkstall Abbey land in 1564 including the reconstituted Manor of Headingley. In 1626 Sir John gave land for the erection of a church at Headingley. St Michael's is the third church to stand on this site. Three owls, taken from the Savile coat of arms, were incorporated into the seal of Leeds in his honour, and remain a prominent Leeds motif.

John Hope Shaw (1792-1864). An eminent solicitor, president of the Leeds Mechanics Institute and Literary Society, trustee of Leeds Parish Church, Alderman of the borough, and twice Mayor of Leeds in 1849 and 1853. As Lord Mayor he laid the foundation stone of Leeds Town Hall. He died aged seventy two at his Headingley residence. His house, complete with 'vinery, hothouse, and fernery', and a further 3.6 acres of building land were auctioned after his death. It had a long frontage to the top part of Monk Bridge Road which was renamed Shaw Lane in his memory.

Thomas Simpson (1829-1898). Solicitor and joint founder of the Leeds law firm Simpson Curtis. He bought Weetwood land from the Englefield estate in 1858 and commissioned his cousin John Simpson to design Bardon Hill on Weetwood Lane. In 1874 he also acquired Far Headingley glebeland at auction, laid out Burton Crescent and sold individual plots for villa development. His brother, William, married a Mary Burton, and this may be the connection with the name Burton Crescent.

His cousin, a brother of the architect John, was Edward Simpson who founded in Leeds, with Edmund Stead, the shoe making and retailing business Stead and Simpson.

Samuel Smith (1828-1880) Built Highbury Works (Meanwood Tannery) in 1856 on the site of Wood Mills. His brother was John Smith, founder of the famous Tadcaster brewery. Samuel Smith lived at Meanwood but owned land

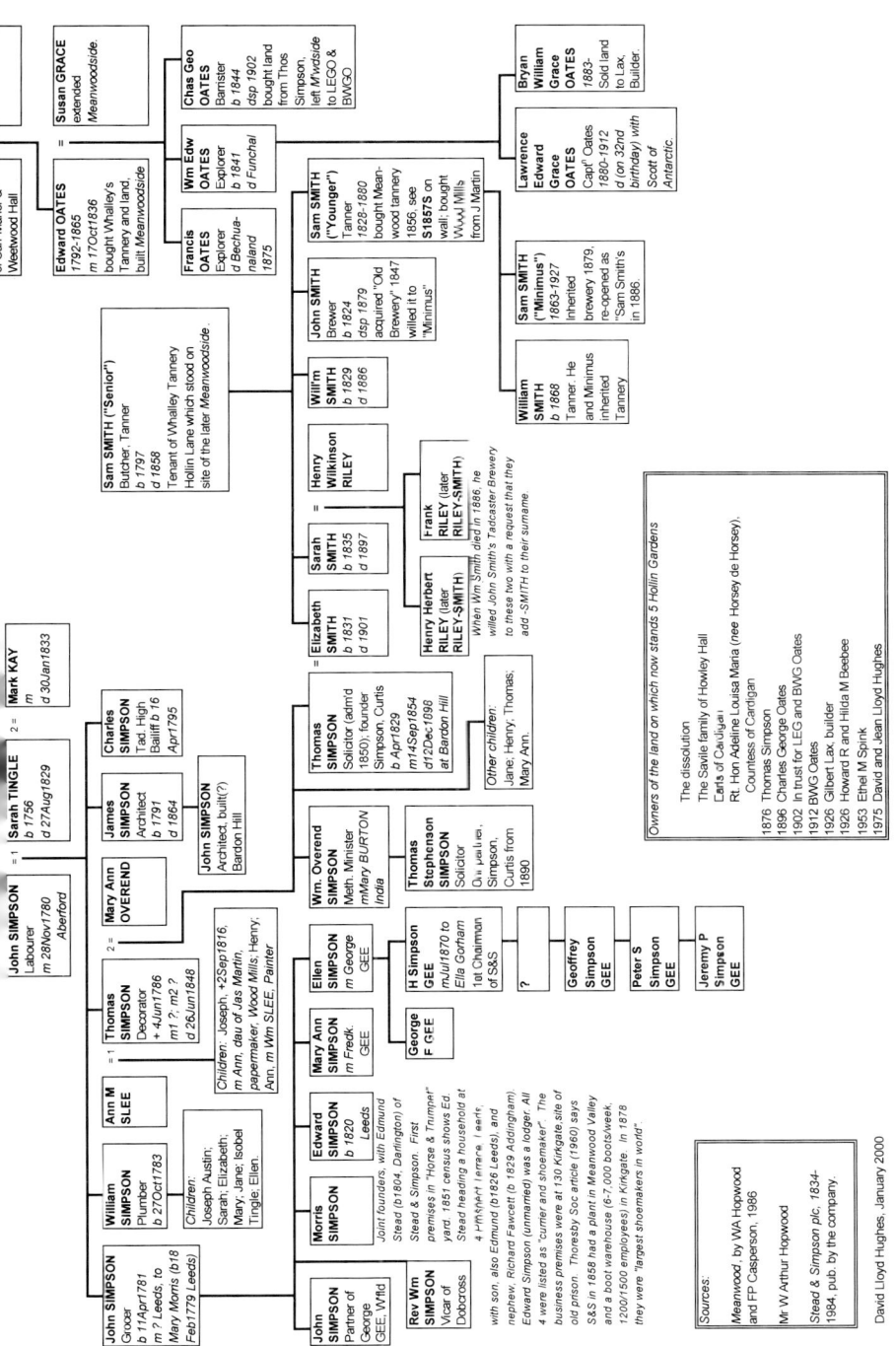

in Moor Road Far Headingley, later sold for house building (Moor Drive and Moor Park Villas). His son, Sam Smith 'Minimus' (1863-1927), moved to Tadcaster when he inherited the Old Brewery at Tadcaster from his Uncle John.

Thomas Spring Rice, Baron Monteagle (1790-1866). Born at Limerick, sent to Trinity College Cambridge, was MP for Limerick between 1820 and 1832, and MP for Cambridge between 1832 and 1839. He became Chancellor of the Exchequer in April 1835 in Lord Melbourne's second administration and held that office until 1839. In that year, he introduced the penny postage scheme and was created Baron Monteagle. Lord Melbourne spoke of him as a man 'too much given to details and possessed of no broad views'.

He married Theodosia in 1811 with whom he had five sons and three daughters. Theodosia died in 1839. In 1841 he married Marianne, the eldest daughter of John Marshall of Hallsteads, Cumberland (and Headingley). She died in 1889 aged eighty nine. His youngest daughter married Henry Cowper Marshall, and he will have been a regular visitor to their home, Weetwood Hall. Baron Monteagle became son-in-law to John Marshall, and father-in-law to his own brother-in-law when Lucy Spring Rice married Henry.

Vita Sackville-West. Popular name of Victoria Mary Sackville-West (1892-1962). Poet and novelist born at Knole, Kent. In 1913 she married diplomat and critic, Harold Nicholson. Her best known novels are *The Edwardians* 1930 and *All Passion Spent* 1931. Her friendship with Virginia Woolf occasioned the latter's *Orlando* (1928). For three years, from 1918 to 1921 she had a passionate affair with Violet Trefusis, the reputed daughter of Ernest Beckett and Alice Keppell, the King's mistress.

Charles Francis Tetley (1848-1934). Eldest son of Francis William Tetley. He grew up at Spring Bank in Headingley Lane, Highfield House (Moor House) in Moor Road and Fox Hill at Weetwood. On the death of his mother he inherited, and moved to, Fox Hill where he lived until the end of his life. He was Chairman of Joshua Tetley and Son between 1902 and 1934. He also inherited Moor House which he sold in 1899.

Charles Harold Tetley, Colonel Tetley (1877-1959). Eldest son of Charles F Tetley. A great benefactor to the University of Leeds. He was Pro-Chancellor for twenty years from 1926. Tetley Hall of Residence in Moor Road was named in his honour. He was Chairman of Joshua Tetley and Son from 1934 until 1953.

Francis William Tetley (1817-1883). Eldest son of Joshua Tetley. Francis was taken into his father's brewing business when he was twenty two. From that time the firm was restyled Joshua Tetley & Son. Francis married Isabella Ryder of London in 1847. They had fourteen children – seven boys and seven girls. The family lived at Moor House (or Highfield House) in Moor Road for a time before Francis commissioned Fox Hill at Weetwood. Interestingly the 1861 census shows a Charles Ryder (39), brewer and malster, living at Sandfield House, Headingley Moor, with his wife Louisa (34) and family.

J R R Tolkien (1892-1973). Philologist and writer, born in Bloemfontein, South Africa. Wrote *The Hobbit* 1937 and *The Lord of the Rings* 1954-5. He moved to the English Department of Leeds University in 1921 and was appointed Professor of English Language in 1924. He lived briefly at Hollybank, then Woodhouse, and later in West Park where bedtime story telling to his children inspired his classic books.

Violet Trefusis (1894-1972). Reputed daughter of Ernest Beckett of Kirkstall Grange and King Edward VII's mistress, Alice Keppel. Violet married Major Denys Trefusis. She became a writer and was close to the Bloomsbury set. Between 1918 and 1921 she had a traumatic lesbian relationship with Vita Sackville-West. Violet wrote several books including *Broderie Anglaise, Don't Look Round,* and *Hunt the Slipper.*

Alfred Henry Vine (1845-1917). Hymn writer, born at Sneighton Nottinghamshire and educated at King Edward's School Birmingham. He became a Methodist Minister in 1867 starting his ministry at Cleckheaton. In 1881 he was at Bradford, 1884 Headingley and 1890 Hackney. Whilst at Headingley he lived at The Manse in Burton Crescent (No 9). He wrote 'The Doom of Saul' (1895), 'Songs of Living Things for Boys and Girls' (1897) and 'Song of the Heart' (1905). He retired to Woodford in 1910 and died on April 20th, 1917. His most enduring hymn was 'O Breath of God, breathe on us now'.

Oscar Wilde (1854-1900). Poet, wit and playwright. Born in Dublin, Oscar Wilde championed the aesthetic movement in the 1880s. He was the guest of Ernest Beckett at Kirkstall Grange c1883. His most famous plays, *Lady Windermere's Fan* and *The Importance of Being Ernest* were produced in 1892 and 1895 repectively. In 1895 he was imprisoned at Reading for 'immoral' (homosexual) acts against his friend Lord Alfred Douglas. On his release he went to France where he died in 1900.

Mr Geoffrey Wooler (Born 1911). Educated at Leeds Grammar School, Giggleswick, Cambridge and the London Hospital. Geoffrey Wooler is one of this country's most distinguished surgeons. During the war he performed more than 3,500 operations, many of them within range of enemy guns. On his return to England he became consultant in cardiothoracic surgery at Leeds General Infirmary and pioneered open heart surgery in the UK earning world wide recognition for his work in heart valve repair and replacement. In 1957 he was featured in the BBCTV series *Your Life in Their Hands.* In later years he briefly, and he maintains, unsuccessfully, ran the Oakbank Restaurant in Shaw Lane before selling it on to his chef. This amusing story and others are told in his autobiography *'Pig In A Suitcase'* published in 1999. He has been a Far Headingley resident since 1987.

Dorothy Wordsworth (1771-1855). Only sister of William Wordsworth and herself a noted writer. In 1805 she visited New Grange with her brother, to stay with her school friend Jane Marshall, the wife of John Marshall.

William Wordsworth (1770-1850) The renowned English poet who succeeded Robert Southey as Poet Laureate in 1843. He married Mary Hutchinson in 1802 and lived at Grasmere in the Lake District with Mary and his sister. He accompanied Dorothy on her visit to the Marshalls of New Grange in 1805.

With apologies to any other worthy people not included here, but who should be.

Sources:

Twentieth Century Authors, Kunitz and Haycraft.
Oxford Dictionary of National Biography.
The History of Meanwood. W A Hopwood and F P Casperson.
The Dictionary of Biography.
Biographia Leodiensis, R V Taylor 1865
Marshalls of Leeds - Flaxspinners, W G Rimmer 1960.
Rosemary Ashton '*George Eliot, A Life*' Hamish Hamilton 1996
Martin Seymour-Smith '*Hardy*' Bloomsbury 1994
Cambridge Biograpical Encyclopaedia
Chambers Biographical Dictionary
Lord Grimthorpe, Peter Ferriday, John Murray 1957
Butlers Lives of the Saints 1981 edition

Bibliography

A Companion of Kirkstall Abbey 1806
Acorn to Oak, Christopher Gardener 1985
A History of Castle Grove, E Richard Vaughan, 1996
A History of Kirkstall Abbey, T Hargreaves, 1848
A History of Methodism, J Stanley Mathers, MA, a pamphlet published in 1970
A History of Modern Leeds, edited by Derek Fraser 1980
An Act for Inclosing Lands in the Manor and Township of Headingley cum Burley 1829
An Act for Repairing, Maintaining and Improving the Line of the Road from Leeds to Otley in the West Riding of the County of York 1837
Anglo Saxon England, F M Stenton, Oxford University Press
Aspects of Leeds, Wharncliffe Publishing 1998
Brass Castles, George Sheeran, Ryburn 1993
Building and Estate Development in the Northern Out-Townships of Leeds 1781-1914, Colin Treen, University of Leeds 1977
Captain Oates - Soldier and Explorer, Sue Limb and Patrick Cordingley, B T Batsford Ltd
Directory of Yorkshire Architects, St Chad's Centenary Year Booklet, Joseph Sprittles 1969
Ducatus Leodiensis, The Topography of Leeds, Ralph Thoresby 1714
Edward Oates and the Making of the Lost American Garden at Meanwoodside, Colin Treen, Thoresby Society, 1995
George Merry: a taped interview with Robert Merry.
Historic Architecture of Leeds, Derek Linstrum, Criel Press, 1969
Jackson's New Illustrated Guide to Leeds and Environs 1889
Kirkstall Abbey, A Descriptive Guide to the Abbey Buildings, J Wreghitt Connon
Kirkstall Abbey, David E Owen, E J Arnold
Kirkstall Abbey, Holy Year Pilgrimage Souvenir 1950
Kirkstall Grange, Joyce N Pogson
Lawnswood High School Centenary Brochure
Leeds Art Calendar 1994
Leeds and Yorkshire Biography (Press Obits) Leeds Library
Leeds City Charter, West Yorkshire Archive 1993
Leeds, Ivan Broadhead, Smith Settle 1990
Leeds Lantern Slides Thoresby Society: Weetwood Mill, F P Casperson
Leeds Transport, J Soper. Leeds Transport Historic Society 1985
Marshalls of Leeds, Flax-Spinners 1788-1886, W G Rimmer Cambridge University Press 1960
Meanwood, W Arthur Hopwood and Frederic P Casperson, 1986
Mrs Keppel and her Daughter, Diana Soutami, Harper Collins 1996
Musical Reminiscences, Dr W Spark 1892
New Grange, J Sprittles, Thoresby Society 1959
Oakfield Terrace 1874-1974 A Short History by Colin Treen
Old Far Headingley, Philip Elston 1976
Oscar Wilde, Frank Harris, Robinson Publishing, 1916
Prince Alamayou of Ethiopia, Lord Amulree
Report to the Trustees of the Leeds to Otley Turnpike Road 1845
Round About Leeds and the Old Kingdom of Elmet, Edmund Bogg 1904
Spenfield, Janet Douglas
Spenfield Yorkshire by Huon Mallalieu. *Country Life* Sept 1992

St Chad's Magazines, collected by A Johnson
St Chad's, A Home for Waifs and Strays: A History of Hollin Hall 1894-1996, Samantha J Fisher
St Oswald's Church Highbury Centenary Booklet, F P Casperson 1989
The Annals and History of Leeds, John Mayhall, Joseph Johnson 1860
The Architect 1896
The Autobiography of Alfred Austin, MacMillan 1911
The Autobiography of Arthur Ransome, Jonathan Cape 1976
The Biographia Leodiensis, Rev R V Taylor BA 1865
The Biography of Lord Grimthorpe, Peter Ferriday, John Murray, 1957
The Conservation of Far Headingley, FHVS, 1973
The Concise Dictionary of English Place Names
The Ecclesiae Leodiensis, Rev R V Taylor BA 1875
The Dictionary of National Biography
The History of Headingley Golf Club, The Centenary Brochure
The Homicidal Earl, The life of Lord Cardigan, Saul David, Little Brown & Co 1997
The Leeds Police Force 1836-1974 Edited by Ewart W Clay
The Life of Arthur Ransome, Jonathan Cape 1984
The unpublished autobiography of Cyril Ransome 1888. Brotherton Library. University of Leeds
Towers and Colonnades: The Archiecture of Cuthbert Brodrick, Derek Linstrum, Leeds
    Philosophical and Literary Society Ltd 1999
Two Leeds Architects, T B Wilson, West Yorkshire Society of Architects 1937
Two Hundred Years of Banking, H Pemberton, Thoresby Society 1959
Victorian Cities, Asa Briggs, Oldhams Press 1963
Victorian Society Journals
Weetwood and the Foxcroft Family, J M Collinson, The Leeds University Review 1987/8
Westminster Bank in Leeds 1966
Writing Home, Alan Bennett, Faber and Faber, 1994
70 Years of Silver Screen Entertainment 1912-1982, Cottage Road cinema booklet

Churchwood Avenue in the 1940s/50s.   *Courtesy: Ian Ballantine.*

Copies reserved for:

Neill and Ann Alexander
Christine Baker
Ian Ballantine
Maggie Barnshaw
Sir Martin Beckett
Richard Beckett Q.C.
N Beecroft
Brian S Beevers
Harold Best MP
Mrs Sonia Bolster
Margaret Bonsall
Jim Brettell
Mr G Brogden
S Claire Brown
Mr and Mrs A F Bryan
Kathleen and Edmund Bush
Ken and Phyllis Butterworth
Frank and Mary Coggill
Canon Peter Cole
John H Coles
Miss N L Cook
Wallace Cooper
R and M Cotton
C A H Cunningham
Mark Dalton
Andrew and Pam Davies
Mr Geoffrey Dilworth
Stanley and Ann Dodd
Andrew Earnshaw
Dorothy Fielding
Mr Barry French
Mrs Shirley Frost
Hon Alderman Douglas Gabb
Mrs Margaret Gledhill
Robert Goring
Carole Grant
Miss Avis Grimshaw
Chris Hammond
Angela Harley
Edward and Doreen Haynes
Mrs L Heald
P Holdsworth
Pauline and Donald Hood
W Arthur Hopwood
Rev Bill and Mrs Judy Hulse
Chris and Ian Jackson
Mrs Win Jackson
Mark Jenkinson
Mr Alfred Johnson
David and Valerie Kaye
John T Kent

Mrs S Langford
Jean Lawson
Dr Eric Lewis
Mr and Mrs Gerard Liston
Freidy Luther and Mark Blamire
Mr R R MacDonald
Kay Mellor
Clive and Marian Marcham
C Milner
Dr A J and Mrs D J Moyes
Rob Murphy
Claire and Chris Nash
Mr and Mrs A C Nield
John and Yvonne Oughton
Margaret Pearson
Mrs Plaiten
D Plews
Mrs Pollard
Colin and Diane Pontefract
R Preedy
Gill Redfearn
Mrs Clare Richardson
Mrs E W Rigg
Mr Martin Rigg
Mrs Margaret Ripley
Mrs Margaret Scally
Mrs P M Schofield
Mr and Mrs John Scott
Mark and Heather Scott
P Simmons
Professor B D Sleeman
Smith Settle
Mr J Soper
Mrs Phyllis Spurway
Mrs Margaret Summerwill
Mr H Sutcliffe
B H Thompson
Mrs Elizabeth Thompson
E Thompson
John and Jean Townsend
Mu and Tom Tucker
Neville and Margaret Verity
Christopher Walbank
Mrs Lucy Warrack
N R Whitaker
David E Whiteley
Beth Williams
Ray Woodcraft
Geoffrey Wooler
Mrs P Woolnough

Index

Adel   1, 8, 14, 25, 40, 56, 126, 140, 181
Adel Church   16, 141
Aire, river   1, 5, 54
Alamayou, Prince   91, 117-122, 202
Albert House   85-6
Albert, The Prince Consort   57, 85
Allbutt, Sir Thomas Clifford,
  physician   121, 202
Ambler, Thomas, architect   91, 202
Annesley-Powys, Vicar of Meanwood   121
Arthington, William   13-14
Askey, John Snr   39, 44, 114, 167, 170
Askey, John and Ann   154, 168
Associated Tower Cinemas Ltd   151
Atkinson, John and William, omnibus
  proprietors   44
Atkinson, Henry & Sons, building
  contrators   151, 172
Avison, William, coach operator   34, 44
Austin, Alfred, Poet Laureate   xxiii, 203

Balfour, Arthur James, Prime
  Minister   131-3, 203
Bardon Grange   97
Bardon Grange Lodge   97
Bardon Hill   26, 99-102, 111, 165
Barre Grange   13
Bateson Thomas, verger of St Chads   156, 164
Bayldon, Richard, road surveyor   41-2, 49
Beckett, Christopher d1847   31, 36, 49, 59,
  61, 86,
[Beckett] Denison, Edmund Sr. d1874   59,
  61-3, 67, 78, 105, 205
Beckett-Denison, Edmund QC, 1st Baron
  Grimthorpe d1905   62, 67, 77, 205
Beckett-Denison, Maria nee Beverley   77, 105
Beckett-Denison, William d1890   61, 65,
  67-70, 72, 205
Beckett, Miss Elizabeth   67
Beckett, Ernest William, 2nd Lord
  Grimthorpe   68, 73, 76-7, 129-30, 141,
  178, 181
Beckett, Frances nee Maynell   61
Beckett, Gervase d1937   131-2, 178, 203
Beckett, Sir John d1826   35, 203
Beckett Lucy nee Tracy Lee d1891   70-2,
  77, 130

Beckett, Miss Mary   59
Beckett, Ralph   70, 72, 138
Beckett, Rupert   68, 132
Beckett, Sir Thomas d1872   61, 67, 72, 77
Beckett, William d1863   27, 35-6, 49, 57,
  59-60, 62-3, 74, 77, 178, 205
Beckett's Bank   35-6, 57
Beckett's Park   9, 35-6, 114, 178, 185
Beckett Park College   132, 134, 173, 178
Bennett, Alan, playwright   xxi, 192, 206
Benyon, Thomas, flaxspinner   33-4
Bodington Hall   128, 139
Bodington, Sir Nathan   114, 127, 164, 206
Botanic and Zoological Gardens, The
  Leeds   54
Bogg, Edmund   xxiii-xxiv
Bolton Abbey   32
Bramhope   41-2
Bramhope Tunnel   49
Briggate   6, 103
Brodrick, Cuthbert, architect   56-7, 87-8,
  93, 97, 138, 165, 206
Brooks, Owen   151, 172
Brown, George William   97-8, 106, 188
Brown, William   97, 111, 188
Browne, John, last Abbot of Kirkstall   10
Brudenell, Adeline, nee de Horsey, Lady
  Cardigan, later Dowager Countess de
  Lancastre   53, 177
Brudenell, Edmund   53, 177
Brudenell, Lord Francis d1698   18
Brudenell, Lady Frances nee Savile   18
Brudenell, Sir George, 3rd Earl of Cardigan
  d 1732   7, 19, 23
Brudenell, Sir George, 4th Earl of Cardigan
  d 1790   29
Brudenell, Sir James, 5th Earl of Cardigan
  d 1811   29
Brudenell, Sir James, 7th Earl of Cardigan
  d 1868   49, 53, 206
Brudenell, Sir Robert, 2nd Earl of Cardigan
  d 1703   18
Brudenell, Sir Robert, 6th Earl of Cardigan
  d 1837   36, 38, 53
Brudenell, Sir Thomas, 1st Earl of Cardigan
  d 1663   18
Bryan's Modern Fisheries   149, 163, 194

INDEX 225

Buck, Samuel, Recorder of Leeds   7, 29
Burley   10, 16, 23, 25, 29, 41
Burton Crescent   48, 50, 86-8, 99, 137
Burton Grange   87-8, 164
Burton Lea (formerly Oak Lea)   87-8, 164
Busby, William and Daniel, The Liverpool Road and Railway Omnibus Co.   44

Cardigan, Earls of, see Brudenell
Castle Grove   39, 42, 79-83, 110
Castle Grove Masonic Hall   80, 127, 185-6, 199
Catholic Care Home, The   161
Cecil, Sir Thomas   13
Charge of the Light Brigade 1854, The   53
Chantrell, William   16
Charles I   16, 18
cholera   40
Churchill, Sir Winston, Prime Minister   131, 206
Civil War   18
Claremont Road   55
Clegg, Mr Marshall   185
Clifton Villas   91
coal, the search for   24
Conversation Club, The   127
Conyers, Joseph   79
Cooke, Alfred, colour printer   105-7, 113, 129, 206
Corson George, architect   51, 90, 95-6, 98, 110, 194, 206
Cottage Road   24, 38-9, 42, 159, 193-6, 199, 201
Cottage Road Dairy   156, 194
Cottage Road Picture House   129, 150-1
Cottage Road Wash House   155
Cranmer Thomas, Archbishop of Canterbury   10, 12, 14, 208
Cranmer, Thomas Jr   12-3
Crossland, William Henry, Architect   63
Curfew Club, The, conversation and reading club   126

Dalwood, Hubert   191, 208
de Bermingham, John   9
de Lacy, Ilbert   5
de Lacy, Henry   6, 7
Deene Park, *Northants.*   18, 24, 53
Denison, Lady Anne   26, 30, 78, 105
Denison, Sir Thomas d1765   26, 208

Dickinson, Joseph, land agent to 3rd Lord Cardigan   22-4

Eccup   40
Eddison, Eric Rucker, author   126
Eden, Anthony, Earl of Avon   131, 208
Edward VI   12
Edward VII   69, 101, 129-30, 208
Eliot, Thomas Stearns, poet, playwright   191-2, 208
Elizabeth I   12-13
Ellis Terrace   36, 98, 199, 200
Elmet, Kingdom of   1-2
Englefield, Sir Henry bt   25-7, 105

Fairfield   51-88
Far Headingley Village/Headingley Moor   179
Far Headingley Village Society, The   176, 198-9, 200
Fairburn, Sir Peter   59
Fairfax, Sir Thomas   18
Fletcher, Valerie, Mrs T S Eliot   191-2
Forster, Major, of Burley   23
Fox Hill   84, 97-9, 106, 136, 200
Fox, James, actor   196, 209
Foxcroft, Daniel (I) d1639   15, 19
Foxcroft, Daniel (II) d1691   19, 20, 25
Foxcroft, Daniel (III) d.1741   26, 105
Foxcroft, Isaac   13
Foxcroft, Martha nee Layton d1688   19
Foxcroft, Samuel d.1713   25-6
Foxcroft, Thomas   13
Frost, Terry   191

Gabb, Hon. Alderman Douglas   209
Geldard, John, tenant of Weetwood Farm and Tannery   26
Glebe House   77
Glebe Terrace   91
Glendor Ltd   152
Great Northern Railway Co   63
Gregory, Eric, Gregory Fellowship   191
Grimshaw, Atkinson   83
Grove Lane   88-90, 111
Grove Road   55, 127
Groves Mill   111

Hawksworth Woods   23, 25, 34
Headingley   1, 25, 40

INDEX

Headingley Golf Club   140-1, 179
Headingley Hill   xxiii, 36
Headingley and Kirkstall Station   49
Headingley Moor/Far Headingley Village   9, 11-13, 18, 23-5, 36, 38-40, 74, 79, 93
Headingley Parsonage/Holly Dene   29
Heathfield Terrace   9, 111, 148, 201
Heenan, Cardinal John   101, 209
Henry VIII   10, 209
Herbert, George, hymn writer   15
Highbury Mount   74
Highbury Terrace   76
Highbury Working Mens Club   76
Highbury Works/Meanwood Tannery/ Woods Mill   11, 74, 110
Hill, William, architect   87, 90, 210
Hillaby, John, travel writer   191, 210
Hobson W A architect   72
Hollies, The   26, 97-8, 188-9
Hollin Lane   24, 36, 50-1, 72, 74, 90-1, 119
Hollin Hall, St Chad's Home for Waifs and Strays   72, 129, 135
Hollin House   91
Holly Dene/Headingley Parsonage   48, 66, 86, 159
Holmes, Samuel   39, 55, 79
House, Archdeacon Francis   196, 210
Hoyle, Rev Joshua, 2nd Vicar of St Chad's   76, 123, 148
Hunslet   107
Husler, Ann   55, 77

Ilkley   41
Inclosure Act 1829   36, 39-40, 159

Jenkins, The Rt Rev David, Bishop of Durham   196, 210
Johnson Alfred   76, 134, 146, 155, 163-4
Joy, William   79

Kensal Green Cemetery, London   59, 61
Keppel Alice, Mrs,   130, 211
Kepstorn   11
Kettle, Prof Arnold   193, 196, 211
Kettle, Martin   193, 196, 211
Killingbeck, John   20-1
Kirk, John   78-80, 129, 151, 185
Kirkstall   16, 23, 25
Kirsktall Abbey   7, 9, 10, 20, 34

Kirkstall Grange see New Grange
Kitson Clarks, of Meanwoodside   109, 110, 188

Lawnswood   13, 41, 175, 180
Leeds – Borough, Parish, Corporation, Town Council   16, 19, 69, 110, 177-8, 181, 188, 198
Leeds Improvement Act   40
Leeds and Liverpool Canal   31
Leeds Modern School   138-9, 192
Leeds and Otley Turnpike Trust   30, 41-2
Leeds Parish Church   59, 61
Leeds Reformed Baptist Church   148
Leeds to Thirsk Railway   41, 49
Leeds Town Hall   56, 62, 43, 193
Leeds Tramways Co   47, 49, 112, 176-7
Leeds University, formerly The Yorkshire College   26, 86, 88, 97, 105, 107, 119, 126-7, 193
Leeds Vicarage Act 1844   77
Liverpool Road and Railway Omnibus Co   44
Lisle, Frank, artist   195, 211
Longbottom, Joseph   39

Manklin's Farm/Snow's Farm   20, 21, 91, 105, 107
Mansfield Garage   152-4
Marshall, Canon Charles, Vicar of St Chad's   139, 145-6, 148
Marshall, John, flaxspinner and industrial baron   32-3, 54, 58, 105, 211
Marshall, Jane   32, 105
Marshall, Henry Cowper   4-5, 105, 107, 211
Martin, James   26
Martin, Thomas   31
Martin, William   26-7, 29, 110
Mary Queen of England   12
Masham Court/Springville   93
Mazebrook   39, 195, 197
Meanwood   9, 13
Meanwood Beck   9, 20, 24, 33, 36, 90, 111, 188-9
Meanwood Church, Holy Trinity   109
Meanwood Hall   59, 61, 67-8, 105
Meanwoodside   20, 50, 98, 107-8, 110, 186, 188
Meanwood Tannery/Highbury Works/Woods Mill   31, 33, 74

Mellor, Kay, playwright   196, 212
Merry, George, reminiscences   112-6, 129
Meynell, Richard   14, 15
Monk Bridge Road   9, 38
Moorfield Lodge   86, 95
Moor Grange   9, 20, 24, 30, 140, 181
Moor Grange (formerly Moor Ham)   86, 164, 179
Moor House   42, 80, 83-4, 185-6
Moorlands School   99, 128
Moorman, Theo, tapestry artist   212
Moor Park Mount   83, 85
Moor Road   9, 24, 36, 95, 129, 154, 193-4
Moor Road Dairy   156-7
Moor Road Wesleyan Mission Room   73-4, 78
Moorville   39, 193, 195-6
Morritt, William, omnibus proprietor   44
Moxon's laundry   155
Murray, Matthew   32

Nandy, Dipak, race relations and equal opportunities campaigner   213
New Grange/Kirkstall Grange   9-15, 23-5, 27, 29, 32-4, 42, 49, 50, 58, 61-2, 67-70, 73, 105, 129-35, 139, 141, 179
New Inn, The   88, 114, 159, 169, 170

Oak Bank   93
Oakfield Terrace   88-90
Oakwood House   56
Oates, Bryan William Grace   91, 109-10
Oates Charles d1902   73, 109, 129
Oates, Edward d1865   27, 91, 105, 107-8, 110, 213
Oates, Joseph d1824   26, 91, 105, 107
Oates, Captain Lawrence Grace d1912   91, 109-10, 213
Oates, Susan, nee Grace   107
Oddy, Willliam   39
Oliver, William T, art critic   195, 213
Original Oak Inn, The   55
Osburn, William, Leeds poet   54
Otley   23, 41
Otley Road, the new turnpike road 1837   24, 41, 49, 63, 72-3, 80, 88, 187
Otley Old Road, the old turnpike road   41, 174-5
O'Toole, Peter, actor   195
Overend, Rev Barry, Vicar of St Chads   148, 196, 214

Oxley Hall (Weetwood Villa)   26, 94, 97, 99
Oxley, Henry d1890   94, 99, 214
Oxley, James Walker d1928   86, 94-7, 110, 129, 141, 183, 214
Oxmoor, the   24, 181

Pakeman, Robert   12
Palmerston, Lord   59, 214
Parkhurst   88, 159
Paynel, Ralph (Paganel)   5, 6, 214
Paytefen, Walter (Peytvin, Peitevin)   6, 7, 215
Pepys, Samuel   21
Perkin and Bulmer, architects   73
Pickersgill, Joseph   99, 101, 103, 165, 215
Police Force, The Leeds Reserve   52
Prokofiev, Oleg   191

Queenswood   58

Railway, The Leeds to Thirsk   41, 49
Ransome, Arthur, author   91, 123-6, 215
Ransome, Cyril, Prof of History and Modern Literature   119, 121-7, 219, 255
Ransome Edith   125-7
Ransome Literary Club   127
Richardson and Watson, estate agents   88, 90
Ring Road, The   139-40, 175
Road tolls   41
Rope, Margaret   145-6
Roughstones   39
Rye Cottage   98

St Agnes' School   137
Sackville-West, Vita, novelist   130, 218
St Chad   65, 206
St Chad's Church, Far Headingley   xxiii, 47, 59, 61, 64-5, 67, 77, 80, 112, 116, 128-9, 143-4, 146-8
St Chad's Church clock   67-8, 148
St Chad's Cricket Club   115, 139, 145
St Chad's Gardens   126, 195
St Chad's Home for Waifs and Strays/Glebe House/Hollin House   71, 129, 132, 135
St Chad's war memorial   134, 145
St Chad's Villas   99, 123, 127-8
St George's Hall, Bradford   56-7
St Giles's Church, Headingley   16-7, 20, 29
St Matthias' Church, Burley   61
St Michael's Church, Headingley   4, 16, 61

St Oswald's Mission Chapel, Highbury   74, 76-7, 143, 164
St Stephen's Church, Kirkstall   34, 49, 61
Savile, Sir John d1630   12, 14-17, 216
Savile, Sir Henry   12
Savile, Sir Robert d1585   12-13
Savile, Sir Thomas d1644   17-18
Savile, Sir William d1644   18, 21
School, The Glebe   50
School, Hollin Lane   50, 51
School, Lawnswood   139
School, Moorlands   136
School, Richmond House   137, 187
School, St Agnes'   137
School, St Chad's Otley Road   137
School, Weetwood Primary   137-8
Scott, William   39
Skipton   23
Seven Arches   46
Shaw Grange   93
Shaw House   55. 93
Shaw, John Hope   55, 57, 93, 216
Shaw Lane   48, 55, 92-3
Shire Oak, the   4, 123, 126
Shire Oak Inn, The   4, 47, 123
Shrewsbury, Rev JVB, Methodist Minister   74
Simpson, Thomas, solicitor   86-8, 94, 99, 195, 216-7
Skyrack Wapentake   4
Smith, John Metcalfe of Kirkstall Grange   67
Smith, Samuel Snr, tanner d1880   74, 110, 216
Smith Samuel Jnr, brewer   85, 110, 186
Smith, William, last man publicly hanged in Leeds   33
Smith, William, Leeds solicitor   56
Smith's Cottages   36, 199, 200
Smithy Mills   9, 11
Smyth, Dr Thomas, first Vicar of St Chad's   51, 63, 66, 74, 148
Snow, Thomas and Betty   21, 91, 107
Sowden's Yard   199
Spark, Dr William, organist, Leeds Town Hall   77
Spenfield   26, 94-7, 129, 141, 183
Spen Lane   14, 140, 175, 181
Spring-Rice, Thomas, Baron Monteagle   107, 218

Springville/Masham Court   93
Stables, Rev Howard, 3rd Vicar of St Chad's   76, 143, 145, 148
Stoppard, Tom, playwright   195
Sullivan, Sir Arthur   69

Tetley, Charles Francis d1934   84, 218
Tetley, Charles Harold, Colonel Tetley   86, 218
Tetley, Frances and Ellen   84
Tetley, Francis (William) d1883 and Isabella   84, 98, 218
Tetley Hall   86
Thompson, Robert   4
Thoresby, Ralph   3, 20, 23, 26
Three Horse Shoes, The   xxi, 39, 42, 44, 52, 112, 114, 116, 123, 141, 154, 161, 163-4, 166-170
Tolkien, J R R., author   126, 190, 218
Torquay Terrace   56
tram and bus depot, The Headingley   47, 177, 180
Trefusis, Violet, novelist   130, 219
Tucker, Captain, cartographer   42
Tuckwell, Rev Henry, Vicar of Headingley   88
Tuke, John, cartographer   26, 30-31

Upper Headrow, The   39

Vicarage, St Chad's   146
Victoria Queen and Empress   53, 57-9, 117-9, 121, 129
Victoria Terrace   55, 159
Vine Rev Alfred H   87, 219

Waddington, Samuel, farm tenant   24
Wade, Ann nee Allanson d1809   29
Wade, Anthony d1683   13, 27
Wade Benjamin d1671 and family   11, 15, 27, 29
Wade, Judith nee Foxcroft   13, 15
Wade, Thompson d1828   39
Wade, Walter d1771   27
Waite, Tommy, Methodist leader   51, 73
Walker, John   20, 25
Walkers Dairy, Cottage Rd   156, 194
War, The Great, 1914-1918   132
War Memorial, St Chad's   134
War, Second World 1939-1945   135-6, 146

Waterworks Company, The Leeds   40, 97, 181
Weetwood   9, 11-13, 40, 56
Weetwood Hall   14-15, 19, 20, 24-6, 41-2, 104-7, 129, 139, 175
Weetwood Lane   24, 47-8, 72, 100, 103, 106, 154, 158, 163, 167, 169, 191
Weetwood Lane Forge   153-5, 163-4, 194
Weetwood Laundry   155
Weetwood Primary School   135
Weetwood Villa   94
Wesleyan Chapel, Moor Road   34, 47
West Grove   79, 161
West Park   126, 141, 161-2, 179-184
Whalley, Thomas and family   20, 21, 107-8
Wheatlands   39, 195
Wilde, Oscar   69, 78, 219
William I   5
William IV   36
Williamson, Rev William, Vicar of Headingley   74
Wilson, Thomas Butler, architect   79, 207
Wood, James, builder   56, 77
Wood, John, stage coach proprietor   39, 44, 52
Woodbine Terrace   56, 77
Woodhouse Moor   18, 25, 40, 42, 57
Woodman Inn, The   114, 169, 171-2
Woods Mill/Highbury Works/Meanwood Tannery   30
Wooler, Geoffrey, surgeon   93, 219
Wordsworth, Dorothy   32-3, 219
Wordsworth, William, poet   32, 219
Wright, Sergeant William   52

Yorkshire College, see Leeds University
Yorkshire Post   195

Zoological and Botanical Gardens, Burley   41, 105, 111

. . . and finally

An evocative photograph *c*1910 which 'surfaced' in recent years in the home of Mike and Julie Smith. Simply inscribed on the back 'Victoria Terrace garden'.   *Courtesy Mike and Julie Smith.*

*Make this book unique.
Put your favourite photograph
of Far Headingley here
and record the significance of it
in the space below.*

....
....
....
....
....
....